S0-APM-949

Behavioral Models for Market Analysis: Foundations for Marketing Action

Behavioral Models for Market Analysis: Foundations for Marketing Action

Francesco M. Nicosia
University of California, Berkeley

Yoram Wind
Wharton School,
University of Pennsylvania

The Dryden Press
Hinsdale, Illinois

To Vardina and the Unknown ♀

Copyright © 1977 by The Dryden Press
A division of Holt, Rinehart & Winston, Publishers
All rights reserved
Library of Congress number: 77-78701
ISBN: 0-03-013616-4
Printed in the United States of America
789 059 987654321

Foreword

Few marketing practitioners or academics would argue with the assertion that buyer behavior models—and their implications for marketing decision making—are where the current action is. One need only look to the scholarly journals and popular press to see plenty of examples of models dealing with buyer motivations, organizational influences, consumer perceptions and preferences, attribute tradeoff processes and the like. As if that were not enough, we are further reminded by the new lexicon of the market place—product positioning, customer psychographics, and benefit bundles, to name a few examples.

But individual research efforts, however insightful or provocative, need organizing and integrating from time to time. Nicosia and Wind, the editors of this volume, have tried to do just that. It is a difficult job to do under any set of circumstances. Fortunately for the reader, the editors have assembled a talented and wise group of scholars to aid them in their task.

The result is an organized look at the current state of the art of behavioral models—what is around, what it seems to be good for, how it has been used and what might be in the offing. The book is a blend of the tutorial, the ruminating, the programmatic and the speculative. As a bonus, we are also treated to insightful discussions (fore and aft) of the *process of model building* and why the whole enterprise might be interesting and worthwhile.

Nicosia and Wind's penchant and skill for organizing the book's presentation leave little room for additional comment. Their introduction in Chapter 1 describes the book's purpose and presentation sequence. Moreover, the editors provide a brief introductory note for each chapter that serves to maintain continuity (and eliminate the need for further embellishment by us).

We can only say to the prospective reader: don't sample, just gorge yourself. The topics are wide ranging and thoughtfully presented. And, unlike most verbal smorgasbords cooked up by multiple contributors, this one has coherence and direction.

Paul E. Green, Philip Kotler

Preface

Basic and applied disciplines consist of people and their thoughts, feelings, and actions. Humans are a heterogeneous lot—everyone is different from everyone else and each changes through time. All this, plus some more, make scientific Truths rather volatile, temporary, and changing. Fashion is inherently human; it is a process whose domain comprehends all social events; it is not limited to the length of skirts or the styling of cars.

The development of marketing has witnessed many fashions—a cascade of discoveries, realizations, enthusiasms, and then, the gaining of perspective and the appreciation of the limited power of any principle, concept, method, procedure, and so-called facts.

In the late fifties, the reports by the Ford and Carnegie Foundations led marketing to accept economics, psychology, some sociology, a little math, a little scientific method, and lots of stat and computer languages.

One of the main consequences of this was that a rapidly increasing number of marketing managers, researchers, teachers, and students began to enjoy the *use* of such words as theory, model, and the like. These words have now become very popular in every marketing textbook—from the basic undergraduate introductory to the advanced marketing management courses and specialized graduate seminars.

We are concerned that the popular use of the words model, theory, and the like has also led to their *misuse*. And misuse may lead to disappointments, which in a classical pendulum fashion, may lead to *underutilization*.

The authors of the chapters in this book feel that theories and models can contribute to marketing managers' thinking and decision making process and to the training of students who want to become marketing managers or who are interested in marketing. At the same time, the authors also illustrate the limitations and dangers of inappropriate development and use of theories and models.

We believe that this book will be useful, not only to teachers and students of marketing, but also to those who play the real marketing roles in private firms, nonprofit organizations, state and federal agencies and regulatory commissions, legislative bodies, and courts. This book builds a bridge between management and research; it suggests to marketing managers how to buy theories and models judiciously; it urges researchers to sell and design theories and models with humility.

Our first acknowledgment goes to the authors of the various chapters. They gave unselfishly of their experience and time, for they are sincerely concerned with the uses and misuses of theories and models in the profession of marketing. Ellen McGibbon managed to keep the many authors on course down to the smallest detail, and Sandy Nykerk helped us, too. Acting Dean Robert Goshay and Dean Earl Cheit provided the necessary support throughout the many drafts. And we would be quite remiss if we did not say thank you to the many clients, colleagues, and students who have helped us over the years to realize both the power and limitations of theories and models in the applied discipline of marketing.

F. M. Nicosia
Berkeley

Yoram Wind
Philadelphia

Contents

Part Three
Models of Market Analysis:
The Competitive Setting

Chapter 1

Introduction

Yoram Wind and *F. M. Nicosia*

One of the central focal points of the marketing system is the marketing manager. He or she has responsibility for selecting the firm's target market segment(s) and for the design of the product, price, promotion, and distribution strategies—all the decisions required to assure consumer satisfaction (the essence of the marketing concept) subject to the achievement of the firm's objectives. In making these decisions, marketing managers need information on the behavior of their current and potential customers and a better understanding of their competitive positions.

In the acquisition, processing, and use of information, managers and researchers rely on some implicit or explicit model of the phenomenon under study. Of special interest are *substantive* models, i.e., models of processes that explicitly state variables and their relationships. These models provide guidelines to marketing action; their description of a phenomenon's process is the basis for explanation and prediction. Excluded from this book are those models that do not describe a process and are intended to provide only predictive information, for example, stochastic brand choice models, such as Markov chains and learning models, and statistical inference models.

In constructing and implementing substantive models, the manager must rely on marketing research, the behavioral sciences (including the emerging discipline of consumer behavior), and management science.

The behavioral sciences—including psychology, sociology, cultural anthropology, economics, political science, and communication research—provide a series of concepts and findings concerning the behavior of customers and competitors. They also provide the basis for operational definitions of relevant variables and measurement and scaling techniques. The marketing manager and researcher have to verify the behavioral hypotheses in the relevant context of the firm's characteristics and market environment. In addition, by using some of the management science tools (such as simulation or optimization procedures), management can obtain more rigorous guidelines for marketing decisions.

Substantive models of customer behavior and competitive setting therefore perform a triple role: (1) guidelines for the firm's research activities; (2) guidelines for the interpretation of market data; and (3) once verified in the specific context of the firm's characteristics and market environment, they provide management with essential inputs for the design of the firm's marketing strategies.

This central role of behavioral models of market analysis in marketing management is illustrated in Figure 1.1. In fact, a stronger understanding of buying processes is necessary if several things are to happen, for example, increasing the efficiency and effectiveness of buying decisions of a family or an organization (i.e., the design of a process that describes which activities are best performed by which subjects). Even more important, an understanding of buying and competitive processes by "sellers" provides the foundation for the design of marketing strategies. Such understanding is a necessary condition, not only for the buyer to be satisfied and thus become loyal, but also for the seller to increase and consolidate its market share over the long run. Finally, understanding of the buying processes and the competitive setting by lawmakers and regulatory agencies may ultimately lead to results that are "better" for the seller, the buyer, and the public interest.

In essence the rationale underlying the study of behavioral models of the market (customers and competitors) is portrayed by the analogy to the driver who "the more he (she) knows of an engine, the better driver he (she) will be." "Better" means, in practical terms:

1. *To provide preventive maintenance.* A seller monitors how a client is getting along; how happy he (she) is with the purchased products or services; what problems he (she) anticipates; and so on.
2. *To improve performance.* A seller continues to study his (her) customers to identify new needs or to satisfy current needs more fully.
3. *To repair sudden breakdowns promptly and satisfactorily.* A seller must be able to determine why a buyer is planning to switch to other suppliers or why products or services fail to meet agreed-upon performance.
4. *To react to changes in the environment that may make his (her) car substandard or dangerous.* A seller who knows his (her) buyers' needs can anticipate their reactions to technological changes and other environmental changes.

So far we have discussed the concept of *behavioral models* but have not defined it operationally. In fact the term "behavioral models of market analysis," as the more general term "model," means different things to different people and has frequently been used and misused in diverse ways. The objectives of this book, therefore, are threefold:

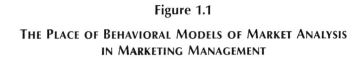

Figure 1.1

**THE PLACE OF BEHAVIORAL MODELS OF MARKET ANALYSIS
IN MARKETING MANAGEMENT**

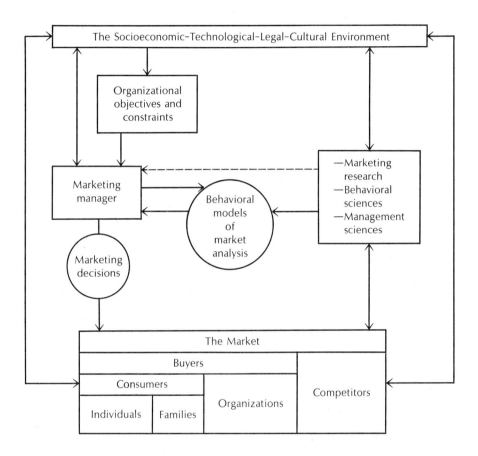

1. To provide an introductory discussion of the fundamental process of constructing models.
2. To discuss the current state of the art with respect to existing models of market analysis, including both the buyers (at the individual, family, and organization level of analysis) and the competitive setting.
3. To suggest possible management uses of models of market analysis for the design of marketing strategies.

To achieve these objectives the book is organized along the following lines.

Part One: Constructing Models

What are the meanings of models? This section includes three chapters by V. Blankenship, G. Zaltman, and L. Dominguez and F. Nicosia. It is commonly accepted that scientific methodology is a way for humans to be "objective." Yet, can a human be objective? And in what ways can knowledge be objective—in an absolute way? The book begins with an incisive discussion of this and related questions by Blankenship. The lesson we learn is modesty. In reading this chapter marketing managers and researchers will appreciate the power and concurrent fragility of the concepts of theory and model.

Zaltman presents the results of his search for criteria external to market (consumer behavior) theories (i.e., meta theory) that can be used to evaluate the "goodness" of any theory and, in particular, theories and models about any marketing phenomenon.

Dominguez and Nicosia come a bit closer to the moment when we roll up our sleeves and go to work. They discuss some of the practical problems faced when we develop an "operational" theory or model. Their chapter bridges the preceding discussion and those that follow.

Part Two: Models of Market Analysis: The Buyers

In the second part, four chapters are concerned with the state of the art in modeling buyer behavior. The first three focus on describing buyer behavior while the fourth examines management use of market segmentation.

J. Lunn begins with an examination of how different theories and models can help or hinder our understanding of the individual consumer.

R. Ferber turns our attention to a small group of consumers—the family. This is a relatively new topic in our field, and we shall see how we are presently at the very early stage of the discourse between mind (theories and model construction) and matter (i.e., the so-called data or facts).

F. Nicosia and Y. Wind ascend the ladder of complexity and tackle the study of large groups—the organizational buyer. They focus on the current literature of organizational buying, a set of activities that have received relatively little attention, and suggest an agenda for future research.

After discussing the role(s) of theories and models in these specific areas, we should be ready to ask the usual question: So what? W. Massy and B. Weitz focus on the decision to segment a market. They discuss why a firm should segment and highlight how models of market analysis can provide guidelines—the more operational, the better—to help managers to identify "heterogeneity" in the input (buying) markets and output (selling) markets with which firms try to establish economic rapport.

Part Three: Models of Market Analysis: The Competitive Setting

The two chapters in this part shift the focus from the modeling of buyer behavior to the understanding of the competitive setting of the firm. J. Carman examines how economic theories can be used (or misused) to describe the environment in which a firm or group of firms operate—in a way that is relevant to management decisions and/or to decisions by legislators, regulators, and courts.

Wind examines the competitive setting from a different point of view, through the eyes of the consumer and other relevant publics (the firm, the intermediate marketing organizations, etc.), i.e., the focus is on the perceived positioning of the firm vis-à-vis its competitors.

Epilogue

Any review of the state of the art can benefit from an insightful reflection on where we are, where we are going, and most importantly where we should be going. C. W. Churchman is eminently qualified to sum up the book's inquiry and to answer these questions. One of the fathers of operations research, a founder of management science, and one of the few researchers who has gone beyond "doing," he has given much thought to the question: "How do we know that we do have some knowledge?" Although the combination of these three qualities is rare, Churchman satisfies a fourth quality also. Since the early fifties he has been concerned with marketing, in both its micromanagerial and its macroeconomic and social aspects.

It is our hope that this book will provide the reader with a better understanding of the current uses (and misuses) of behavioral models of market analysis and will stimulate their necessary further development and implementation.

Part One

Constructing Models

Chapter 2

The Social Context
of Science

*L. Vaughn Blankenship**

Editors' Note

In this chapter, the author questions the notion of objectivity. He argues that objectivity in measurement is not sufficient. Values and concepts intrinsically determine the "validity" of a research project, its results, and the results' meaning to managers and researchers.

A major purpose of empirical research in marketing is to produce information about the "existential" world which can serve as the basis for action. Since the information produced is symbolic in one form or another, its effects on action are, at best, indirect. It affects what men do by changing the "pictures in their heads" of what is out there and how it relates to them in their roles as scientists or managers. Because men act on the basis of information produced by a process called research, the characteristics of that information (its persuasiveness, its internal and external validity, its reliability, its episte-

*L. Vaughn Blankenship is a professor of Political Science, SUNY/Buffalo, on leave to the Division of Social Systems and Human Resources, National Science Foundation, from 1973 to 1975. The views stated herein are those of the author alone and should not be considered to represent in any way the views of the National Science Foundation.

mological structure) and the process by which it was created are of crucial importance.

The major theme of this chapter is that the characteristics of information and the way in which men react to these characteristics cannot be dealt with separately from the process by which the information is created and presented to the decision maker. The typical course in research methodology presents the student with a series of disembodied, impersonal rules and formulas for collecting, ordering, evaluating, and giving meaning to something called data. Seldom is the context in which these operations are done made clear, nor is it clear exactly who is doing it, why it is being done, or why anyone should take the results seriously. The process of scientific research, i.e., the production of information, is treated as separable from the psychology of the individual performing it, the incentives and politics of the social/organizational system in which it is being performed, and the interests and perspectives of the "reception system" to which its results are directed. The student merely memorizes the rules, gets some experience in applying them to empirical problems, and then goes out and does his damndest! Furthermore, he is taught—implicitly or explicitly—that he is operating in an unconstrained environment where resources are free, motivations are uncontaminated and unambiguous, and scientific information is highly valued (Blankenship 1974).

A number of consequences follow from this view of the nature of empirical inquiry. There is a failure to recognize that successful research is as much a problem in management and the structuring of communication systems as it is a problem in the application of disembodied logic to bits of data. Thus one needs to be at least conscious about the structure and management of research operations. (Similar points have been made by Churchman 1968.) Perhaps even more troublesome is the failure to recognize that the concept of successful research depends very much upon the social system in which the researcher is embedded. This can lead to the misapplication or selection of irrelevant criteria in the allocation of scarce resources or evaluation of results and a misguided emphasis by the researcher.

To illustrate these points more forcefully and demonstrate their implications, I would like to examine three somewhat different models of empirical inquiry in detail.[1]

The first, the *positivist* model, comes closest to what is probably most widely understood as empiricism in social science—experimental procedures involving data which can ultimately be measured objectively. It enjoys wide support in both social science and philosophy, and for many it constitutes *the* model (or the only *legitimate* model) of scientific inquiry. It approximates most closely how social scientists *believe* physical scientists feel about and proceed with their work.

The second model has ties with phenomenology and clinical investigations and rests on a rather different set of assumptions about the nature of knowledge concerning social phenomena. In terms of traditions, it is probably closer to that of the *humanist*.

---

1. The line of reasoning developed in this part of the paper draws heavily on a previous paper by the author (Blankenship 1971).

The third, for want of a better title, might be called the *value-centered model.* Its most basic attribute is that it posits a different starting point and a different set of appropriate behaviors and motivations for empirical inquiry and theorizing.

I propose to compare them, more or less systematically, in terms of certain interrelated themes:

1. The aims of research. What does each model assume about the reasons for undertaking empirical inquiry? What sets of goals serve to guide activities, including the selection of problems to work on? What is the information each model generates supposed to do, i.e., what is its wider function relative to what reception system?
2. The relation with data. What are the relationships between the investigator and his data (any social object of study)?
3. The relation with the researcher's audience(s). Who are his audiences—the scientific community, the subjects, the marketing manager?

Throughout the chapter we shall ask: What is the meaning of objectivity in each model? What is the role of theory, and how are results verified, i.e., how does the empiricist come to believe that what he says is true and that he has done what he set out to do in the first place? Finally, what does each assume about the organization of research itself?

The Positivist Model

The Aims of Research

This world or, more accurately, the behavior and outlook of the scientist *qua* scientist in this world, is believed to be governed by a distinctive set of universalistic impersonal norms. These specify appropriate attitudes toward self, work, and colleagues as well as toward the scientific enterprise itself, and a listing of them might include the following:

1. *Universalism.* Acceptance or rejection of the theories or findings of science depends on certain objective, rational standards generated by the community of science itself and not on the personal attributes, e.g., motives, personality, social class, religion, ethnicity, sex, age, or kinship of the scientist. These are public standards to be applied equally to all offerings made in the name of science.
2. *Communality.* The output of science is not owned by any individual but is the property of the community, and reward for scientific achievement should be limited to collegial esteem and recognition.
3. *Disinterestedness.* It is inappropriate for a scientist to take a proprietary attitude toward his work or to make the search for recognition an explicit goal. Only in this way can he maintain the necessary objectivity toward his own work and the work of others.
4. *Organized skepticism.* Each individual and the community of science itself

should be appropriately skeptical of all findings and theories. An open-minded posture, a posture expressing doubt, is to be maintained. (Boguslaw n.d., pp. 57–58)

Though there is much evidence to demonstrate that researchers do not adhere to such idealistic standards, they constitute an integral part of the positivist model with significant implications for some of the other dimensions which we shall consider next.[2] It is also clear that they have been widely accepted by social scientists as a statement of ideal orientations and behaviors. The researcher is supposed to be neutral and open-minded with respect to his data and the data of others, and he perceives knowledge, per se, to be both an end in itself and its own reward.

Differences among scientists are resolved by open debate and the use of agreed-upon, rational standards of measurement and evaluation. In the long run, the truth wins out and error loses without the intervention of any kind of authority or power structure. Even if individual scientists are corrupt or their motives and methods suspect, the enterprise itself has a life of its own and will survive and eventually filter out universal objective truth.

Thus, as in the dogma of the medieval church, a distinction is drawn between the *institution* and the behavior and ethics of *individual actors* at a point in historical time. Though the latter may be corrupt, misguided, or in severe error, the former is *ultimately* correct and can make only true judgments and pronouncements. For the church, faith in its ultimate ability to produce the truth is rooted in its relationship to God, a perfect being who would not allow his church to be less than equally perfect. For science as represented in the positivist model, faith in its ultimate ability to produce the truth rests on the twin pillars of a belief in the possibility of making unbiased empirical observations and the postulated existence of a Platonic ideal, a "perfect" scientific community that will guarantee the results of these empirical efforts.

The Relation with Data

Two other characteristics of the positivist model of empirical inquiry are the relation between the observer (scientist) and the object observed (which may be an individual or individuals, small groups, communities, organizations, or some other social object or unit), and the relation between the scientist and his audience (the decision maker). To begin with, the observer looks at his subject as a "thing" from which he must maintain a social and emotional distance. Personal involvement is to be avoided as it will stand in the way of objective, rational judgments. He is interested only in externalities that can be directly detected as sense-data (i.e., data perceived through the sensory organs). He is concerned with objective "social facts" which need to be explained at that level without reference to the inner world of the object(s) being observed.

In this the social scientist would be like the physicist studying atomic particles without reference to how the particles may feel or how they might view

2. For a rigorous criticism of these "norms" of science, as the sociologist is wont to call them, see Mitroff 1974.

him as a scientist. Concepts, categories of analysis, indicators, hypotheses, and research problems *are generated not with reference to the perspective of the objects or social systems being studied, but from the universalistic theories developed by social science.* Much of the so-called behavioral research in marketing tends to be of this type.

The purpose of this activity is not to particularize findings to individuals or classes of individuals but to contribute further information to the scientific enterprise and the disciplinary specialty with which the investigator is identified. The researcher seeks to test theory, to generalize to universal truths independently of the particular attributes of his objects. He is interested only in those attributes which his theory tells him are relevant, and verification of his findings depends on a series of "objective" procedures, the existence of a community of scientists to judge them, and the observance of a number of norms having to do with such things as full public disclosure, replication, and professional honesty. His moral obligations to his subjects are quite limited, with the only commitment being to science. There is no personal responsibility either for the effects of research or findings on subjects or the uses that might be made of his work by others.

As we can see, in this model there is the assumption that in the observer-observed relationships wisdom and power lie with the former, and it is only in the former that learning takes place. The observer establishes the rules of the game in the form of hypotheses, research designs, measuring devices, data collection, and analysis techniques. His interests in the observed are defined and circumscribed by this apparatus, and he "forces" subjects to respond to him in terms relevant to it. Learning then occurs within the observer as he looks at responses (sense-data) and interprets them in terms meaningful to him, e.g., in terms that fit within his universalistic theories. The subject is in a dependent, almost childlike relationship to the (adult) researcher. The possibility that subjects may learn from the research—from observing the investigator at work, or from participation in or reading about other research—and consequently adjust their responses either to take into account what they have learned or what they want the scientist to learn is either ignored or else dealt with as a problem in subject (or data) manipulation and control. It is illegitimate for subjects to influence the scientist, in terms of either what *they* want or what they *think he wants* out of the study. Influence is the prerogative of the scientist alone. Such influence might bias the scientific quality of the results! (For a further incisive analysis of these characteristics of the positivistic model of research, see Argyris 1968.)

Subjects might be controlled in a variety of ways: by feeding them misleading or intentionally ambiguous information about the investigator's purpose, by physically manipulating the environment or the experimental situation, by limiting contacts between observer and observed so that chances for learning (on the part of subjects) is minimized, by searching for unobtrusive measures, by looking for naive subjects, or by statistical or logical manipulation of the data so as to rule out the biasing effects of learning. That there is in reality a highly complex game in which the observer and the observed seek, consciously and unconsciously, to con each other is glossed over, in the belief that power and wisdom rest with the scientist and that all (or most) unwanted influences can ultimately be controlled, randomized, or exorcised by appropriate qualifying phrases. This helps the investigator to sustain the picture of himself as objective, observing his passive data and reporting on it publicly to his scientific colleagues.

When we strip the positivist model to its essence in this fashion, a rather grim, dehumanized picture of theory, the scientist, and the scientific enterprise emerges. The notion that there is a considerable gap between the expert and the layman on the subject being studied is built into it as is the idea that one can discover truth in a piece of reality without disturbing the whole or without creating the reality observed through the very process of observing it. One is reminded at this point of an observation attributed to Bertrand Russell in the 1920s that the apes used in learning experiments by the German Gestalt school typically sat around and "thought out" solutions, while those used for similar purposes by American behavioralists were constantly on the move and "solved problems" by trial and error (Merton 1957, p. 486, n. 85). According to the assumptions of the positivist model, of course, it is perfectly clear who is studying whom: the scientist is objectively observing and describing the behavior of monkeys. (Perhaps German apes have a genetic structure that differs significantly from their American counterparts. This might account for the differences that Russell observed.) Those of a different persuasion would have greater doubts on the matter.

The spirit of this aspect of the positivist orientation is perhaps best captured by a statement that I have heard uttered with great profundity on numerous occasions by practicing researchers who find their ideas or conclusions challenged: "That is ultimately an *empirical* question!" This presumably puts the issue beyond useful debate until another rigorous study can be mounted to collect the objective information to answer it authoritatively once and for all. The data, we are being told, lie "out there"; they can be collected independently of the motives, wishes, hopes, or assumptions of the investigator according to the universalistic theories of science; once collected, they will speak for themselves through the impartial scientist to resolve clearly the disagreement. If they fall short and an area of uncertainty remains, the answer is further specification of the problem, more empirical data, better measuring techniques, improved statistics, and greater rigor. Given enough time, infinite resources, better measures, and enough data, we can, according to this view, answer every question definitely.

The Relation with the Researcher's Audience(s)

In the positivist model of inquiry, the primary audience for the researcher is not the marketing manager, but a collective body—the community of specialists with whom he identifies. They set the boundaries for the acceptable language and format that he can use for meaningful communication (frequently known as jargon to those outside the group); establish rules of logic, reasoning, and measurement; frame and define relevancy of problems; and serve as the ultimate judge of the individual's performance according to these criteria. They decide which information to accept, i.e., to add to the "growing body of relevant literature" on the problem; which to treat as more or less significant, more or less fundamental; and which to act on, i.e., which to use as the basis for further discussion, specification, and research.

Typically this collective is organized into separate disciplines and specialties, with these divisions institutionalized in the form of academic departments, degree programs, government research-funding activities, scholarly journals, and professional associations. Decision making within this autonomous community is supposed to be decentralized and nonhierarchical with all members recognized as equals. The status orderings that do exist are, ideally, based on group assessments of past performance. In fact, differential status, i.e., group recognition and deference, is the major reward that is held out to members to ensure conformity to its expectations and standards. Identification with the collective and acceptance of its standards and definitions of relevance and significance is the result of selective recruitment and the intensive socialization process that the individual undergoes to become a specialist (Hagstrom 1965, ch. 1).

Who provides the resources to support these activities and institutional arrangements? The model has nothing to say on this issue, though it implicitly makes a number of assumptions about it. The researcher presumably operates in an unconstrained environment, an environment in which resources such as time, energy, attention span, talent, manpower, technology, and wealth are unlimited. His only concerns are logic and measurement, and a partial truth today is not nearly so valuable as a slightly better truth tomorrow, or an even more complete version in five years. There are no resource limitations, no moral uncertainties, no nasty choices, no motivational or communication problems.

A similar condition presumably holds at the level of the scientific community. This assumption can be illustrated in a number of ways—the denial that the value of science can or should be judged relative to other demands on scarce resources according to utilitarian or economic criteria; the belief that the pursuit of ideal, generalized truths is and must be separated from the question of the uses to which knowledge is put and the value of that knowledge to nonscientists; the position that the scientific community alone is qualified to define significant problems for research and the assertion that others must acquiesce to these definitions and willingly provide the needed resources because knowledge, as an end in itself, is a great good; the denial of responsibility for the uses of science and its technological products.

What is it, finally, that guarantees that this marvelous enterprise will operate according to this model? The guarantee lies in two things: the character and socialization of the individual scientist, and the fact that interference with or imperfections of the process will result in erroneous "truths" that will eventually catch up with the perpetrators and punish them through individual, system, or societal failure. Thus like the inexorable workings of the marketplace of classical economics, the invisible hand of scientific truth allocates resources, guides decisions, and ensures success to those individuals and societies who play by its rules and failure to those who don't. The model of inquiry is self-starting and self-operating; its rules are somehow self-enforcing both on the participants in the game and on those who are admonished to watch from the sidelines.

The Humanist Model

The Aims of Research

There are difficulties in attempting to characterize the humanist model of empirical inquiry precisely—difficulties, as we shall see, *inherent in its very nature as a way of generating theory and empirical knowledge.* Its philosophical and social roots are not so visible to social scientists raised on the positivist model, and many would deny it equal legitimacy as a way of proceeding to do science. With the positivist model we can point to the physicist as the ideal type and everyone intuitively grasps the essence of what we are talking about. The rules of the humanist model are less well articulated, partly because they rely heavily upon the insight and emotional experiences of the individual investigator and partly because social scientists report the results of their research as it should have been conducted, i.e., according to the canons of "reconstructed logic," rather than describing how they actually went about their work.

In some important ways the methods of the humanist model approach those of the artist, poet, or psychotherapist more closely than they do those of the natural scientist. Involving as they do the personality of the investigator and his experiences in a particular setting, they defy rationalization beyond a certain point. The knowledge and theories they produce have a particularistic flavor, and validation of results (if it occurs) may require a set of assumptions and procedures quite different from that in the positivist model.

The Relation with Data

The relation between observer and observed in the humanist model is characterized by closeness and intimacy at least during a major portion of the research. This occurs because the concern of the observer is to gain an understanding of the world through the eyes of the subject. He wants to comprehend the inner, subjective reality of the observed, the moral and ethical meanings he attaches to his acts, the way in which he makes decisions, the way in which he confronts and deals with his environment, the pressures he feels, the aspirations he has.

The extreme form of the humanist model is the case of the clinical psychologist, who in contrast to the cultural anthropologist and the historian, seeks intimate, private knowledge through a series of interactions between observer and observed in which both learn about each other. The scientist abandons his impersonal stance to become a partisan in events since this is a way of creating within himself the same feelings that move his subjects and give meaning to their world. *They* rather than *he* are the experts. He may argue with them, point up inconsistencies in their values and behavior, inject himself into conflicts. By participating he learns from his mistakes since his subjects react to them, and, at the same time, his behavior may force them to become reflective about their own orientations and values.

The humanist may enter this relationship with certain general theories or concepts, but these are explicitly in a state of tension with the subjective world he is studying. In a very real sense he is searching for a problem, waiting for one to emerge from his interactions, testing his initial hunches as he proceeds. (For an elaboration, see Bensman & Vidich 1960.) Testing in this context may involve several things: logical operations with data or symbols, injection of the scientist directly into the system on an experimental basis to see how it responds, feeding ideas back to the subject to see what sense they make to him. Data and evidence are produced along the way, always subject to reinterpretation, as the researcher gains new insights into the inner world of his subjects and they gain new insights about themselves or him, which they in turn reflect back to him.

Communication of findings to others moves back and forth between different levels of abstraction and experiencing. First, the meaning attached to terms or concepts by the observed must be conveyed. This requires the use of words, models, analogues, etc., which, insofar as possible, will recreate within the audience subjective *feelings* similar to those emotional, perceptual, or cognitive states experienced by the observed. A second level of communication involves relating subjective orientations to political, economic, or social structures.

The purpose of such generalizations may be to account for the emergence of certain institutional forms in a particular culture. Thus Weber (1958), for example, related capitalism as a unique orientation toward economic activities to the subjective world view of particular Protestant sects and explained the *initial* emergence of the former and the organizational arrangements to which it gave rise in terms of the latter orientation. Or, conversely, the purpose may be to demonstrate how structure gives rise to certain subjective experiences, frustrations, or styles of decision making (see Gerth & Mills 1964). In either case, the knowledge is not so much a contribution to abstract universalistic theory as it is a contribution to an understanding of the human condition, the relation between the inner and outer world of man in a particuar historical and cultural setting.

These insights may, of course, be communicated back to the subjects— individuals, groups, organizations, communities—enabling them to come to grips with the conditions producing their experiences. In such a case the social scientist slips into the role of clinician, and his theories and interpretation of data are a function of their usefulness to subjects either in controlling or changing their environment or in alleviating anxiety and uncertainty with respect to it and its relation to their inner world. Once more the observed is drawn directly into the process of inquiry in the humanist model, and the boundary between scientist (expert) and subject (layman) becomes blurred.

The need to move back and forth between involvement and withdrawal creates a number of dilemmas for the scientist that may not be present (or at least not as visible) in the positivist model. It requires facility in a number of different roles in the course of research. Problem selection, data collection, theorizing, and even validation involve close relationships betwen observer and observed. The location of wisdom, the flow of influence, the boundaries between expert and layman are blurred and unstable. At some point, however, the researcher must retire from the relationships, insulate himself from the observed, reflect on the meaning of his experiences, and search for ways to organize them so that they can be communicated to others.

The Relation with the Researcher's Audience(s)

Following the humanist model implies some problems of communicating research results to audiences. The observer's role as a social scientist with a commitment to a community *outside of that in which he and his subjects are participants* must reassert itself. As in the positivist model, data and findings emerging from his research are now subject to treatment in a "secular" fashion despite the fact that they have been generated in a way that implies a much more intimate and extended *human* relationship. Conversion of the relationship between the scientist and his subjects into a commodity for use in public exchange between the scientist and his colleagues clearly changes its meaning.

The ethical obligations of the social scientist (or lack of them) in the positivist model are reasonably clear. They become confused in the humanist model where a whole new dimension of human meaning and communication is opened up. Even if an effort is made to protect the identity of the subject as a way of depersonalizing knowledge and reducing its emotional overtones, this is extremely difficult to carry out given the very nature of that knowledge. The researcher may be insulated from the consequences of these facts if he lives in a different culture from that of the subject. The ivory tower of academia may serve the same purpose and ease the inner tension involved or else submerge it completely. Likewise, subjects may ease the problem by defusing the relationship of some of its personal, human meaning, discounting the importance of any findings and erecting barriers between themselves and the world of the social scientist.

All in all the complexity of the research subjects' interaction in the humanist model is higher and, in some ways, more demanding than it is in the positivist model, therefore making it difficult to communicate useful findings to the marketing manager.

The Value-Centered Model

The Aims of Research

The major feature distinguishing this from the preceding models is the existence of a fourth party to the earlier triad of scientific community, observer, and observed—a client who is explicitly purchasing the knowledge generated by the researcher. The exact nature of the contractual relationship between client and scientist may vary. The client may be an employer, so that the relationship is embedded in a larger set of employer-employee obligations, or he may hire the social scientist as a consultant, contracting for an explicit piece of research for which money is to be exchanged.

In the value-centered model the problem emerges from the interaction between researcher and client rather than from the concerns of universalistic empirical theory (as in the positivist model) or in the interaction between researcher and subject (as in the humanist model). Obviously, the researcher does not enter the negotiations preceding problem definition without ideas of his own about what needs to be done, what he would like to do, or what the goals of the client ought to be, and these ideas may be informed by general theoretical concerns and experience with other clients. Conversely, the client seldom has a clear idea about the nature of his problem. Nor are these issues resolved once and for all at an early stage in the negotiations. As in the humanist model, they emerge out of the total research process in which there is a continual testing of hunches, hypotheses, theories, and conclusions—testing that includes communication with the client. Learning is continuous, in both the researcher and the client, and where the cultures are substantially different, a good deal of energy must be devoted to mutual education and the development of a common language.

Even more fuzziness is introduced into the picture when the role of client and funder becomes split, when the ostensible user of research output is not the same (or only partially the same) as the individual or institution providing resources for the research. A number of federal programs involving value-centered research have this character: an agency is approached by, or approaches (through program solicitations, requests for proposals, program announcements, etc.) an individual researcher with a proposal. The agency has as its mission the support of research which has a high usefulness potential to some client—itself or other federal programs, local communities, private agencies, businesses, voluntary associations, etc. The client has his own needs, his own perceptions of the organizational and political constraints within which he operates and within which he must implement (or ignore) any research results. Thus problem definition involves very complicated patterns of communication among several parties with frequently conflicting needs: the obligation of the funding agency to maintain accountability for its expenditure of public funds; the desire of the researcher to maintain his professional integrity, some degree of autonomy, and his identification with a scientific community; the interest of the user in obtaining practical, relevant findings—findings which do not come too late to do any good and which can be implemented in real time in a real organizational environment. It is easy to understand how the social scientist, caught in the midst of a complex system such as this, can yearn for the simplicity of the positivist or even humanist model of research!

The Relation with Data

The design and conduct of inquiry itself may be patterned after the traditions of either the positivist or humanist models. Thus the scientist may be primarily concerned with the externalities of behavior and rely upon objective techniques for measuring them while maintaining an appropriate distance from his subjects and assigning meaning to his findings in terms of universalistic theories. Concern for the inner meanings of terms or problems to subjects would, as we have seen, result in a different design and set of procedures. In either case the general boundaries of research are set by the interests of the client, and at some point he must confront the issue of communicating findings in a way that makes their relevance to these interests clear.

When access to the subjects for research may be fully or partially controlled by the client, a number of problems arise. Some of these problems are highlighted in the context of the value-centered model, although they may apply to the other two models as well. Here the client is able to place stipulations on the researcher, limiting the data he can collect or review and subjecting analysis and/or findings to clearance. In such a situation, a series of moral and legal issues becomes highly salient. Does the client *really* have the right to control access to the subjects (data), and what are the reciprocal rights of the subject and the scientist? In the case of private businesses, the courts have generally recognized their right to control information deemed proprietary, i.e., information which *may* have a market value, which they have purchased or produced themselves. Does the same enterprise, however, have the right to make employee records available or insist that employees cooperate with a researcher? What rights do employees and unions or students and parents have under such circumstances?

Such questions may take on a different character when the client has little or no control over access to the subjects. In both cases, however, the basic point is the same: the relation between the *purposes of the client and the uses to which he intends to put information,* and the right of the subjects to privacy and to know *how the information they are being asked to provide will serve their own purposes and needs.* This critical problem is sublimated in the positivist model of inquiry by the claims that (a) information serves the abstract ends of science, and (b) no one stands to profit by it directly. (At best, someone may get promoted to a tenured position or receive a salary increase because of the research he has done!) It cannot be avoided in the value-centered model, however, since the client wants information that he can exploit directly in pursuit of his own interests. These interests may or may not correspond to those of the observed.

The Relation with the Researcher's Audience(s)

The organizational, moral, and scientific environment with which the researcher must cope in the value-centered model is infinitely more complex and troublesome than in the two previous models. The introduction of a fourth party with some proprietary interest in research findings has clearly changed and complicated the rules of the game. In addition to the process of mutual education, the problem of values must be confronted directly—those of the researcher, the client, the subjects, and under some circumstances, the funder. Implicit in a contractual relationship is the assumption that the product is going to be used in some fashion by the buyer. This implication is reinforced by the fact that research is frequently conducted in an action-oriented environment or designed in action-oriented terms and categories. The language of research and generalizations takes its direction, at least in part, from the problems of the client rather than from universalistic empirical theory. Thus the use to which knowledge is likely to be put, i.e., the goals (values) of the client, is of critical concern since the social scientist shares (moral if not legal) responsibility for the results.

Furthermore, until now we have been talking as if the client were a single, easily distinguishable individual or social unit. *It is probably more typical, however, for the client to be a variable rather than a given in the value-centered model,* and consequently it becomes necessary to expend considerable thought and energy in specifying who (or what) the client is. This is obviously crucial for problem definitions, the location of interests that are to guide research, and the communication of results. It is here that the researcher must once more confront his own values and perceptions.

The validity of findings in this model of inquiry presents some special problems. In the two previous models, the researcher was, at least to some extent, insulated from direct pressures from laymen to modify his work to meet their tastes and preferences. Especially in the positivist model, power and wisdom remained with him and the community of scientists who would judge his work according to certain universalistic standards. This power relationship was further reinforced by the fact that the definition of problems for research tended to correspond to the organization of academic specialties and the structure of professional societies. These social and operational mechanisms had a self-interest in enforcing the canons of the positivist model and in guaranteeing the objectivity of the scientist and the validity of his findings. Though the researcher in the value-centered model does not give up his membership in the community of science or his right and ability to do a careful, craftsmanlike job, the direct involvement of a client's interest in his work clearly places the question of his objectivity in a different light. Since the definition of the research problem may not correspond to preexisting disciplinary distinctions, it is not even clear which part of the scientific community he is supposed to be responsive to.

Under such circumstances what guarantees his objectivity and the validity of his findings to his client? Suppose, for example, that the client is his employer. There is some evidence in the literature on organizational behavior that status differences have a marked influence on the flow of information in organizations and that what bosses tell subordinates, and subordinates tell bosses, is shaped by perceptions of these distinctions as much or more than it is by any so-called reality factors. Is there any reason for believing that information generated by the value-centered model of inquiry would be less subject to such influences, especially when it may also be used as a strategic weapon in the internal political struggles that occur in any organization? How does the boss know that he is not being told what is "safe" or what will put the researcher (or his party) in the best light, rather than what is, in some objective sense, true and valid? The problem is similar where the relation is that of consultant, contractor, or grantee and client, and the client is in a position to give or withhold future contracts, grants, or the right to publish findings. How does the client then guarantee himself that he is being told the truth rather than what he wants to hear or what the consultant thinks will maximize his own future earnings or research opportunities?

What guarantees his objectivity and the validity of his findings to his colleagues? Or, perhaps more accurately, how can the community of science be involved so that it can guarantee his work, especially if the problem overlaps the boundaries of more than one discipline or if there are implicit or explicit restrictions on what can be made public? Furthermore, if findings are reported according to the canons of reconstructed logic, there is no opportunity for an independent assessment of the impact of client (and researcher) values on the various stages of the research process. This suggests that questions of validity in this model may require a much more elaborate description of the actual process of research, including the choices confronted and the value environment of confrontation, than is the case with research conducted in the traditions of the other models. Only then (and perhaps not *even* then) can we begin to say that, from the perspective of the community of science, the knowledge and generalizations produced in value-centered research have been validated.

Participation, Objectivity, and Inquiry

Though these models of inquiry have some things in common, they clearly are different in several important ways. They all create empirical knowledge about some reality, but they do so by rather different processes. In each we find the concept of a scientific community, some group of scholars with whom the researcher has a particular relationship, a group that serves as both a frame of reference for and a participant in *some* portion of the process whereby knowledge is produced and evaluated.

In one case, however, this community claims for itself the exclusive monopoly to determine what is or is not truth, what is or is not significant knowledge, what is or is not relevant at a particular point in time; the distance between those who possess this marvelous wisdom and those who do not is at a maximum. Truth, relevance, and significance, however, have a social meaning particular to this model, just as they do in the humanist and value-centered models.

Likewise, the opportunity for participation by nonexperts in the decision-making process by which knowledge is generated and evaluated varies from model to model. As would be expected it is most restricted in the case of the positivist model, where the layman's role is at best a passive one and he is asked to support the scientist on faith alone. Power rests with the researcher and his community. Changes in the theoretical structure, methodology, or understanding of some particular empirical phenomenon are produced internal to the system of inquiry. In contrast, participation is most open in the value-centered model, where a fourth party both has a base of power independent of the researcher and becomes directly involved in identifying the purpose of inquiry and evaluating the goodness of the results. Here the danger is that the researcher will, in fact, *not* inquire into the values of the fourth party and their relation to his own. Nor will he ask whether or not they are good relative to some larger frame of reference, some larger system of values. Instead he merely accepts them as given (objective functions) and defines his role as that of providing information to aid in their achievement.

Finally, let me suggest that the objectivity of the knowledge that is produced in each case is guaranteed, not by the ultimate neutrality of the investigator where neutrality refers to some inner state of mind, but by the range of points of view (values) that must be taken into account in the conduct of inquiry and by the range of interests represented in the audience to whom the researcher is accountable.

Objectivity, the conviction that knowledge is not false, either because it has been distorted by the private perceptions and values of those reporting on it or by groups evaluating it, is the result of complex social and intellectual processes characteristic of each of our models of inquiry.

The individual may believe that observation (sensation) is simple, that the relation between observation and conviction is obvious, and that objectivity arises simply as a result of measurement precision, the proper controls, a careful use of reason, and inner toughness and rigor. Each of these, however, is based on a whole series of prior, untested assumptions and social arrangements. Sensation, for example, is hardly simple, as the experimental psychologists have made us aware; the connection between the physical process and the mental state of being convinced something is so is a mystery, as is the process by which a group—e.g., administrators, scientists, or lawyers—decides something is so.

Somehow knowledge of the empirical world arises from the interaction between private experience and the pictures in our heads. Concepts shape observations of *and* reports about empirical reality. In the positivistic model these pictures presumably arise from the problem-solving experience of the observer, experiences that occur within the particular paradigm generated by the scientific community. A brief example of this interaction between theory, experience, and reporting is provided by a rather provocative study in experimental psychology (Sherman 1951). Two groups of graduate students were shown identical pictures of babies in various physical states. They were asked to suggest the cause or stimulus that most likely produced the pictured condition. The medical students mentioned diseases or physical conditions like colic or hunger most frequently. The clinical psychology students most often referred to psychological states—anger, fear, or frustration!

There is much more interaction between observer and observed allowed for in the humanist model and between observer and client in the value-centered model. Consequently, there are *explicit* opportunities for concepts to be intimately connected to and profoundly shaped by the larger social and political environment in which the observer is conducting inquiry at a particular point in time. Sutherland, for example, demonstrates how different social definitions of what is and is not crime can determine what kind of behavior will be considered criminal, who will be classified as a criminal, and the types of statistics that will be collected to measure crime rate. (Sutherland 1949. For a similar point on the concept of violence, see Skolnick 1969, especially pp. 4–5.)

In conclusion, then, objectivity—the conviction that knowledge is not false because it has been distorted by either the private perceptions and values of those reporting on it or by groups evaluating it—*begins* when information must be shared with others. Objectivity, in this sense, means expanding rather than narrowing a view of reality, our view of the total system and how it works; it means recognizing the necessity of drawing other groups, other values, and other points of view into the process of inquiry; it means being prepared continually to question purpose, examine values, and redefine categories of thought, recognizing that at any point in time they are tenuous, subject to challenge, *and dependent upon* existing social and political arrangements; it means developing better ways of presenting expanded views of reality to different audiences and of drawing them into the process of evaluating (and changing) them as opposed to drawing lines between expert and layman more and more narrowly.

References

Argyris, C. 1968. "Some Unintended Consequences of Rigorous Research." *The Psychological Bulletin* 70 (September):185–197.

Bensman, J. and Vidich, A. 1960. "Social Theory in Field Research." *American Journal of Sociology* 65 (May):577–584.

Blankenship, L. V. 1971. "Public Administration and the Challenge to Reason." In *Public Administration in a Time of Turbulence*, ed. Dwight Waldo. San Francisco: Chandler Publishing Co.

———. 1974. "Management, Politics, and Science: A Nonseparable System." *Research Policy* 3:245–257.

Boguslaw, R. (n.d.). "Values in the Research Society." In *The Research Society*, ed. Evelyn Glatt and Maynard W. Shelly. New York: Gordon and Breach.

Churchman, C. W. 1968. *The Challenge to Reason*. New York: McGraw-Hill Book Co.

Gerth, H. and Mills, C. W. 1964. *Character and Social Structure*. New York: Harcourt Brace Inc.

Hagstrom, W. O. 1965. *The Scientific Community*. New York: Basic Books.

Merton, R. K. 1957. *Social Theory and Social Structure*. Glencoe, Ill.: The Free Press.

Mitroff, I. 1974. "Norms and Counter Norms: A Case-Study of the Ambivalence Scientists." *American Sociological Review* 39 (August):579–595.

Sherman, M. 1951. "The Interpretation of Emotional Responses in Infants." In *Readings in Clinical Psychology*, ed. Wayne Dennis. Englewood Cliffs, N.J.: Prentice-Hall.

Skolnick, J. H. 1969. *The Politics of Protest*. New York: Ballantine Books.

Sutherland, E. H. 1949. *White Collar Crimes*. New York: Dryden Press.

Weber, M. 1958. *The Protestant Ethic and the Spirit of Capitalism*. New York: Charles Scribner.

Chapter 3

The Structure
and Purpose of
Marketing Models*

Gerald Zaltman

Editors' Note

Realizing the difficulties in achieving objectivity in research, we now consider explicitly some of the operations discussed in the previous chapter: How can a manager arrive at a useful picture of the behavior, for instance, of suppliers, competitors, or current and potential buyers? Most marketing decisions (e.g., change a package design or introduce a new brand) are based on some picture of the behavior of interest. Such a picture may be very intuitive. But the author of this chapter shows how it can be made clearer—by a set of operations called model building. The author also points out some of the major difficulties that must be considered for a model to be useful to a decision maker and suggests guidelines to cope with these difficulties.

Introduction

A model is a simplified but organized and meaningful representation of selected attributes of an actual system or process. The attributes are represented

*This paper is adapted from Chapter 3 in G. Zaltman and P. Burger, Marketing Research: Fundamentals and Dynamics, *Hinsdale, Ill.: Dryden Press, 1975.*

intially by concepts which are then linked to form propositions, which in turn are linked to form a model or theory. This paper examines some of the salient issues concerning the validity of concepts, propositions, and models. It also examines some basic concerns the marketer must have in mind with regard to one of the most important tasks a model can perform, the task of explaining marketing phenomena.

Concepts

Concepts are the fundamental units researchers employ in thinking about and trying to solve marketing problems. Examples of frequently used concepts in marketing research are product positioning, market segmentation, brand loyalty, innovation, retailing, convenience goods, and loss leaders. A concept refers to certain characteristics or to phenomena that can be grouped together; it is a symbol representing similarities in otherwise diverse phenomena. Likewise, the term "variable" can be defined as a measured concept. For example, the concept "consumer," as it is used in most marketing contexts, identifies and groups together at least three characteristics related to (1) people in the act of (2) consumption of (3) ideas, goods, and services.

The market researcher must be sensitive to the fact that different concepts are often expressed by the same word. An example is provided by the term "market." In some instances market refers to a set of potential customers, while in another instance it may refer to a place where buyers and sellers congregate.

Another example is the concept of a reference group that is frequently employed in consumer behavior research (Ostlund 1973). A reference group (1) may or may not involve a group of which the consumer is a member, (2) can ever be a member, or (3) ever wants to be a member. Thus it is necessary to be explicit in defining terms and identifying the phenomena to which they refer. This is especially important when comparing research performed by different investigators. Although different investigators may use the same term, we must always ask: Do they refer to the same concept?

Apart from the problem of identical terms being used to refer to different concepts, there are problems of abstraction and operationalization. Concepts may be very specific or highly general, and they can vary with respect to their operational definition. For example, consider opinion leadership, a concept sometimes used in new product research.

At least three operational definitions are possible. Researchers might collect consumer responses to the statement: "My friends or neighbors often come to me for advice." Alternatively, they might use as a stimulus the statement, "I sometimes influence what my friends buy." Still another statement might be, "People come to me more often than I go to them for information about brands." These statements may be considered as alternative operational definitions of opinion leadership for one or more conceptual definitions of opinion leadership. The first definition stresses particular people seeking out the respondent; the second definition stresses influence without indicating whether the information given by the respondent is solicited or unsolicited; the third alternative stresses both the giving and seeking of information. Do all three

Exhibit 3.1

CONCEPT-RELATED QUESTIONS FOR THE MARKETING MANAGER

1. What are the basic concepts relevant to the problem?
2. What are the principal components of the concepts?
3. Are the same concepts used by different researchers? That is, do different researchers identify different concepts as being relevant?
4. Do different researchers use different terms to label the same concept? Conversely, do different concepts have the same term applied to them?
5. Is the concept specific enough to be reliably and validly operational?

operational definitions equally reflect all aspects of the concept of opinion leadership? Obviously not. Thus it is very important to understand the particular bias inherent in an operational definition of a concept. The bias should be evaluated in terms of what aspect of a concept it emphasizes and whether that aspect is the most relevant one for the research problem at hand.

Exhibit 3.1 suggests some basic definitional questions marketing managers could ask of various ideas and research findings that might be presented to them as a basis for decision making. Each question corresponds to a basic concern that various philosophies of science have raised about concepts.

Propositions

Propositions specify relationships among concepts. In this section, after a brief comment on specificity in propositions, emphasis will be placed upon the various forms of relationships among concepts. This section concludes with a discussion of sources of doubt in propositions.

Specificity

Propositions involve statements of relationship among concepts. These relationships may be stated with varying degrees of specificity. Specificity may be relevant in at least two ways. First, there is specificity in terms of the explicitness of the intervening mechanism connecting two variables in the proposition. For example, at a very general level, we may have the proposition "advertising increases sales," while at a more specific level a proposition might state that a certain level of advertising will produce a critical level of interest (intervening variable), which in turn will yield a certain level of sales.

Second, specificity also requires identifying the conditions affecting the propositional relationship. What variables can we specify as being relevant to the proposition? Seasonal variations may be a factor influencing the impact of advertising on sales of certain foods, types of clothing, and so forth. Or the level of advertising necessary to produce a critical level of interest that is satisfied by a purchase may be affected by the nature and extent of general industry advertising.

In addition, in specifying propositional relationships we must deal with the problem of the "form" of any functional relationship. We can specify only the sign of the function's derivative (e.g., increasing or decreasing relationship). Or if we have theoretical or empirical reasons to make stronger commitments, we can hypothesize the specific form as being linear or nonlinear and, in this latter case, which specific nonlinear relationship. By specifying the form of a relationship, we explicitly make commitments about intercepts (i.e., the so-called threshold level) and saturation levels and so on.

The Meaning of Relationships

In evaluating the meaning of a theoretical or empirical relationship, a number of potential pitfalls and bouts must be kept in mind:

Prediction. If a relationship is used for predictive purposes, we must be aware that we make the *ceteris paribus* assumption. For example, if we know from past data that a 10 percent increase in the advertising budget leads to an increase of 15 percent in sales, in using this knowledge to increase our advertising budget we assume there is no change in competitive environment, consumer behavior, or other factors.

Generalization beyond Known Cases. For example, the literature in the diffusion of innovations contains two widely cited generalizations—"early adopters have a greater intelligence than later adopters," and "stimulators of collective innovation decisions are more cosmopolite than other members of the social system"—which are respectively based on only five cases and one case.

A Proposition May Cite an Inferred Variable. The statement that "people who buy new products soon after they are placed on the market are more novelty oriented than people who adopt only after the product is on the market a long time" may imply a third variable—namely, openness to communication. That is, to adopt early, novelty-oriented people must place themselves in a situation to hear about the new product early. This is not stated in the propositions, but it is obviously implied.

A Proposition May State or Imply a Cause-Effect Relationship. The issue of causality has been aptly described as an extensive philosophical thicket. Many people in the marketing discipline as well as in other disciplines argue that, except in a very few real-world situations or in highly artificial situations, causality is impossible to prove. There is always a competing explanation, including one not thought of, that could have produced a given effect. This of course is true. Nevertheless, we can establish highly probable causes, and marketers who do not attempt to establish highly plausible causes of marketing events lose insight that could be of great benefit in their attempts to shape those events to their advantage. Thinking in causal terms provides clues as to what the relevant marketing decision variables are in a given situation. This in turn indicates to marketers what variables or phenomena they can manipulate directly to help

28

bring about a desired situation. The discussion below presents· a few basic requirements for propositions of the nature, "*A* causes *B*."

First, the idea of "cause" is a theoretical concept. It is inferred from observations. Second, *A* and *B* must be defined or operationalized independently so that the indicators involved for each are mutually exclusive. (If the same item is used in operationalizing two concepts, there is bound to be some covariation between the two concepts when the item common to both varies.) A third but somewhat controversial point is that *A* must be temporally prior to *B*. This ignores, however, the fact that the anticipation of an event may bring about its own causes. In some contexts this is referred to as the self-fulfilling prophecy. Fourth, causal links cannot necessarily be inferred, even with perfect correlation between *A* and *B*. Fifth is the determination that variable *X* does indeed cause *Y*, and that the relationship between *X* and *Y* is not simply due to the fact that they are both related to some third variable, *Z*. In this case, a change in *Z* would cause a change in *X* and *Y*, so that it would appear that a change in *X* is actually the cause for a change in *Y*, or vice versa, when in fact they are not directly connected.

Finally, when we say "*A* causes *B*," there are three possible situations involving condition *A*: Condition *A* is a necessary and sufficient condition for *B* to occur; condition *A* is necessary but not sufficient for *B*; and *A* is sufficient but not necessary for event *B*. A *necessary condition* is a state of affairs which, if absent, would result in *B* not happening.

Thus we always want to ask whether the particular variable or concept viewed as the causal factor is a necessary condition. Furthermore, we would want to ask whether there are other variables whose absence or presence constitute necessary conditions for the so-called causal factor to have its impact. For example, store images may have an impact on perceived product quality only when price is high—that is, a relatively high price may be necessary before store image can have an impact on perceived product quality (Stafford & Enis 1969). Second, we must consider *sufficient conditions*, which are states of affairs justifying the prediction of an event: ". . . if *A* is a sufficient condition, then given that we have observed *A* we would automatically expect to observe *B*" (Harvey 1969, p. 87).

Exhibit 3.2 contains several questions relating to propositions suggested by some of the issues discussed in this section. The list is only a representative one. The reader should try to formulate additional questions, such as those associated more explicitly with sources of doubt in propositions.

Models

Types of Models

The terms "theory" and "model" are often used synonymously, with models being the somewhat more frequently employed term in marketing. In this chapter we shall use the term "model."

A model is a *simplified, organized,* and *meaningful* representation of an actual

Exhibit 3.2

Proposition-Related Questions for the Marketing Manager

1. What propositions are implicit but not clearly stated in the research report?
2. For all propositions, how clearly stated is the nature of the relationship between concepts contained in the propositions? For example, does the stated relationship provide insight into the social, psychological, or economic mechanisms connecting the concepts in the proposition?
3. Are there clear cause-and-effect statements embodied in the proposition?
4. Is information provided that describes the condition under which cause and effect may actually take place?
5. Are the data collected to test the propositions based on data gathered at the ranges of the phenomena relevant to the problem at hand?
6. Does the proposition assume information that is not known or not easily interpreted?
7. Are there hidden concepts or variables in the stated propositions?

Exhibit 3.3

Uses of Management Science Models

I. **Understanding Problems—Descriptive and Predictive Models**
   A. Descriptive Models
      1. Transform data into more meaningful forms
      2. Indicate areas for search and experimentation
      3. Generate structural hypotheses for testing
      4. Provide a framework for measurement
      5. Aid in systematic thinking about problem
      6. Provide bases of discussion that will lead to common understanding of problem
   B. Predictive Models
      1. Make forecasts of future events
      2. Validate descriptive models
      3. Determine sensitivity of predictions to model parameters
II. **Solving Problems—Normative Models**
   A. Provide framework for structuring subjective feelings and determining their decision implications
   B. Provide a tool for the analysis of decisions
   C. Assess system implications of decisions
   D. Yield solutions to problems
   E. Determine sensitivity of decision to the model's characteristics
   F. Provide a basis for updating and controling decisions

Source: David B. Montgomery and Glen L. Urban, *Management Science in Marketing,* © 1969. Reprinted by permission of Prentice-Hall, Inc., Englewood Cliffs, N.J.

system or process. As far as marketing research is concerned, there are two major benefits from working with models. First, constructing a model of the phenomena that one is concerned with (*a*) sensitizes researchers to the assumptions they are making about the variables they intuitively feel are important, (*b*) forces researchers to scrutinize the range of possible variables and select those they feel are most important, and (*c*) forces researchers to think about relationships that may exist among the variables deemed relevant. Second, having a model facilitates (*a*) the structuring of research activity, (*b*) the collection of information, (*c*) the organization of information, and (*d*) the interpretation of information. Exhibit 3.3 is a more detailed classification of uses of management science models.

Many kinds of models can be found in the literature. For example, there are "literary" models, sometimes called "implicit" models, i.e., pictures of the world held in our mind. These models may become very explicit in the form of physical models as represented by toy guns, architectural mockups, etc. They are sometimes referred to as iconic models; they have the appearance of reality but do not behave in real ways.

The literature frequently refers to "symbolic" models, which employ some set of symbols to replicate the system or process of concern. Symbolic models may be verbal, schematic, or mathematical. Figure 3.1 illustrates the translation of a verbal model into a logical-flow model and a mathematical model. Moreover, symbolic models may be descriptive, predictive, or normative—the focus being on, respectively, describing how a system functions, predicting future states of a system under specified conditions, and prescribing optimal managerial action vis-à-vis a system.

Another classification of models distinguishes between stochastic and deterministic models, which differ with respect to their explicit consideration of probabilities bearing upon the behavior of variables or relationships among variables.

It has been proposed that it may be useful to distinguish the three types of mathematical models (based on Nicosia & Rosenberg 1972.) First, there are *substantive* models, which must express the structure of consumer thought process and behavior mathematically. The structure being modeled must also contain properties believed to be inherent to consumers. These properties could be elements of the social situation surrounding consumers at the moment of their exposure to an ad—psychological elements, such as consumers' previous experience with the advertised brand, etc. In addition, the relationship among the variables must be stated in a formal language. In this context substantive mathematical models are devices for the translation of known and/or postulated causal relationships into structures with more clearly defined theoretical and/or empirical implications.

A second type of mathematical model is a *statistically based* model. These differ from substantive models in that they do not represent knowledge or hypotheses about elements of consumer thinking mechanisms and behavior. They do, however, predict consumer behavior. For example, Markov models are used to predict brand switching and changes in market shares. Being able to predict brands' market shares is useful but does not provide behavioral insight.

Figure 3.1

Simple Examples of Three Types of Models

Verbal model:

"If I change my price, my competitor will match my price unless it would cause him to lose money."

Logical flow model:

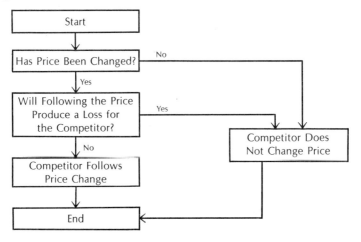

Mathematical model:

$$\bar{P}_c = (1 - I)P_c + IP_n$$

$$I = \begin{cases} 0, \text{ if } P_nQ_c - C_c < 0 \\ 1, \text{ if } P_nQ_c - C_c \geq 0 \end{cases}$$

$\bar{P}_c$ = competitor's new price
P_c = competitor's old price
P_n = price of firm ("my" firm)
Q_c = quantity of sales competitor could sell at P_n
C_c = competitor's total cost of producing and selling Q_c

Source: *David B. Montgomery and Glen L. Urban,* Management Science in Marketing *(Englewood Cliffs, N.J.: Prentice-Hall, 1969), p. 11.*

A third type of mathematical model is the *estimation-inference* model. There are two subtypes. The first is not addressed to problems of possible causative relationships, but rather to the search structure or dimensions underlying a set of manifest data. Factor-analytic models, cluster analysis, and multidimensional scaling models fall into this category. These models are used to measure psychological variables such as brand image and perceptual maps of different products. The second subgroup—which includes correlation, regression analyses, and canonical correlation—is used to infer relationships between a set of explanatory variables and one or more dependent variables.

There is an underlying dimension of desirability concerning symbolic models. The researcher should start with verbal models and translate them into schematic or logical-flow models which in turn are ultimately to be converted into quantitative models. An illustration of this is presented in Figure 3.1. For many marketing research problems, it is often sufficient to develop only the schematic or logical-flow model. We shall consider below some of the criteria and processes involved in building models.

Model-Building Process

Keeping in mind the problem and the manager's perspective, the first step is to select variables for the model and determine what other possible variables were omitted and why. The next step is to hypothesize the relationships among variables in the model. Also, it is useful to establish what other relationships might exist but which were rejected, and why they were rejected.

Models can be made more complex or simpler by altering just a few parameters, as indicated in Table 3.1.

Exhibit 3.4 presents several basic questions marketers must be sensitive to in their use of models. As with earlier sets of questions, these are derived from a sample of some of the basic issues raised in the philosophy of science.

Explanation

One very important function of models in marketing is to assist both the researcher and manager in understanding market phenomena. This understanding is partly reflected by the ability to explain the dynamics of the phenomena of concern. Explanation is defined here as the ascription of causes to an event. Having a good explanation of an event provides a very powerful basis for predicting changes in or occurrences of the event and for attempting to manipulate or control that event.

Systematic Requirements

Scientific explanations must meet two systematic requirements. These have been labeled the requirement of explanatory relevance and the requirement of testability. Explanatory relevance means the account of some phenomenon provided by an explanation would constitute good grounds for expecting that the phenomenon would appear under the specified circumstances. Explanatory

Table 3.1

MODELS CAN BE MADE MORE

Complex by:	Simple by:
• making constants into variables	• making variables into constants
• adding variables	• eliminating variables
• using nonlinear relations	• using linear relations
• adding weaker assumptions and restrictions	• adding stronger assumptions and restrictions
• permitting randomness	• eliminating randomness

Exhibit 3.4

MODEL- OR THEORY-RELATED QUESTIONS FOR THE MARKETING MANAGER

1. Are all the relevant concepts and propositions included in the model? Is there some systematic exclusion of relevant ideas that may bias the results of the research?
2. Are the underlying assumptions of the model used made clear by the researcher?
3. Does the researcher state the various limitations of his model?
4. Does the model provide the necessary description of the situation being researched if description is the goal or purpose of developing and testing a model?
5. Does the model provide the necessary predictions if prediction is the goal?
6. Does the model provide the desired explanations if that is the goal?
7. Are normative guidelines provided where desired?
8. If a verbal model is involved, how readily can it be quantified?
9. Is the model rich enough in terms of concepts and propositions to allow logical deductions of certain outcomes, given certain hypothesized beginning conditions?

relevance is achieved when "the explanatory information adduced affords good grounds for believing that the phenomenon to be explained did, or does, indeed occur. This condition must be met if we are to be entitled to say: 'That explains it—the phenomenon in question was indeed expected under the circumstances'" (Hempel 1966, p. 91).

An explanation is devoid of empirical content; no empirical findings could support it or disconfirm it, and consequently it provides little or no grounds for expecting a particular phenomenon—it lacks what Hempel calls objective explanatory power. Thus the requirement of testability is that scientific explanations must be capable of empirical test. An explanation that meets the first requirement (empirical relevance) also meets the requirement of testability, whereas the converse does not hold.

Causality in Explanation

The definition of an explanation employed here relies heavily on the concept of causation discussed earlier. A very brief return to the notion of "cause" will be helpful. For the researcher, the object of explanation should be to provide, with as high a degree of certainty as possible, information about what variables influence, produce, or affect other variables. It is necessary to determine the nature of the marketing decision variables (causes) so that procedures can be established for manipulating them. Only when hypotheses are presented in this way can they be of maximum utility in deriving market implications. It will be useful to formulate a causal statement in a marketing context and use this statement to discuss the properties of causal laws.

Managerial Implications and Scientific Causal Statement

If customers feel that the salesperson really cares about them and spends time on them which could otherwise be spent on other "prospects," they may feel indebted to the salesperson and will want to give him or her some business. Stated more formally: *Norms of reciprocity experienced by customers will affect the personal selling situation.*

The two variables in the above statement are norms, or feelings of reciprocity, and the outcome of a selling effort. The connecting mechanism at the individual level might be that feelings of obligation (in turn explained by social exchange theory) develop within consumers as they come to perceive that the salesperson is investing in the selling situation resources valuable to him or her. Because of the apparent opportunity cost incurred by the salesperson (as perceived by the prospect) in the relationship with the consumer, the latter will reciprocate by rewarding the salesperson with a purchase. A number of things in the causal sentence that are properties of causal statements should be noted:

1. The statement assumes, for example, that high levels of reciprocity experienced by customers should be found in most successful personal selling situations.
2. Changes in the level of experienced reciprocity will produce changes in the frequency of successful personal selling.
3. Successful selling efforts by salespeople do not produce feelings of reciprocity among customers. (This may at first glance seem contradictory, but salespeople may only activate or stimulate this variable, not create it.)
4. There can be contexts where the causal relationship does not apply. Presumably it would not apply to "order-taking" personal-selling situations but would apply to "creative" personal-selling situations.
5. Other variables, such as changes in level of disposable income or advertising, could cause a change in sales without invalidating the causal statement.
6. Most important, we do not know that a given change in sales is in fact caused by a change in reciprocity (either among a given group or by

exposure of other groups to the sales effort). Even when variations in reciprocity are associated with variations in sales, controlling for all other variables, one cannot conclude with absolute certainty that the causal statement is true. There is always the chance that a variable or a set of variables (including measuring errors and problems in the research design) we have not thought of has produced the change in sales.

Levels of Explanation

There are at least four levels of explanation in the behavioral sciences (Doby 1969). These are presented in Table 3.2.

A good illustration of these four levels of explanation involving behavioral phenomena of relevance to marketing is presented by H. G. Barnett's (1953) theory of innovation as a basis for cultural change. Only elements of this theory, his notion of basic wants as necessary conditions for innovation, will be discussed. At level one of explanation, adoption is actually observed; it is known—not just assumed—to have occurred.

At level two, the phenomenon is observed to be of a certain nature, Q, in this instance the purchase of an ultramodern architectural blueprint for a permanent home or possibly the actual purchase of such a home. Thus the nature of the event, Q, consists of a purchase (a particular behavior) of an object perceived as new with new being defined in terms of qualitative distinction rather than in terms of time. Q, then, is composed of three factors: (1) purchase behavior, (2) perceptual processes, and (3) an object having qualitative distinction from other objects in the same general class of objects. Q may have been produced by, or be a result of, central subliminal wants (a type of self-want) and creative wants (a type of want that we relabel as autotelic wants). These two wants represent x_1 and x_2 in Table 3.2. Central subliminal wants are those that relate to the individual's need for self-preservation and self-definition. They influence how we structure and organize our environment. Creative wants emphasize accomplishment with the process or act of being creative as impor-

Table 3.2

LEVELS OF EXPLANATION

Level of Explanation	Description
One	A certain phenomenon (sales) has an empirical existence.
Two	The phenomenon is of the nature Q and is produced by factors $x_1, x_2, \ldots, x_n$. x_1 might be customer characteristics, x_2 salesman characteristics, and so forth.
Three	Factors $x_1, x_2, \ldots, x_n$ are interactive or have interacted in manner $y_1, y_2, \ldots, y_n$ to produce in some past or present time a phenomenon of the nature Q. y_1, for example, could be a norm of reciprocity.
Four	Factors $x_1, x_2, \ldots, x_n$ interact in a manner $y_1, y_2, \ldots, y_n$ for reasons $w_1, w_2, \ldots, w_n$, thus producing a phenomenon of the nature Q. w_1 would be the reason why reciprocity exists.

tant as—and possibly more important than—the resultant innovation or objects. In general, wants of this nature result from dissatisfaction with the accepted way of doing things.

Level three is concerned with explaining how central subliminal wants (x_1) and creative wants (x_2) interact in manner y_1 to produce the adoption of the innovation in question. Explanation in this case takes the form of describing what y_1 is. In our example, creative wants interact with central subliminal wants. The need to define oneself as unique, avant-garde, etc., together with dissatisfaction with existing modes of architecture as means of achieving this self-definition, lead to the adoption of radical architectural style. But in level three the emphasis is upon the manner of interaction. It could be explained that creative wants stimulate (the manner of interaction) central subliminal wants and that, for reasons of congruence or cognitive consistency, the central subliminal wants are expressed in creative ways, i.e., the individual establishes a self-definition of being an innovator. Being interested in doing innovative things and being dissatisfied with existing conditions bring about the idea that he or she is an innovator, which becomes expressed in such behavior as the acquisition of a radically or at least a significantly different home.

At level four explanation goes beyond the relationship of the x's to each other and attempts to account for the reasons $(w_1, w_2,$ etc.) why factors x interact in manner y_1. An explanation at this level has already been given. It was stated above that for reasons of cognitive consistency, creative wants (factor x_1) cause central subliminal wants (factor x_2) to express themselves in innovative, i.e., creative, ways. The notion of cognitive consistency in this illustration constitutes the reason, w_1.

Evaluating Explanations

There are four basic criteria for evaluating explanations that will be presented here. These are: scope, precision, power, and reliability. Each is discussed briefly below.

Scope. Scope refers to the range of events to which an explanation can be applied. A number of hypotheses and theories relevant to marketing and having broad scope can be cited briefly. The two-step flow of communication hypothesis is a good example of an explanation of marketing-relevant communication behavior. Exchange theory, as articulated by George Homans and Peter Blau, is a theory of wide scope and relevant to marketing. E. T. Hall's theory of culture as communication is another explanation with extremely broad scope, although difficult to test empirically.

Precision. "The precision of an explanation refers to the exactness with which the concepts used in explanation are related to empirical indicators, and the precision with which the rules of interaction of the variable in the system are stated" (Meehan 1968, p. 117). Note that there are two areas of precision referred to in this quote. The first concerns the relationship between a concept and its empirical indicator. The second concerns precision in the statements concerning the relationships among concepts.

With regard to precision in the first case, there is always an unavoidable gap, a lack of precision, between a concept and its empirical operationalization. "In a very real sense no theoretically defined concepts can be directly translated into operations nor can theoretical propositions be tested empirically" (Blalock 1968, p. 14). In an article largely devoted to this problem of precision, Zaltman concludes: "Perhaps one of the greatest obstacles inhibiting the effective application of the behavioral sciences to marketing problems is that this very important quality of isomorphism (between theoretical and operational systems) can only be determined intuitively" (1970, p. 32).

The second aspect of precision concerns precision in the stated relationships between concepts. Blalock (1968, p. 18) argues vigorously for specifying relationships in the form of direct causal links stated in terms of covariations and temporal sequences for reasons of explication, testing, and measurement.

Exhibit 3.5

EXPLANATION-RELATED QUESTIONS FOR THE MARKETING MANAGER

1. Is the explanation of a market phenomenon provided by researchers and others capable of being tested so that insight can be obtained concerning its accuracy? Can the ideas be measured in the real world?

2. Are marketing decision variables—those capable of manipulation by the marketer—clearly identified?

3. Are the variables affected by the marketing decision variables clearly identified?

4. What is the level of explanation provided? Can it be moved to a higher level of understanding?

5. What is the scope or variety of market events encompassed by the explanation?

6. How closely related are the concepts or variables used and the empirical indicators employed to describe the state of the concepts or variables? In other words, how precisely are the basic ideas in an explanation related by real-world phenomena?

7. Are there possible interrelationships between the marketing decision variables or concepts and between the resultant variables? Are these possible or actual interrelationships clearly identified and described?

8. Does the explanation enable the manager to intervene in the market process effectively? Alternatively, is the information provided in such a way that the action implications for the manager are clear?

9. Is it likely that concepts other than those contained in the explanation will be active and disrupt or render useless the explanation?

10. Marketers are able to intervene in the marketplace more effectively, thus increasing the likelihood of marketing objectives being attained.

11. A more constructively critical approach can be pursued in the evaluation of the overall research process.

This last factor—measurement—is a key factor influencing precision. In the first case it affects the accuracy of the operationalized concept: the smaller the measurement error, the more isomorphic the relationship between theoretical concepts and their empirical indicators. In the second place measurement affects the detection of such things as interaction effects which influence the interpretation of relationships among explanatory variables.

Power. Power refers to the degree of control over the environment an explanation provides. Power depends upon the precision of the description and explanation, and upon the completeness of the variables. An explanation encompassing all, or many, relevant variables and providing linking statements, as discussed in the preceding section on precision, is considered more powerful than an explanation that involves few variables inarticulately expressed and relies heavily on the clause, "other things being equal."

Reliability. Reliability refers to the frequency with which factors not included in the explanation interrupt the situation the explanation concerns. It would be unusual, of course, to have complete reliability in marketing and the behavioral sciences in general. Reliability must be considered as a relative thing and not in absolute terms. In some ways reliability is related to the degree of precision. We can say that a certain behavior is accounted for—or explained by—the life-style of the actor. This statement is rather reliable, given its vague all-inclusiveness, but it is not very precise—certainly not as precise as breaking life-style down into principal component parts and explaining behavior in terms of these parts.

Exhibit 3.5 presents several questions a marketing manager would want to have in mind when considering explanations.

Conclusion

This chapter discussed some of the issues involved in the design and evaluation of models. Consideration of these issues may provide marketing management with some of the following benefits:

1. Problem definition is made more accurate.
2. Research questions related to the marketing problem become more focused and precise.
3. Marketing research becomes clearer and more precise with regard to the statement of behavioral and marketing concepts and their measurement.
4. Marketing research is conducted in a more methodical and systematic way.
5. Ideas and hypotheses are tested under circumstances where their credibility is more readily established or desired.
6. The accuracy and completeness of description and explanation are enhanced.
7. Better marketing predictions can be made.

References

Barnett, H. G. 1953. *Innovation: The Basis of Cultural Change*. New York: McGraw-Hill.

Blalock, H. M., Jr. 1968. "The Measurement Problem: A Gap between the Languages of Theory and Research." In *Methodology in Social Research*, ed. H. M. Blalock, Jr., and A. B. Blalock. New York: McGraw-Hill.

Doby, J. T. 1969. "Logic and Levels of Scientific Explanation." In *Sociological Methodology*, ed. E. F. Borgatta. San Francisco: Jossey-Bass.

Harvey, D. 1969. *Explanation in Geography*. London: Edward Arnold Publishers.

Hempel, C. G. 1966. *Philosophy of Natural Science*. Englewood Cliffs, N.J.: Prentice-Hall.

Meehan, E. J. 1968. *Explanation in Social Science: A System Paradigm*. Homewood, Ill.: The Dorsey Press.

Nicosia, F. M. and Rosenberg, B. 1972. "Substantive Modeling in Consumer Attitude Research: Some Practical Uses." In *Proceedings of the 4th Attitude Research Conference*, ed. R. I. Haley. Chicago: American Marketing Association.

Ostlund, L. 1973. "Role Theory and Group Dynamics." In *Consumer Behavior*, ed. S. Ward and T. Robertson. Englewood Cliffs, N.J.: Prentice-Hall.

Stafford, J. E. and Enis, B. M. 1969. "The Price-Quality Relationship: An Extension." *Journal of Marketing Research* 6:456–458.

Zaltman, G. 1970. "Marketing Inference in the Behavioral Sciences." *Journal of Marketing* 34 (July):32.

Chapter 4

Some Practical Problems in Building Substantive Marketing Models

Luis V. Dominguez and *F. M. Nicosia**

Editors' Note

The authors discuss some advanced steps toward the development of "strong" theories and models. They suggest that marketing research and management should move beyond the current use of statistical estimation of one or more verbal propositions—a theory—describing a marketing phenomenon. The authors argue for mathematical representations of a theory *and* for analyses of these representations *prior* to empirical work.

The chapter encapsules both the evolving interaction between a researcher's mental picture of what is "reality" and what reality seems in fact to be, and above all, the practical advantages for researchers to capture their learning about reality by precise formal representations of it. In many ways the authors tell us that classical mechanics and useful models could not have evolved from the empirical work by Galileo and others without the use of calculus.

Indirectly, the authors also want us to remember that the behavior of

Luis V. Dominguez and F. M. Nicosia are from the Graduate School of Business, Indiana University, and Graduate School of Business Administration, University of California, Berkeley, respectively. The authors acknowledge the helpful criticisms of Marcel Corstjens.

so-called random variables is very predictable. They remind us that the substantive model of the behavior of a free particle is "deterministic" in the sense that the Shroedinger equation, even though it contains neither random variables nor the notion of randomness, has many practical uses.

Introduction

Terms like "model" and "model building" have become a regular part of the jargon of social and administrative science, but their meanings vary considerably from one field to another. Various taxonomies of models have been proposed in marketing and in other fields (e.g., Kaplan 1964, Lipstein 1965, Montgomery & Urban 1969, Nicosia & Rosenberg 1972, and Sheth 1967). The focus of this chapter, however, is on the features of one particular type of model and model-building process that Nicosia and Rosenberg (1972) have labeled "substantive." Specifically, we shall examine a sequence of steps for gaining as much insight as possible into complex systems without necessarily engaging in highly complex research designs. Our objective is to point out ways of designing and analyzing substantive models for their usefulness to managers and researchers.

Criteria of Substantive Modeling

The growing skepticism toward words like "model" and "model building" is a healthy development that points to a greater maturity in contemporary research. In marketing, as in other fields, the practical value of a model must receive a high order of priority. This value depends partly on how much thought has been put into steps geared to facilitating use and implementation, but it also depends in a major way on the very *substantive* content of the model.

There are several criteria to be met for a model to be substantive. For the purposes of this chapter, a model is said to be substantive to the extent that it meets four specific criteria:

1. As in Kanter (1957), it is a view that offers an explanation of *how* and/or *why* a phenomenon occurs. An example is Simon's (1957) model of social interaction.
2. It meets the criteria of "decision relevance" and "realism." In other words, a substantive model seeks answers to the types of questions that managers are interested in. Thus it conceptually and operationally defines those aspects (critical variables) of the phenomenon and those relationships among such variables that are relevant to managers.
3. The chief focus is on the *inherent properties* of the process being studied. One would like to be able to generalize as far as possible.
4. The model is or can be reduced to mathematical expression. A mathematical expression *and* analysis is not only necessary for statistical estimation, but it is also a vehicle for *extending* the results of the model. By means of its analytically or otherwise derived properties, one can lay down further hypotheses.

These criteria allow one to distinguish substantive models from statistically based models and estimation-inference models in which the emphasis is, for example, on prediction, detection of association, classification, and data simplification. (For a classical discussion of such distinctions, see Morgan & Andrews 1974 and Einhorn 1974; see also the description of the new Ph.D. program in the methodology of behavioral sciences at the University of Chicago.) These criteria underlie two themes of substantive model building that are at the core of all "hard" sciences: (1) suitable and powerful explanations of empirical phenomena derive only from unified theoretical schemes, and (2) if a theoretical scheme is to be useful, it must be reducible to symbolic, mathematical expression. It follows that substantive model building is most apt to succeed in the physical sciences and, in general, in those behavioral disciplines where researchers are willing to state their understanding of a process in a mathematical form of representation (see Matthews 1964, Lipstein 1965, Nicosia 1966, Papandreou 1958, Sethi et al. 1973, and Simon 1957 for a few examples).

In the following sections we shall discuss two of the more salient features of substantive models—namely, (*a*) those operations that are necessary in the building of one, and (*b*) those operations that involve the explicit derivations of the properties implied by the theory the model represents.

As an introduction to this discussion, it will be useful to consider briefly how substantive model building relates to current work in quantitative marketing. An examination of Figure 4.1 indicates that substantive models are a further step in the natural evolution of the contributions that research can make to management—from simple insights into the nature of a given marketing phenomenon to gradual refinements of initial insights into more precise and stronger representations of the structure and processes governing the behavior of such a phenomenon (for an examination of this trend in consumer research, see Nicosia 1977).

In Figure 4.1 we begin with a meaningful management question. Deciding what to do about a marketing phenomenon is explicitly or implicitly relying on some "hypotheses" about what makes the phenomenon behave the way it does and how it will react to the decision. Research contributes to decision making by progressively specifying and strengthening initial insights. To illustrate, in an almost historical sequence, we see that the first insight (theory) into why consumers do the things they do is to speculate that they react to price or that they are driven by some Freudian sexual need. These images of buyers—as Kanter (1957) noted long ago—guide empirical research, the results of which lead to revisions (see step 1 in Figure 4.1).

Not only in marketing, but in many other disciplines, one of these revisions consists of refining the early images into more complex ones, especially because of the realization that marketing phenomena consist of multivariable processes. For instance, we learn that the demand for cars is not only a function of car prices, but also of several other variables (e.g., income, general price level, assets, and intentions to buy). To illustrate, Ferber and Nicosia (1976) speculate that car purchases are not only a function of intentions to buy cars but also of intentions to buy other durable goods and that, in turn, these intentions may be a function of the age of, and satisfaction with, the presently owned car. Such

Figure 4.1

SUBSTANTIVE MODEL BUILDING:
THE NEXT STEP IN DEVELOPING RESEARCH CONTRIBUTIONS TO MANAGEMENT

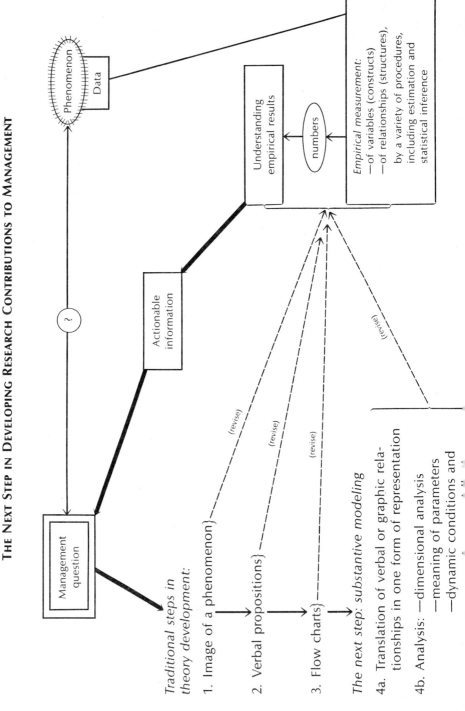

Traditional steps in theory development:

1. Image of a phenomenon}

2. Verbal propositions} ——

3. Flow charts}

The next step: substantive modeling

4a. Translation of verbal or graphic relationships in one form of representation

4b. Analysis: —dimensional analysis
—meaning of parameters
—dynamic conditions and

speculations or verbal propositions are usually "tested" by a variety of inference procedures, and the results lead to revisions—i.e., some learning about the phenomenon under study may be occurring (see step 2 in Figure 4.1).

Note that at this stage of possible research contributions, propositions are stated verbally, and when they tend to interact with each other, they are tested only in a recursive fashion.

The next step, of course, is to recognize explicitly the interdependence among a set of propositions. Thus researchers begin to represent a set of interacting propositions by "causal" flow charts. Here too, we turn to a variety of empirical tests, from traditional to newer procedures, such as path analysis (for an application of path analysis in marketing, see Monroe and Guiltinan 1975). From the tests' results, we tend to learn and thus revise the original specification of the theory, i.e., the representation of the structure and process of a phenomenon (see step 3 in Figure 4.1).

As is known, even at this level of specification, "mistakes" can be made (for example, see the discussions concerning the empirical "tests" by Farley & Ring 1969 of some aspects of the flow charts proposed by Howard & Sheth 1969 or the specific examples in Arbuckle 1971). The term "mistakes" above is used in a very specific sense—it refers only to the fact that the specification of any theory is not sufficient for purposes of empirical measurement unless two further steps are taken: (*a*) encoding such theory into a substantive model, and (*b*) analyzing such a model in manners traditional in many other disciplines.

In the following sections we shall share some of the technical knowledge that illustrates why these two steps—(*a*) and (*b*)—are at least necessary for learning from empirical measurement what are, in fact, the structure and processes governing the behavior of a phenomenon. As in many other disciplines, improving research contributions to marketing decision makers depends partly on our ability and willingness to move beyond the traditional steps listed in Figure 4.1.

Building a Substantive Model

A model, like the conclusion of a reasoned argument, is no stronger than its weakest link. Marketing research has put the bulk of its emphasis on the design of data-collection schemes and the properties of estimation techniques, especially inference of possible relationships; but perhaps the most difficult problems relate to the definition of the model. Part of the difficulty lies in a comparative lack of use of mathematical forms of representation in behavioral science and marketing and lack of explicit concern with the dynamic aspects of behavior. This is in clear contrast to economics, where mathematical analysis of the behavior of dynamic economic systems has been a primary concern of researchers and, indeed, has anteceded and spurred the development of estimation techniques that could handle the theoretical implications of those models (for a discussion of this, see Blalock 1969 and Nicosia and Rosenberg 1972).

Since the starting point in substantive model-building efforts is a *per force* tentative statement of a theory, it becomes essential to derive testable implications from a model of such theory. As will be seen, it is the detailed analysis of the implications of a model that separates substantive from purely numerical, situation-bound expressions (e.g., $y = a + b_1x_1 + b_2x_2 + \cdots + b_nx_n + \varepsilon$), from which generalization is rather hazardous.

The first model-building step is to define the system according to its intended use: the units of description (whether consumers, market segments, or entire markets), the endogenous variable(s) whose behavior is to be explained, the exogenous or external variables from other systems, the functional relations among variables that determine the system's behavior, and the boundaries that separate the system from others.

Clearly, this is more art than science. But the criteria of realism and decision relevance are highly useful: *a model ought to portray what theory, managerial expertise, and the researcher's own insights* indicate about the behavior of a system, and it should explain *how* and *why* a system acts as it does, at a level of detail consistent with the inputs that the model is supposed to make into users' decisions. Although precise rules for determining the acceptable ranges of realism and decision relevance cannot be stated, one can suggest four substantive levels. They are illustrated in the context of a marketing planning model.

Level 1: Specification of How Individual Components of the Real Systems Operate. For example, how marketing decisions at the factory level influence channel demand for a product.

Level 2: Relations among the System's Components. That is, the network of actions and reactions of manufacturers, intermediaries, and final users of a line of competing products. This is the structure of the core marketing system.

Level 3: Behavior of the Entire System. That is, its character as an operating unit. This encompasses the stability of the system, its competitive character, and the rules of control and management that stem from its analysis.

Level 4: Interaction with Higher-Level Systems. For example, it may be that as a by-product of level 3 it becomes possible to characterize both the demand for raw materials, labor, and capital inputs of this industry sector and its outputs to other sectors and the causal relationships that govern these interactions. An example of this is Cohen's pioneering study (1960) of the shoe, hide, leather sequence.

Before the higher substantive levels can be contemplated, problems at levels 1 and 2 must be tackled. Loosely stated theories that are not easily translatable to operational form or that are remotely connected to or describe only a small fraction of a system provide the shakiest foundation for substantive model building. There are four questions that are crucial in the beginning of a model-building effort:

1. Does the model incorporate reputable theory and managerial expertise?
2. Do the model's parameters capture the meaning intended by a theory and/or a user's question?

3. How well does the model describe concrete empirical cases?
4. How well does it compare with simpler as well as more complex models?

We shall discuss below the first two of these questions, for they relate to the nature of building substantive models. The other two—numbers 3 and 4—involve complex issues concerning not only statistical inference but scientific methodologies and cannot be considered in this chapter.

Focus of the Model

Most outstanding models employ theory mainly as a *focus*, an integrative scheme into which are incorporated factual observations and opinions of informed people (notably, decision makers and other personnel of an organization, trade, or industry). An outstanding behavioral science example of this is Simon's (1957) model of group interaction. It is based on the notion that exchange is motivated by profit. Simon extended this idea to the process of interpersonal communication and influence in a functioning group, combining it with casual observation, behavioral science evidence, and some deductive reasoning. Note that while the starting point was static microeconomic theory, the resulting model was dynamic in character. It was also a much more parsimonious statement than would be expected from someone else who would have started without a unifying theoretical framework. Despite its parsimony the model describes attitudinal and behavioral mechanisms (level 1), their interdependencies (level 2), and their joint operation (level 3). The model might more properly be termed "a family of models" (more about this point later) that may be enriched with exogenous variables that are specific to concrete settings (size and cohesiveness of a group, for example) in order to make it applicable to a given case. But its inherent structure becomes both the hypothesis and the mathematical model.

Marketing examples are found in the development of consumer decision making models by Lipstein (1965), Nicosia (1966), and Sethi et al. (1973). If one starts with the premise that consumer behavior is an ongoing process of adaptation to the environment, a model of communication effects must be addressed to *dynamic* response behavior. How the response mechanism is defined is a matter of interpretation. For instance, any interpretation of empirical findings from the point of view of basic social psychology (from Tolman's sign-gestalt to Lewin's gestalt and Simon's problem-solving approach) led Nicosia to adopt three verbal propositions:

Level 1. Communication effects begin to operate through a "funneling" scheme. Attitudinal effects are brought into a more specific focus (motivation to buy) and thereby to choice behavior followed by feedbacks into attitudinal/ motivational states.

Level 2. Attitude and purchase behavior follow a mutually adaptive, dynamic process.

Level 3. The dynamic process is described by a disequilibrium between the attitude level and the purchase behavior rate. Disequilibria can be induced by advertising stimuli.

Clearly, this is a parsimonious statement that oversimplifies features of thought processes other researchers will regard as essential. But a key aim of substantive model building is to arrive iteratively at a more efficient balance between parsimony and general explanatory-predictive ability, i.e., between simplicity and ability to reproduce the behavior of the system under study. Another aim of substantive model building is to extract maximum information from the model. For this it is necessary to turn to its operational form.

Operational Form and Its Interpretation

A prerequisite to extracting substantive content is to operationalize the model, i.e., to translate verbal propositions into quantitative, *and then* empirical terms. The first step toward quantification is to *map* the system by means of a *causal* diagram. For example, the possible impact of various communication stimuli ($C = C_1, \ldots, C_t$) on brand attitude (A), motivation to buy (M), and buying (B), and the dynamic interactions may be graphed as in Figure 4.2.

Numerous equations will satisfy that graph. The second step, translating the graph into a system of equations, involves deciding what variables go into which equations and what the functional form ought to be. But equally important, it must reflect one's premises about the character of the system. A plausible *quantitative* representation of the three verbal propositions above is in Nicosia (1966, p. 209):

$$\frac{dB(t)}{dt} = b[M(t) - \beta B(t)] \tag{1}$$

$$M(t) = mA(t) \tag{2}$$

$$\frac{dA(t)}{dt} = a[A(t) - \alpha B(t)] + cC(t). \tag{3}$$

The next operation in substantive model building is to examine the meaning of a model's coefficients. In the model above, each coefficient in the

Figure 4.2

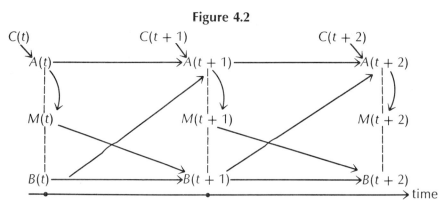

equation system has a precise psychological meaning. For instance, $1/\beta$ represents the rate at which motivational changes are released into behavior changes. Thus if

$$0 < 1/\beta < 1,$$

"an increase in the level of motivation leads to a smaller increase in the level of buying" (Nicosia 1966, p. 210). On the other hand when $\beta < 0$, the more motivation, the less buying. If this last case is considered unreasonable, then other mechanisms of behavior must be considered.

This examination of the meaning of a model's coefficients must be *conducted prior to estimation,* for it allows one to state the behavioral bounds beyond which the model would be an inadequate representation of a marketing phenomenon. Presumably, as the model succeeds or fails in making sense of behavior in selected settings, a clearer idea is gained of the realism and generality of the model.

Dimensional Analysis: A Measurement and a Theory-Interpretive Device

The construction of substantive models requires two additional operations prior to empirical work. From engineering to advanced econometrics, these operations are referred to as dimensional analysis (see, e.g., Bridgman 1963 and DeJong 1967).

First, given the tendency in quantitative marketing to emphasize only empirical estimation, dimensional analysis is crucial, for it is one of the necessary foundations of empirical measurement. In any case of "strong" inference, and especially in cases where we depend on statistical inference to estimate relationships among n variables, the use of dimensional analysis assures that the numerical estimates of the values of a model's parameters are "real."

To illustrate, given the model in equations (1) to (3), we could succumb to the temptation of proceeding directly with the estimation of its parameters (a, b, c, m, α, and β). If we do this, we may read "numbers" in a computer output but will not know whether such numbers are "measures," for we have not determined the dimensional constant(s) of each parameter. In the case of the coefficient β, the dimension is $[1/\$]$; the dimensions of b are $[\$]/[t]$; m is a scalar; and so on. Whenever we cannot determine the dimensional constants of a model's parameters, we do know that the proposed model is not yet a model of anything.

It is in this latter sense that dimensional analysis is fundamental to the modeling of marketing phenomena. When theory and experience suggest only vaguely what should be the operational form of a model, there is little assurance that a particular representation is correct, *even if* its basic verbal propositions are upheld empirically. In particular, a model builder would want to know:

1. whether there are one, several, or no possible representations of a theory as stated;
2. whether more than one theory can result in a specific operational model;

3. what some of the derived properties of a model are, such as that represented by equations (1)–(3), above.

Dimensional analysis offers the model builder a number of checks that are instrumental in answering these questions and that, in some circumstances, can even be of direct help in estimation of response equations (Dominguez 1973). The analysis starts with an assumption about the functional form among the n variables in a model (e.g., linear or Cobb-Douglas) involving r primary dimensions, such as advertising dollars, number of retail outlets served, and time. A rule of thumb is that there are a maximum of $s = n - r + 1$ solutions. The obvious value of this rule is to check whether a "theory" can be operationalized ($s > 0$), and if so, what its alternative expressions are and whether one that has been proposed agrees with the "theory." Furthermore, it could be used to reconcile models, i.e., do alternative formulations express the same theory? It can also be used to tighten a theory so that only one or a few solutions are possible (see DeJong 1967 and Drhymes 1970, pp. 210–211).

Illustration

Suppose that an advertising agency wants to estimate the level of advertising expenditures by one of its large accounts. It is known that the account uses advertising (A) to increase sales (U); that sales respond exponentially to advertising and distribution effort (N); and that if A and N increase by any factor $K > 0$, sales increase in the same proportion. The sales response function is:

$$U = cA^\alpha N^{1-\alpha}. \tag{4}$$

The dimensionalities of the variables are (see DeJong 1967, pp. 35–51):

$$U\varepsilon[ST^{-1}] \tag{5}$$
$$A\varepsilon[DT^{-1}]$$
$$N\varepsilon[Q].$$

The primary dimensions are S (quantity sold), T (time), D (advertising gross impressions), and Q (number of outlets carrying the product). The dimensional constant c is:

$$c\varepsilon[SD^{-\alpha}Q^{\alpha-1}T^{\alpha-1}]. \tag{6}$$

Dimensional analysis may now be applied to determining the function for the demand for advertising. The demand will depend on the productivity of marketing effort, the price of the product (P), the number of outlets (N), and the cost per advertising gross impression (a). Now, the constant c is a scale factor that affects the rate of sales that will be produced by any (A, N) level of effort and, hence, may be used as a productivity measure. Thus advertising demand will be:

$$A_D = f(P, N, a, c), \tag{7}$$

with dimensionalities:

$$A_D\varepsilon[DT^{-1}] \tag{8}$$

$$P\varepsilon[MS^{-1}]$$

$$a\varepsilon[MD^{-1}]$$

$$C\varepsilon, \text{ as in } (6)$$

$$N\varepsilon, \text{ as in } (5),$$

where M represents the dimension "money." There are a total of five primary dimensions and five variables, so there is only one solution.

To obtain the solution, seek a ratio whose dimensionality is [1]. This ratio is:

$$\frac{C_A PN^{1-\alpha}}{aA_D^{1-\alpha}} \varepsilon \frac{[SD^{-\alpha}Q^{\alpha-1}T^{\alpha-1}] [MS^{-1}Q^{1-\alpha}]}{[MD^{-1}][D^{1-\alpha}T^{\alpha-1}]} = [1] \tag{9}$$

From this, the demand for advertising is derived as:

$$A_D = \left(\frac{C_A P}{\gamma_a}\right)^{1/(1-\alpha)} N. \tag{10}$$

This equation has been derived solely from the sales response equation (3) and the use of dimensional analysis. It is the theoretically correct expression of the demand for advertising, in contrast with any arbitrary estimation specification—commonly referred to as model—such as:

$$A_D = b_0 + b_1 S + b_2 \frac{P}{a} + b_3 N. \tag{11}$$

Note that if (11) corresponded to another interpretation of the sales response and advertising demand processes, then comparison of results of (4) and its counterpart (11) would be much more meaningful than merely fitting (11) without any prior framework. Recall that, generally, for each expression like (11), there may be $n > 1$ structures (theories) that may satisfy the estimated values of b_i. Thus, one ought to seek the greatest possible amount of explicit information as to the specific structure governing the behavior of a phenomenon.

Extending the Model

Once a substantive model has been stated formally and values' boundaries of its coefficients hypothesized, the next step is to explore derived properties of the model. Some of the derived properties may include additional models as in the preceding illustration. But here the chief concern is with mathematical manipulation of the model to derive further testable properties of a phenomenon's structure.

Analysis directed specifically to dynamic properties is particularly desirable. It is usually dynamic models that are the most substantive because they vastly increase the number of tests that can be made and the number of properties that can be derived from them. In addition, most marketing processes are dynamic in any case, and the elimination of dynamic features can lead to important distortions (see, e.g., Nicosia & Rosenberg 1972, Palda 1970, and Wold & Strotz 1960). There are three ways in which a mathematical model can be extended.

Tests of Hypotheses about Derived Properties

Sometimes a "theory" is much more explicit about derived (especially dynamic) properties than about structure. For example, Howard and Sheth (1969) limited specification of their buyer behavior model to a graph but were fairly explicit about the effect of the interaction of perpetual and learning subsystems on the dynamics of the extent of problem solving. Thus it would be interesting to infer whether, in such studies as Farley and Ring's (1969), the operational model behaved dynamically as Howard and Sheth postulated.

In other cases, the properties are derived directly from the mathematical model. For example, Nicosia (1966) ascertains that if a consumer behaved according to the structure in (1)–(3), then the psychological properties expressed by the model's parameters *must satisfy* the quantitative relationships ($\beta\alpha > m, \alpha > 1/\beta$) for brand loyalty to be observed empirically. Nicosia can also determine that, for certain combinations of parameters' values, a *linear* model produces specific nonlinear buying behaviors. Economic growth models are also analyzed, for instance, to ascertain different trajectories (Matthews 1964). In yet other cases the question is how the model will behave if underlying conditions follow a certain dynamic path rather than stay constant. For example, if it is known what are the cyclical patterns of advertising and sales, a model of sales behavior must be able to reproduce the oscillatory response of sales. Techniques of econometric and spectral analysis are available for these tests of derived properties (Drhymes 1970).

Family of Models

It would be most startling if the same numerical values of all parameters in a model such as (1)–(3) applied to all individuals and time periods. For example, as individuals become convinced that one or more brands are acceptable alternatives, the coefficient m should move closer to unity. But if the individual is uncertain that the alternative(s) in question is (are) acceptable, he may be motivated to buy less-preferred brands. Hence, m could be close to zero, or even negative. Therefore, m is likely to vary through time and cross sectionally, depending on the problem-solving mode being used by each consumer.

This suggests two research approaches. One is to hypothesize a stochastic evolutionary process according to which m changes, possibly subject also to cross-sectional variations (see, e.g., Rosenberg 1973). The second approach begins with an analysis of the ranges of possible values a model's parameters can take. As it should be known, this leads to stating the boundaries for the underdamped, oscillatory, overdamped, and critically damped cases. For instance, this analysis allows Nicosia (1966) to identify a *family of models*, all of which are consistent with the original equations (1)–(3) and yet cover a wide assortment of dynamic responses (i.e., time-path characteristics).

The next step in this approach is *to observe* whether there are consumers who, in fact, behave according to one or another type of dynamic response. For instance, using the results of a dynamic clustering procedure (Myers & Nicosia 1970), Arbuckle (1971) *observes* that different consumer groups behave according to one or another type of time-path characteristics of the Nicosia model. Moreover, for the critically damped case, Arbuckle (1971) *observes* that even minor differences in the parameters' values differentiate consumers' behavior over time.

The significance of these empirical observations is that they could not be made without an a priori analysis of derived dynamic properties of a substantive model. The reason for this is simple: The "minor" differences in parameter values could not be recognized by any statistical inference method (Arbuckle 1971).

To recapitulate, the idea is that a single model can exhibit widely different behavior patterns while satisfying basic structural premises (such as $0 < 1/\beta < 1$). The ability to catalog the possible behaviors into a "family of models" is one of the payoffs of substantive model building, for it guides social research by providing a base for strong inference.

Decision Rules

If a model explains behavior (Y) as a function of X, and if some goal Z is a function $Z(Y)$, the next logical step should be to find a function $f(X)$ by which goals can be attained or perhaps maximized. If the model is substantive, that control process is based on and enhanced by increased ability to understand the system it represents. This is particularly so if Y is part of a circular system—i.e., let Y = sales and let sales be related to attitudinal-motivational factors, as in equations (1)–(3). Then the problem of manipulating sales involves also accounting for this realistic and decision-relevant relationship among advertising, attitude, and choice behavior.

A simultaneous-equation model, such as (1)–(3), can be solved for the relation between advertising (C) and sales (B):

$$B(t) = \frac{cm}{a(\alpha\beta - m)}\bar{C}(t)$$

in order to find, say, profit-optimal levels of advertising communication expenditures in the short and long terms. Derivations of the system of equations would also allow one to find the best multiperiod budget by means of control-theory methods. (For an early application, see Samuelson 1939.)[1]

Thus substantive models have managerial relevance, for they provide an analytical structure of the phenomenon of concern. Just as in the case of the

1. For a specific application to equations (1)–(3), see chapter 7, section 4, in Nicosia 1966, the extension by Sethi et al. 1973, or the approach in Nicosia 1968.

behavior of a falling body, $s = 1/2\,gt^2$, any analytical structure is concurrently a description and an explanation. Accordingly, such a structure becomes the basis for prediction and prescription (i.e., normative applications).

Projecting the Model: Coping with Structural Changes

Once a model has been specified, the question remains whether it can be applied as is. The preceding section explained one way in which the model can vary: structural coefficients may change. But other changes can occur.

1. *New equations may have to be added (or old ones deleted)*. For example, if advertising for one or more brands is set by an adaptive decision rule, the decision-rule equation will have to be added to the model (1)–(2).
2. *New variables may have to be added (or some old ones deleted)*. An example is the use of seasonal dummy variables or indices of buying power when data are time series or cross sectional, respectively.

Whenever any of these phenomena occur, the specification of the model will change, of course, and so will its derived properties. New tests, families of models, and decision rules will be required. *But the same basic model can still be used as the starting point on which modifications are to be incorporated.*[2] The reader is directed to Dominguez (1973) for a more detailed discussion of types of changes that expand the scope of a model's empirical applicability.

Conclusions

This chapter has discussed the following points:

1. Building a substantive model is more than (indeed, it may not even involve) a statistical-inference exercise.
2. A substantive model captures "theory" derived from the managers' perceptions of a process, the content of one or more theoretical propositions, and the researcher's own insights from previous knowledge, empirical and/or theoretical.
3. The more loosely stated the theory, the less strongly the model may be held and, hence, the more critical it is to test this model, particularly by comparing it to alternative formulas.
4. Numerical expressions such as (11) are not a model in the specific and quantitative sense that more than one structure may yield the estimates in (11). Generally, alternative formulas may derive from one theory or

2. The changes listed in points 1 and 2 are not in degree but in kind. Until very recently only empirical methods (e.g., iterations or stochastic parameters procedures) could be used; it now appears that mathematical developments in topology will allow us to model mathematically also structural changes in kind (Zeeman 1976). For suggestions on applications to consumer behavior, see Childley 1976.

from more than one theory. Dimensional analysis provides help in clarifying whether a model is meaningful in terms of one theory, whether other theories can yield the same model, and whether other models can stem from the same theory. It can also be used to derive properties of a model, as in equation (8).

5. A model's most basic requirement is that it make sense for its intended use. Thus boundaries should be stated within which its results make sense, i.e., beyond which it is not a reasonable interpretation of phenomena.

6. A model's meaning can be extended by deriving (usually dynamic) properties; by categorizing behavior into distinct types, all consistent with the same structure; and deriving complex decision rules that take advantage of the model's dynamic properties.

7. A model so framed will be realistic, useful, and parsimonious; i.e., it will reflect complexities that decision-making users feel are important, and it will provide numerous insights that relate to the types of usually complex and multiperiod questions that decision makers ask, without unnecessary complexity.

It is hoped that by laying down these rules, the attention of researchers will be directed more heavily toward greater use of substantive model building *and* analysis prior to empirical research. This is one of the most pressing needs and least developed phases of quantitative marketing and management processes at this point in time.

References

Arbuckle, J. M. 1971. "On the Role of Mathematical Models in Statistical Models." Master's thesis, Graduate School of Business Administration, University of California, Berkeley.

Blalock, H. M., Jr. 1969. *Theory Construction, from Verbal to Mathematical Formulations.* Englewood Cliffs, N.J.: Prentice-Hall.

Bridgman, P. W. 1963. *Dimensional Analysis.* New Haven, Conn.: Yale University Press.

Childley, J. 1976. "Catastrophe Theory in Consumer Attitude Surveys," *Journal of the Market Research Society* 18 (April).

Cohen, K. J. 1960. *Computer Models of the Shoe, Leather, Hide Sequence.* Englewood Cliffs, N.J.: Prentice-Hall.

DeJong, F. 1967. *Dimensional Analysis for Economists.* Amsterdam: North-Holland Publishing Co.

Dominguez, L. V. 1973. "Experimentation, Market Performance, and Econometric Model Building." *Proceedings of the American Marketing Association,* ed. Thomas V. Greer. Chicago: The Association.

Drhymes, P. J. 1970. *Econometrics: Statistical Foundations and Applications.* New York: Harper & Row.

Einhorn, H. J. 1974. "Reply to Morgan and Andrews." *Public Opinion Quarterly* 37 (Spring).

Farley, J. U. and Ring, L. W. 1969. "An Empirical Test of the Howard-Sheth Model of Buyer Behavior." *Journal of Marketing* 7 (November):427–438.

Ferber, R. and Nicosia, F. M. 1977. "The Use of Configurations of Buying Intentions for Predicting Auto Purchases: Some Explorations." In *Attitude Research Goes West*, ed. W. Wells. Chicago: American Marketing Association.

Howard, J. A. and Sheth, J. N. 1969. *The Theory of Buyer Behavior.* New York: John Wiley & Sons.

Kanter, D. L. 1957. "The Way You Test Advertising Depends upon the Approach the Advertising Itself Takes, Says Researcher." *Advertising Age*, July 15.

Kaplan, A. A. 1964. *The Conduct of Inquiry.* San Francisco: Chandler Publishing Company.

Lipstein, B. 1965. "A Mathematical Model of Consumer Behavior." *Journal of Marketing Research* (August).

Matthews, R. C. O. 1964. "The Theory of Economic Growth: A Survey." *Economic Journal* 74 (December):779–795.

Monroe, K. B. and Guiltinan, J. P. 1975. "A Path Analytic Exploration of Retail Patronage Influence." *Journal of Consumer Research* 2 (June).

Montgomery, D. B. and Urban, G. L. 1969. *Management Science in Marketing.* Englewood Cliffs, N.J.: Prentice-Hall.

Morgan, J. N. and Andrews, F. M. 1974. "A Comment on Einhorn's Alchemy in the Behavioral Sciences." *Public Opinion Quarterly* 37 (Spring).

Myers, J. G. and Nicosia, F. M. 1970. "Time-Path Types: From Static to Dynamic Typologies." *Management Science* 16 (June).

Nicosia, F. M. 1966. *Consumer Decision Processes: Marketing and Advertising Implications.* Englewood Cliffs, N.J.: Prentice-Hall.

————. 1968. "Advertising Management, Consumer Behavior, and Simulation." *Journal of Advertising Research* 8 (March).

————. 1977. "Brand Choice: Behavioristic-Behavioral Models." In *Management and Behavioral Sciences in Marketing,* ed. Harry Davis and Alvin Silk. New York: Ronald Press.

Nicosia, F. M. and Rosenberg, B. 1972. "Substantive Models in Consumer Attitude Research: Some Practical Uses." *Proceedings of the Fourth Attitude Research Conference,* ed. Russell I. Haley. Chicago: The Association.

Palda, K. S. 1970. "A Moving Cross-Section Analysis of the Demand for Toothpaste." *Journal of Marketing Research* 7 (November):439–449.

Papandreou, A. G. 1958. *Economics as a Science.* Philadelphia: Lippincott Publishing Co.

Rosenberg, B. 1973. "The Analysis of a Cross Section of Time Series by Stochastically Convergent Parameter Regression." *Annals of Economic and Social Measurement* 2 (October):399–428.

Samuelson, P. A. 1939. "Interactions between the Multiplier Analysis and the Principle of Acceleration." *Review of Economic Statistics* 21 (May):75–78.

Sethi, S. P., Turner, R. E., and Neuman, C. P. 1973. "Intertemporal Model of Market Response to Advertising." Research paper. School of Business, Queen's University, Kingston, Ontario, Canada.

Sheth, I. N. 1967. "A Review of Buyer Behavior." *Management Science* 13 (August):718–747.

Simon, H. A. 1957. *Models of Man.* New York: John Wiley & Sons.

Wold, H. O. and Strotz, R. 1960. "Recursive versus Non-Recursive Systems: An Attempt at Synthesis." *Econometrica* 28 (July):417–427.

Zeeman, E. C. 1976. "Catastrophe Theory." *Scientific American* 234 (April):65–83.

Part Two

Models of Market Analysis: The Buyers

Chapter 5

Applications of Behavioral Models to the Study of Individual Consumers

*J. A. Lunn**

Editors' Note

Many, if not all, marketing decisions are based on some "views" (implicit or explicit models) of how consumers go about making choices. How do the considerations developed in Part One apply to the study of consumer decision processes? This chapter does not intend to provide an exhaustive review of consumer behavior models and their applications. It begins with a review of some of the models that have been developed and used. Then it focuses on applications of a few specific models in the context of management action. For managerial applications of comprehensive models—e.g., those by Lipstein, Nicosia, and Howard and Sheth—and of models concerning specific aspects of consumer behavior—e.g., learning, attitude formation and change, and choice models—the reader may consult the voluminous available literature.

Introduction

During the past decade, consumer models have generated a high level of interest, especially among marketing scholars. Many different approaches have been developed, ranging from specific submodels, such as those of Fishbein (e.g.,

*J. A. Lunn is from the Research Bureau (Research International) Ltd., London, England.

Fishbein & Ajzen 1975) and Bettman (1974), which focus on particular aspects of the consumer decision process, to the comprehensive schemata of Nicosia (1966) and Howard and Sheth (1969), which specify a large number of variables and interrelationships. Several overviews can be found in the literature (e.g., Lunn 1974, Bettman & Jones 1972, and Hughes & Ray 1974) as well as in an increasing number of consumer behavior texts.

The central theme of this chapter concerns the practical value of this large volume of work. Are consumer models mainly of academic concern, or do they have a part to play in management decision making? It has to be admitted that several researchers engaged in the modeling activity have expressed pessimism about the extent to which models are in fact used by management (e.g., Little 1970 and Palmer 1973), and the literature contains relatively few positive case histories.[1] However, recent experience with a variety of approaches has convinced the writer that models do have considerable practical potential. This potential has been increased by developments in computer simulation, which enable research to move from descriptive and explanatory accounts of markets to predictions of the effects of different marketing strategies.

Some Definitions and General Considerations

Models

Models serve to specify both the key variables in a system—such as consumer beliefs, situational factors, and purchasing intention—and the relationship between these variables. Models differ in type, scope, and level of explanation (see Chapters 3 and 4).

A more colloquial definition, and one that has proved valuable in communicating with management, is to regard models as views of how things work. As such, we all use models all the time. In everyday life we need models to act at all, and effective models to act successfully—in preparing a meal, catching a train, etc. Likewise, every market research project implies a model or series of models of one kind or another. Researchers assume that their questions reflect phenomena in the real world—that the variables cross-analyzed are linked in a meaningful way, that both questions and analyses have relevance to the problem in hand. All of these assumptions imply models, views of how consumers operate, and how they are affected by marketing action.

In most cases the assumptions underlying research remain implicit and untested. They are often hidden by the techniques and jargon to which researchers are only too prone, or by the preconceptions of marketing men. Bringing assumptions into the open should be the starting point for any modeling exercise and not the least part of its value. Once assumptions have been made explicit—once they are in open view—they can be readily criticized,

---

1. It should be borne in mind, of course, that publication of successful marketing case histories is restricted by proprietarial considerations.

tested, and developed. They can also be understood more clearly by both researchers and marketing people. By making assumptions explicit, we are providing a more efficient route to problem solving.

Consumer Models

Many consumer models are based upon theory drawn from the behavioral sciences, and some provide quantitative estimates of the relationships postulated between the component variables. Some researchers have argued the need for models (Nicosia & Rosenberg 1971 and Dominguez and Nicosia in this book), and a few (e.g., Nicosia 1976) have shown the advantages of developing models that incorporate both substantive theory and sophisticated quantitative methodology.

For the purposes of this chapter, consumer models are taken to refer to representations of the ways individual consumers acquire and process information, of how they use this information in making purchasing decisions, and of consumption and other postpurchase processes. A useful distinction, referred to above, is between these specific submodels that focus upon particular aspects of the decision process and the more comprehensive approaches that attempt to encompass all relevant aspects within a single framework.

Specific Submodels

To concentrate upon the potential of specific behavioral science theories has been referred to as the "a priori approach." In another publication (Lunn 1974), the writer has discussed certain of its strengths and weaknesses. Some of these are summarized below.

Consumer behavior, of course, is a specific aspect of general human behavior, and the strength of the a priori approach lies in its attempt to harness existing knowledge and insights. But as traditionally applied, there are severe limitations. Many of the concepts adopted are still somewhat speculative. They have often been developed in contexts remote from consumer behavior—for instance, in laboratory situations with students as experimental subjects. Moreover, they have usually been developed to account for restricted aspects of human behavior, e.g., learning and perception. Nevertheless, protagonists of different theoretical positions have been all too ready to represent them as rival rather than complementary explanatory systems and to overgeneralize their areas of application. This narrowness of perspective may help the advancement of academic knowledge but can be destructively limiting in a problem-oriented field such as marketing.

The benefits and dangers of the a priori approach are highlighted by McGuire (1970), who gives a fivefold classification of what he calls the guiding theories behind attitude change research and indicates some of their applications for the marketing area. These five theoretical paradigms are labeled perceptual, consistency, learning, functional and information-processing. McGuire argues that the various so-called rival theories are supplementary rather than conflicting. "Their assumptions about man and persuasions are quite different, but the difference resides in the tendency for each of the approaches to stress aspects of man and the social influence process which are neglected by other approaches." The danger is to represent a partial view of man as though it were a complete explanation of behavior.

Comprehensive Models

A distinguishing feature of the comprehensive approach is the attempted synthesis of two sets of information: on the one hand those theories, concepts, and findings in the various behavioral sciences that appear relevant to consumer behavior; on the other hand the rapidly escalating results of market research and consumer-behavior studies, whether stemming from the specific context of marketing problems or the more generalized context of academic research.

The exponents of *comprehensive models* recognize that human behavior is complex and, as mentioned above, attempt to represent this complexity through an integration of several different theories and models. In this they have generated a rich series of hypotheses about consumer behavior applicable to a wide range of problems. However, comprehensiveness is also a potential source of weakness, for it imposes a herculean task upon researchers. It is hard enough to establish an agreed outlook among specialists within a discipline (e.g., learning theorists within psychology), harder still among representatives of different aspects of a major discipline (e.g., learning theorists and psycho-linguisticians), and difficult indeed among representatives of quite different disciplines, such as psychology, sociology, and economics.

The inclusion of a large number of variables and interrelationships runs the danger of leading to highly complex structures that are difficult both to test (Farley & Ring 1970) and to apply in practical situations (Bettman 1974).

In a recent overview (Hughes & Ray 1974), Hughes is especially critical of the comprehensive approach. Referring to certain leading contributors, he comments:

> Each assembles bits and pieces of behavioral concepts from a variety of sources to explain buyer behavior. Perhaps this build up approach should be replaced by a method which dissects buyer behavior. Such an approach would begin with behavior and study the causes of changes in behavior. Dissection would go only as far as the study required. Predictive models would probably require less dissection than explanatory ones. The dissection approach would focus on changes in behavior, so that it would at least be comparatively static in its treatment of time.

In the writer's opinion, there is no necessary incompatibility between these two alternative approaches. Specific submodels may be regarded as core representations of the detailed-choice mechanism. Where appropriate it is possible to build large models representing the effects of marketing variables, such as advertising and in-store factors, and add these to the core model—that is, to aggregate specific submodels into larger ones. The theoretical benefit of this has been discussed by Bettman (1974); practical benefits demonstrated by Faivre and his colleagues (e.g., 1973, 1975) are discussed later in the chapter.

The essential richness of comprehensive models makes them relatively unsuitable to be applied in their entirety for particular marketing problems. Nevertheless, they can provide a valuable backdrop for the classification of research needs. They can indicate what variables should be measured, how these should be analyzed, and what (by default) is being ignored. In addition, they have potential for generating more specific submodels. Illustrations are given later in the chapter.

Functions and Requirements of Consumer Models

Functions

The value and functions of consumer models have been the subject of considerable discussion. At a general level, a central function is an explanatory one, i.e., to increase the understanding of the phenomenon being studied. Additional features described by Howard and Sheth (1969) are:

1. *delimitation:* to help confine research to important and relevant areas.
2. *integration:* to integrate within a common framework the wealth of disparate concepts and findings in the area of consumer research.
3. *generation:* to highlight topics where further research and conceptual clarification is necessary.

More specifically, models have an important role in guiding research projects, at the stages both of *input* (e.g., clarifying assumptions, indicating variables to be included or excluded) and of *output* (e.g., indicating how the results should be analyzed and interpreted).

Requirements of Consumer Modeling

None of the different approaches to consumer modeling are right or wrong in themselves. They may, however, be more or less relevant to a given problem, and *decision relevance* is an especially important characteristic of any model. A related and equally important characteristic is *comprehensibility.* It can be argued that a major reason for the rejection of models by some marketing men is that researchers have, in effect, been talking to each other—presenting in their own jargon, and with a daunting array of equations, concepts that are not seen as relevant to the marketing problem in hand because they are not understood. A further important requirement is *validity,* which may be defined as the similarity the model bears to the real world. This similarity may be hard to establish completely in practice. An excellent discussion of some conceptual and theoretical problems linked with the validation of simulation models is given by Faivre and Sanchez (1975) in a paper which also describes a case history of a successful validation exercise.

A particular challenge to the modeling activity is to strike a balance among decision relevance, comprehensibility, and validity. This applies especially where the system being modeled is complex and would ideally require a large number of variables and interrelationships to be specified.

Models, Modeling, and Structures

It can be argued that an additional requirement from models is that they should have general application across a range of problems and situations. However, a cautionary note should be sounded here. Models built for one purpose may have little or no relevance for another. They may omit important components or contain unimportant ones. This applies both to models built for particular market situations and those built for the basic understanding of consumer behavior or human behavior in general.

As a means of dealing with these and other requirements, the writer and his colleagues have found it useful to distinguish between "models," "modeling," and "structures" when dealing with management problems.

As stated elsewhere (Westwood et al. 1974):

> We use the term *model* to refer to a representation of specific aspects of the consumer decision process: for instance, the process whereby exposure to advertising leads to brand awareness, or beliefs about a brand lead to an intention to purchase it, or use of a brand leads to a modification of beliefs about it, and so on. [For example, in communication research, the work by Lazarsfeld, Hovaband, and, more recently, Fishbein is an example of models in this sense.]
>
> Modeling (or structuring) is the process whereby one or more models are linked together with such other inputs as existing research data and management experience and opinion. These linkages create a representation or "structure" of the particular marketing situation under study. Such structures may be effectively produced by a task force which draws from both management and researchers' experience.
>
> Structures, the output of the modeling process, are a means of examining several aspects of consumer decision making simultaneously. Given the wide differences in marketing problems and circumstances that hold in the real decision-making world, we have, in our own work, adopted the practice of tailor-making each structure to a particular manufacturer's problems. Thus, whilst a structure has a broader focus than a model—it takes more aspects of consumer decision into account—it should not necessarily be expected to have broader application than the solution of the particular problem being tackled. [At the same time there will often be common elements between structures built for particular situations, which can facilitate the model-building process.]
>
> In summary, we see models as research tools of general application which, through a modeling exercise, can contribute toward the creation of structures or representations of specific markets.

Obstacles to Practical Application

The previous sections have touched upon some of the obstacles which inhibit management's use of consumer models. These are pulled together and briefly outlined below.

Academic Irrelevance

The very terms "theory" and "model" are anathema to many business-men—and to some research practitioners as well. To "pragmatic" people the terms have connotations of impracticality and irrelevance; they sound like academic indulgences rather than problem-solving aids. Unfortunately this impression may all too often gain substance from the manner in which modelers have presented themselves to management. Some protagonists of particular approaches have advocated these with almost messianic zeal, regardless of their decision relevance.

Formidability

Models are often regarded as formidable—as being highly complicated both conceptually and methodologically, requiring large and costly data-collection procedures, needing several years to build, and being difficult to apply in practice. Again it must be admitted that these impressions are not without substance. Some models have been presented in these ways, especially the stochastic forecasting models developed in operations research. For some problems a certain level of complexity may be essential if the model is to be an adequate and actionable representation of the process under study. But researchers should, nevertheless, strive for parsimony (Dominguez & Nicosia in this book) and should recognize that complex issues can often be communicated in simple terms. Similar considerations apply in areas such as market segmentation.

Overcoming the Obstacles

Although not totally exonerating management from responsibility, it is up to researchers to take a major initiative in ensuring that more is obtained from the potential offered by consumer models. Much will be gained by paying more attention to decision relevance and comprehensibility. But the writer would place particular emphasis upon the modeling approach referred to above. Experience has shown that even relatively large and complex structures can be actionable, given the close and continuing collaboration between researchers and management in the task-force situation.

Some Practical Applications

Practical Problem-Solving and Basic Research

So far, application has been discussed in the context of practical problem solving, and some illustrations are given in this section. However, the value of basic research into the understanding of consumer choice behavior should not be ignored. As has been pointed out elsewhere (e.g., Lunn 1974 and Sheth 1974), such understanding helps to make consumer research a scientific discipline in its own right, and also provides a setting for methodological development. Consumer models have an important part to play in this more fundamental area.

The remainder of the chapter is devoted to a discussion of four practical applications of consumer models; the first is given in some detail, the others in outline.

Belief Importance and a New Product Development Project[2]

Some Background Considerations. Beliefs about brand and product attributes are widely acknowledged to form a key component in consumer choice behavior. Other variables, such as habit, curiosity, and situational effects, also need to be taken into account (Sheth & Raju 1973). Nevertheless, the hypothesis that under certain circumstances changes in beliefs either precede or follow changes in behavior both accords with common sense and has support in the literature. Not all beliefs will necessarily have equal power to change or reinforce choice behavior. In other words, not all beliefs are equally important, and assessment of the relative importances of beliefs is of fundamental concern in marketing strategies. A large number of models have been developed in this area. For instance, Wilkie and Pessemeir (1973) review forty-two. Most of these are based upon value-expectancy theory and embody some kind of *linear-additive* format; e.g.,

$$Ax = \sum_{i=1}^{n} Bxi \ Ci,$$

where:

Ax = a subject's evaluation of (attitude toward) brand X
Bxi = his belief about brand X in terms of characteristic or outcome i
Ci = his evaluation of characteristic or outcome i.

In other words, it is assumed that consumers will like a brand to the extent to which they associate it with characteristics that they value highly; also that in the evaluation process, a low value on one attribute may be compensated by a high value on another attribute.

Results from using different variants of this class of model are mixed, and it would appear that the linear-additive format is not always an adequate representation of the consumer choice process. For instance:

1. No allowance is made for an unwelcome characteristic that can cause a brand to be rejected outright; instead, it is assumed that this could be

---

2. For a fuller description of this section, see those papers by Westwood et al. 1974*a, b* and *c.*

compensated for by an accumulation of other advantages. For example, no combination of speed, comfort, and economy can make a soft-top automobile desirable if it is perceived as unsafe.

2. Although an attribute may be expressed as a continuum, it may not be continuously related to purchase intention; only some levels of an attribute may be relevant to the explanation of consumer choices. For example, for some people there is a level of quality in the sound reproduction of hi-fi equipment beyond which they put no additional value on improvement.

It is not suggested that these limitations preclude the use of the linear-additive model in all instances—in many circumstances it may be of singular value.

Moreover, there is evidence that the linear-additive model can be improved by taking into account:

1. The fact that consumers do not evaluate brands singly, but rather do so within the framework of an evoked set of considered brands (Nicosia 1966, ch. 7, sect. 3.1.2.5 and Van Raaij 1975)
2. The confidence of the consumer in his ability to discriminate between and evaluate brands and the extent to which he can tolerate risk (Van Raaij 1975 and Cox 1967)

Different markets and situations may well require different types of importance models. Several alternative approaches have been suggested in the literature (e.g., Sheth & Raju 1973 and Wilkie & Pessemier 1973). Two that have been extensively explored by the writer and his colleagues are the threshold and trade-off models.

The *threshold model* suggests that brand choices are made by a sorting procedure: consumers mentally sort through the brands attribute by attribute, rejecting some each time until a decision is finally reached. The procedure may result in the adoption of either a single brand or a small subset of brands from within which the individual makes purchases by means of other decision criteria.

The consumer is assumed to use beliefs essentially as dichotomous scales rather than as continua of evaluation. Instead of looking for the best brand on each attribute, he divides brands into those that are "good enough" and those that are not. Implicit in this sorting procedure is a "threshold level of acceptability" on each belief: brands are good enough if above this threshold, not good enough if below it. Thus the model suggests that chosen brands are the least rejected rather than the most accepted. Illustrations can be found in Lunn and Beazley (1975).

The *trade-off model* contends that consumers, as a rule, are not faced with products that they can meaningfully judge against some hypothetical idea. Instead they usually have to choose among a series of imperfect options. Obtaining a desired product quality (say, efficiency) will require the consumer to sacrifice (trade off) some other desired quality (say, gentleness). In such situations rather than looking for ideal product characteristics, it is more realistic to study the trade-offs that consumers make and to attempt to account for these.

If this approach is to be adopted, it is necessary to study beliefs in more depth than with other importance models. It is not sufficient to regard product attributes as whole entities; instead they must be measured at specific levels. This enables the model to move the crucial step beyond saying "efficiency is more important than mildness" to saying *how much* mildness the consumer is prepared to trade off to gain *how much* efficiency.

The model can be operationalized in several ways. Methods of data collection are relatively straightforward and are based on simple rank orderings or ratings of multi-attributes or concepts. The data are analyzed by a form of conjoint measurement (see, e.g., Green & Wind 1973, 1975), where the objective is to discover the utility of each level of each attribute—i.e., its value in terms of how prone it is to being traded off against various levels of the other attitude. (For a more detailed description of the various approaches of trade-off methodology, see Green & Wind 1973, Johnson 1974, and Westwood et al. 1974a.)

It is worth noting that linear-additive, threshold and trade-off, along with additional markets, such as disjunctive and lexcographic, are receiving considerable attention from marketing scholars. In addition, they are also increasingly being incorporated into commercial modeling projects. Early interest was particularly concerned with which of the various models provided the best representation of the consumer choice process. Perspectives are broadening in several respects. For instance, it is increasingly recognized that the same consumer may use different rules under different circumstances, and that rules may sometimes operate in combined and/or sequential manner. Discussion of these issues can be found in Van Raaij (1975). Gunter and Beazley (1976) describe a successful simulation project for an electrical product in which consumers were found to use several decision rules in combination.

A Research Application. The following discussion refers to a study which used the trade-off model as a component in a structure that was developed both to explain and to simulate a particular market. It was carried out on a European basis.

The study was conducted for a major manufacturer of a form of durable products purchased mainly by commercial establishments. The structure was designed to guide the manufacturer's future new-product development. Since he was already dominant in most of the submarkets in which he competed, this expansion was to be achieved by entering a submarket which—although already highly developed by potential competitors—was new to the manufacturer.

Since the structure was to be used primarily for product development purposes, it was decided to exclude marketing variables (e.g., distribution, sales effectiveness, etc.) at least until a later date. To this extent it was clear that research would be used to describe and then simulate an "artificial world." The challenge was to identify an artificial world which would be of maximum relevance to product development while still retaining a sufficient level of similarity to the real world to ensure that its estimates of sales implications were trustworthy.

Following comprehensive discussions of the basis for modeling with the manufacturer, it was decided that the structure should represent a world where each customer possessed full and accurate knowledge about all competitive products in the marketplace and made logical choices between them on the basis of their abilities to satisfy his requirements.

The simulation model was to be designed so that the product planner could specify a possible future market in terms of the features of both his own products and those of his envisaged competition. Each member of a sample of "electronic" consumers would consider the features of each product in terms of his requirements and then choose whichever was "best" for his purposes. Sales estimates would be made by aggregating choices across the sample. However, initial exploratory research indicated that potential customers considered features in three different ways:

Threshold features. Some features could lead to a product's being deemed totally inappropriate for a customer's purposes and hence rejected. Different customers used different features in this way.

Trade-off features. Choices between nonrejected products were made on the basis of whichever seemed "best" over all remaining "central features" (those that were closely related to the product's basic function). Since no product was likely to supply all possible advantages in these terms—or even to be free of all possible disadvantages—this seemed to be very much a trade-off decision.

Added-value features. Some noncentral features, however, could increase the likelihood of a customer's purchasing a product—these may be thought of as nonessential but desirable features and could be identified as such.

The structure was, therefore, designed to deal with all of these types of features. After careful initial phases of exploratory research and discussion with the manufacturer, a survey was conducted among decision makers in the target market of commercial enterprises. The project, as a whole, provided information of two distinct types. First, by looking at the structure's *explanations* of choice behavior within various market subgroups, the manufacturer was able to generate new product ideas that he would expect to compete favorably in the market. Second, by using it to *simulate* the market, he was able to evaluate these ideas in various competitive contexts.

The manufacturer has used this simulation model to assist in a wide range of decisions. The common theme across these is that he is always checking the sales implications of a new product idea in a specified market configuration.

To take an example, at one stage of his planning, the manufacturer was pursuing an idea we will call "product X." He felt he would not be able to make that product available immediately and that, by the time he would be ready to launch, his competitors might well have developed products A, B, C, and D. To check the viability of product X, he first simulated a market composed of products A, B, C, and D, with the following results:

Product	Simulated Brand Share
A	52%
B	4%
C	33%
D	10%

Having observed that product A and, to a lesser extent C, would dominate this market in formulation terms, he then simulated the market again—this time with product X also included:

Product	Simulated Brand Share
A	30%
B	3%
C	16%
D	8%
X	43%

These results suggested that product X was a very promising idea—it appeared to have the potential for becoming the dominant product in this market.

The manager next questioned his assumptions about future market developments and decided to investigate what might happen if manufacturers developed products B and D into superior formulations N and P. When product X was entered into this market, the following results were achieved:

Product	Simulated Brand Share
A	28%
N	20%
C	13%
P	25%
X	14%

Thus he could see that product X would be very susceptible to developments in B and D, and he looked for formulation changes he could make to counter such developments. He tried out various changes that could be readily engineered in practice, and he eventually discovered a reformulation of X that could perform relatively well in this market:

Product	Simulated Brand Share
A	27%
N	12%
C	15%
P	21%
X MK 1	25%

The planner continued the investigation of product X after this fashion by looking at a range of other possible future developments, seeing the potential of X MK 1 when competing in these contexts, and investigating ways of increasing its competitive appeal when necessary.

This example shows how the manufacturer is able to build his planning decisions around a structure incorporating the trade-off model. (For a somewhat different approach, see Wind et al. 1975.) By on the one hand identifying ways of competing successfully in a range of possible market configurations and on the other hand monitoring market developments as they occur, he is able to take a very flexible approach to his product planning. Having initiated and evaluated a series of product plans at this point in time, he also knows how to modify some of their objectives in the light of market developments. And as the competitive developments become clearer, he learns which of his own developments are likely to prove most effective and which could be shelved. Should any unexpected changes occur in the competitive structure of the market, he can immediately check out their implications by simulating their effect.

This example illustrates a number of issues. For instance:

1. The market structure was evolved through close and continuous collaboration between researchers and members of the manufacturing company, including design engineers as well as marketing men. Although the methodology used was novel to the client and relatively complex, no problems of communication were encountered, and the potential of the model was exploited to the full.
2. Computer simulation (Kotler & Schultz 1970) played a major role in the application of the model.
3. The model was deliberately constructed from an artificial point of view to ensure its relevance to management. In the market under study, customer choices are not usually based on full and accurate information processed in a logical manner. But any attempt to increase the "real-world" validity of the structure—for instance, by attempts to portray the influence of salesmen or by studying "intangible" images rather than objective product characteristics—would have decreased its reality for the design engineer. This relates to the issue of model specificity discussed above. Given a different problem, quite different considerations would have guided the modeling process.

A Product Developmental Marketing Monitoring Project

A series of projects of a similar but more elaborate nature have been carried out by Faivre, with the principles behind them reported in two publications (1971, 1973). Much of the inspiration for these projects derives from the microanalytical approach as exemplified by Amstutz (1967). In one of these projects, Faivre used a linear-additive model of belief importance. Along with the concepts of "brand awareness" and "overall evaluation," this was taken as the basis of a core model of brand choice. Market segments were defined in terms of both general attitudes (e.g., economy mindedness) and consumer requirements in the product field in question. Following a large-scale market segmentation study, computer simulation was used to identify market gaps for new-product development.

This study differs from the one reported in the previous section in several respects. First, it was begun several years ago. It has, therefore, already been possible to use the model at various stages of the marketing process, including the monitoring of a new brand launch. Second, the model was not restricted to the design engineer's point of view; it also brought in the needs and assumptions of marketing, sales, and advertising management. Third, the core model of brand choice was supplemented by a number of peripheral models representing, for instance, the communication process and shopping behavior. These were based on a combination of research and management experience, empirical data, and relevant consumer theory. Their inclusion made it possible to simulate the probable effects of different marketing forces, including media and point-of-sale strategies.

The study resembles the earlier one in its adoption of the task force procedure. Regular meetings of researchers and management, in which assumptions were spelled out and experiences shared, ensured the decision relevance of all stages of the project and its incorporation in management strategies. Comparisons between the forecasts given by the model and results in the marketplace have been very favorable (Faivre & Sanchez 1975).

Comprehensive Models and Point-of-Sale Research

Background. For several years, the writer has been concerned with a program of basic market-research development carried out on behalf of a multinational corporation. In the mid-1960s, it was decided that the program would benefit from guidance by a framework specifying key elements in the consumer decision process and ways in which these can be influenced by marketing activity. A first draft was produced in 1968, based upon a review of the market research literature and unpublished basic research studies (Lunn 1968). The conceptualization of the framework was subsequently extended by incorporating the work of Nicosia and of Howard and Sheth.

This comprehensive perspective has been invaluable in the planning of the program and in interpreting the findings of specific projects in areas as diverse as price research, brand loyalty, and the relationship of attitudes and behavior. Some of these have been reported elsewhere (Lunn 1974). A set of general propositions derived from the comprehensive approach has been especially useful in guiding basic research. Some of these are summarized below:

1. The consumer is not the defenseless creature portrayed by some theoreticians but rather is purposive and goal-oriented.
2. He actively seeks information to satisfy his various needs and structures it in terms of these needs.
3. He is assailed daily by vast quantities of information, only some of which is relevant to his choice behavior. As a result, he screens out much

of this information and adopts selective strategies in relation to exposure to, attention to, structuring, and retention of this information.

4. The consumer's view of what constitutes a market is not necessarily the same as a manufacturer's. Brands from a variety of product fields may be regarded as equally suitable for a given purpose.

5. The decision process will be complicated or continued at different stages of a consumer's life cycle and in the light of experience. Similarly, the evoked set of brands considered as suitable for a given purpose will vary over time.

6. Situational and environmental factors are an important element both in determining purchasing intentions and in influencing their implementation.

These and other propositions are discussed in more detail in Lunn (1974).

Point-of-Sale Research. Attempts to influence the consumer at the point of sale are a major feature of marketing strategy. Two large-scale projects were carried out early in the history of the basic research program in an attempt to provide some guidance in this area, but the results were inconclusive. A fresh series of projects, guided by the comprehensive schemata referred to above, have proved much more successful. They have increased understanding of the mechanisms that determine how shoppers make purchasing decisions and have led to the development of a research structure for measuring in-store influence.

The research is discussed in a paper by Beazley and Lunn (1974). Some of the main results are summarized below:

1. A number of shopper types were identified in terms of general attitudes, e.g., "the inefficient and extravagant shopper," the "anxious muddled shopper," the "efficient model housewife." These types discriminated among differences in shopping behavior.

2. The shopping list is not a reliable predictor of planned shopping.

3. All housewives plan shopping to some extent, and brand-specific planned purchases are the major category of purchases.

4. The majority of unplanned purchases are more meaningfully categorized as "reminder" or "suggestion," rather than "impulse."

5. Unexecuted purchase intentions are quite frequent.

6. Subsidiary trip shopping is more flexible and less planned than main trip shopping.

7. The shop's own price reduction is the single most effective in-store factor.

8. Product fields differ in the degree of planning exhibited.

The Building of an Advertisement Pretesting System

Advertisement pretesting is a major field of market research which has been the center of innumerable controversies and disputes between rival methodologists. This is not only because of deficiencies in particular techniques, but because few pretesting systems have been based upon a systematic conceptualization of how advertising might work. All too often, where any underlying model has been adopted, it has been simplistic, as illustrated by the hierarchy-of-effects system.[3] In recent years, this area has been examined more systematically. For instance, Joyce (1967) attempted syntheses of knowledge about how advertising works. McGuire (1969) has evolved an eclectic theory of the advertising process based upon a variety of standpoints in the attitude change, persuasion, and communication fields. Sheth (1974) has applied the Howard and Sheth theory to a specific examination of the advertising process. Both McGuire and Sheth point out that, providing the hierarchy-of-effects paradigm is not regarded as irreversible or the sole form in which persuasion takes place, it can, in fact, provide a valuable structure for assessing advertisements. But they also emphasize that different advertisements will probably have different effects at each point of the hierarchy; e.g., an advertisement with high attention value may have little persuasive power. However, quite different measuring instruments will be necessary at each stage.

Similar points have been made by Twyman (1969, 1970, 1971), who has evolved a new and flexible pretesting program widely used in the UK. (See also Bloom et al. 1976.)

Twyman argues that it is sometimes wrongly assumed that the role of theory in the methodological development must be in creating a rigid and oversimplified structure. The method becomes a model of a single theory. By contrast, it is possible to use "theory" in general rather than "a specified theory" to widen the range of concepts used in developing methods and also to eliminate as well as to construct hypotheses.

The project referred to above, which was concerned with establishing a set of principles for pretesting advertisements, involved both a survey of current methods and direct findings in the field together with a review of theory and findings in a wide range of related areas. Theory was then used to supplement direct findings in guiding judgment as to the practical steps to be taken in formulating pretesting principles. For example, a number of existing approaches popular at that time relied heavily upon a theory of advertising effectiveness based on not only the hierarchy-of-effects paradigm, but also factual learning and verbal attitude change. A review of theories of communication and learning in related areas makes it clear that this is highly unlikely to be the only basis for advertising effectiveness. It also helps one to assess the potential importance of emotional and associational processes of learning which are much harder to demonstrate in conventional advertising research.

A requirement was thereby set up for a method that would enable advertising effects to be measured from processes other than through the intermediate steps of factual comprehension and learning. Such a method might also distinguish cases where the facts have registered but have not added up to a favorable response for the brand.

To meet these requirements, the indirect-measurement approach was adopted of testing reactions to the brand from matched exposed and nonex-

---

3. E.g., attention; comprehension; attitude change; retention of change; behavior.

posed groups, in addition to checking on the comprehension and learning of and reactions to elements in the advertising. This approach is not incompatible with factual learning theory. But it is incompatible with a much wider range of hypotheses about advertising effectiveness that theory has suggested. Similar recourse to theory has to be made in advertising research when considering issues such as the importance of attention and the meaning of recall results.

Conclusion

In concluding this chapter, the writer would like to strike a balance between undue pessimism and optimism. On the negative side there are still relatively few published case histories of successful consumer modeling projects. And many marketing men and research practitioners continue to harbor doubts about their practical value on grounds which include relevance and feasibility. At the same time, successful case histories are known to exist (e.g. Westwood et al. 1974 and Gunter & Beazley 1976), although proprietarial considerations inevitably restrict publication.

Moreover, a growing interest on the part of those concerned with marketing decisions is being accompanied by a burst of enthusiasm on the part of academic researchers: both conferences and the literature provide evidence of serious attempts to increase our understanding of consumer models of different kinds and levels. The writer fervently hopes that this area will not turn out to be yet another passing fashion. He believes that considerable promise lies in the adoption of an eclectic and flexible approach to different theoretical positions on the part of academic researchers, and in the adoption of the modeling approach referred to in the chapter, whereby relevant theory can be combined with management insights in the development of actionable models for specific markets and problems.

References[4]

Amstutz, A. E. 1967. *Computer Simulation of Competitive Market Response.* Cambridge: MIT Press.

Beazley, D. and Lunn, J. A. 1974. "Shopping Styles and Strategies and Their Relationship to In-Store Factors." *Proceedings of ESOMAR Seminar on Management Information for Retail Organizations.* Lucern, Switzerland.

Bettman, J. R. 1974. "Decision Net Models in Buyer Information Processing and Choice." In *Buyer/Consumer Information Processing,* ed. D. Hughes and M. Ray. Chapel Hill: University of North Carolina Press.

Bettman, J. R. and Jones, J. M. 1972. "Formal Models of Consumer Behavior: A Conceptual Overview." *Journal of Business* 45, no. 4:544–562.

Bloom, D., Jay, A., and Twyman, W. A. 1976. "The Validity of Advertising

4. The Proceedings of seminars organized by the European Society for Opinion and Market Research (ESOMAR) do not have a named editor. They are available from the following address: ESOMAR Central Secretariat, Raadhuisstraat 15, Amsterdam, Netherlands.

Pre-Testing." *Proceedings of the Nineteenth Annual Conference of the Market Research Society.* Brighton, United Kingdom.

Cox, D., ed. 1967. *Risk Taking and Information Handling in Consumer Behavior.* Cambridge, Mass.: Harvard University Press.

Dominguez, L. V. and Nicosia, F. M. "Some Practical Problems in Building Substantive Marketing Models." Chapter 4 of this book.

Faivre, J. P. 1971. "Micro-Analytic Behavioral Simulation Models." *Proceedings of the ESOMAR Annual Conference.* Helsinki, Finland.

————. 1973. "Consumer Models as a Way of Improving Management Decision Making." *Proceedings of ESOMAR Seminar on Developments in Consumer Psychology.* Maidenhead, United Kingdom.

Faivre, J. P. and Sanchez, C. 1975. "The Validation of Marketing Models." *Proceedings of ESOMAR Seminar on Market Modeling.* Part 1.

Farley, J. V. and Ring, W. L. 1970. "An Empirical Test of the Howard-Sheth Model of Buyer Behavior." *Journal of Marketing Research* 9 (August):427–438.

Fishbein, M. and Ajzen, I. 1975. "Attitudes and Opinions." *Annual Review of Psychology* 23:487–544.

Green, P. E. and Wind, Y. 1973. *Multi-Attribute Decisions in Marketing: A Measurement Approach.* Hinsdale, Ill.: Dryden Press.

————. 1975. "New Way to Measure Consumers' Judgment." *Harvard Business Review* (July–August).

Gunter, P. and Beazley, D. 1976. "An Application of Micro-Simulation Modeling to the Marketing of a Consumer Durable." *Proceedings of the ESOMAR Annual Conference.* Venice, Italy.

Howard, J. A. and Sheth, J. N. 1969. *The Theory of Buyer Behavior.* New York: John Wiley & Sons.

Hughes, G. D. and Ray, M., eds. 1974. *Buyer/Consumer Information Processing.* Chapel Hill: University of North Carolina Press.

Johnson, R. M. 1974. "Trade-Off Analysis of Consumer Values." *Journal of Marketing Research* 11:121–127

Joyce, T. 1967. "What Do We Know about How Advertising Works?" *Proceedings of the ESOMAR Seminar on Advertising Research.*

Kotler, P. and Schultz, R. L. 1970. "Marketing Simulations: Review and Prospects." *Journal of Business* 43, no. 3:237–295.

Little, J. D. C. 1970. "Models and Managers." *Management Science* 16, no. 8:466–485.

Lunn, J. A. 1968. "A Consumer Framework." Unpublished paper.

————. 1972. "Constructing and Segmenting Markets." In *Consumer Market Research Handbook,* ed. R. M. Worchester. New York: McGraw-Hill.

————. 1974. "A Review of Consumer Decision Process Models." In *Models of Buyer Behavior,* ed. J. N. Sheth. New York: Harper & Row.

Lunn, J. A. and Beazley, D. 1975. "The Role of the Threshold Model in the Assessment of Belief Importance and in Consumer Information Processing." *Proceedings of the ESOMAR Seminar on Market Modeling.* Noordwijk van Zee, Netherlands.

McGuire, W. J. 1969. "An Information Processing Model of Advertising Effectiveness." Paper given at the Symposium on Behavior and Management Science in Marketing at the University of Chicago.

_____. 1970. "The Guiding Theories behind Attitude Change." *Proceedings of the Third Annual Attitude Research Conference.* (Mexico, March.) Chicago: American Marketing Association.

Nicosia, F. M. 1966. *Consumer Decision Processes: Marketing and Advertising.* Englewood Cliffs, N.J.: Prentice-Hall.

Nicosia, F. M. and Rosenberg, B. 1971. "Substantive Modeling in Consumer Attitude Research: Some Practical Uses." In *Attitude Research in Transition,* ed. R. I. Hally. Chicago: American Marketing Association.

Palmer, J. B. 1973. "Structures of Buyer Behavior." *Proceedings of the ESOMAR Seminar on Developments in Consumer Psychology.* Maidenhead, United Kingdom.

Sheth, J. N. 1974a. "The Future of Buyer Behavior Theory." In *Models of Buyer Behavior,* ed. J. N. Sheth. New York: Harper & Row.

_____. 1974b. "The Measurement of Advertising Effectiveness: Some Theoretical Considerations." *Journal of Advertising* 3, no. 1:6–11.

Sheth, J. N. and Raju, P. S. 1973. "Sequential and Cyclical Nature of Information Processing Models in Repetitive Choice Behavior." *Proceedings of the Fourth Annual Conference of the Association for Consumer Research,* ed. S. Ward and P. L. Wright.

Twyman, W. A. 1969. "The Structure of the Advertising Process." Unpublished paper.

_____. 1970. "The Pre-Testing of TV Commercials." Unpublished paper.

_____. 1971. "Non-Rational Advertising Effects in Relation to Theory and Practice." *Proceedings of the ESOMAR Seminar on Translating Advanced Advertising Theories into Research Reality.* Madrid, Spain.

Van Raaij, W. F. 1975. "Evaluation Process Models: An Overview." *Proceedings of the ESOMAR Seminar on Market Modeling.* Noordwijk van Zee, Netherlands.

Westwood, R., Lunn, J. A., and Beazley, D. 1974a. "The Trade-Off Model and Its Extensions." *Journal of Market Research Society* 16, no. 3:227–241.

_____. 1974b. "Models and Modeling, Part 1. New Approaches to Belief Importance." *European Research* 2, no. 3.

_____. 1974c. "Models and Modeling, Part 2. Models and Structures." *European Research* 2, no. 4:152–158.

Wilkie, W. L. and Pessemier, E. A. 1973. "Issues in Marketing's Use of Multi-Attribute Attitude Models." *Journal of Marketing Research,* no. 4:428–441.

Wind, Y., Jolly, S., and O'Connor, A. 1975. "Concept Testing as Input to Strategic Marketing Simulation." In *Proceedings of the American Marketing Association,* ed. E. Mazzie.

Chapter 6

Applications of Behavioral Theories to the Study of Family Marketing Behavior

Robert Ferber*

Editors' Note

In his selective review of consumer behavior models, Lunn focuses on the individual. Much consumer research is indeed about *individual* decision processes. For years, scholars such as Nelson Foote and Wroe Alderson have recognized the need to understand the *family* as the unit of decision making, and yet only in recent years have some conceptual and methodological developments begun to emerge.

Most behavioral sciences can be brought to bear on the study of a two-or-more-person decision unit. Hence, no single chapter can provide a comprehensive review of all possible inputs relevant to the construction of models of family buying-decision processes. This chapter illustrates the relevance of the behavioral sciences by proposing an integrative framework and by discussing the applications of three major concepts.

The purpose of this chapter is to discuss and illustrate some applications of behavioral concepts to the market behavior of the family. The discussion is

Robert Ferber is Research Professor and Director of the Survey Research Laboratory, University of Illinois.

based on a conceptual framework of the factors entering into family decisions. (For applications of this framework to family finance decisions, see Ferber 1973*b*.) Although the focus is on the behavior of the family, we cannot lose sight of the fact that a family is a group. The study of family behavior can be approached at three levels: (*a*) the individual level, (*b*) the aggregate level, and (*c*) the level of the family as a system of interpersonal interaction. Most conceptual and empirical work has been at the first level. This will not affect our discussion, except that in our case the objective in studying the behavior of individuals is to obtain better insight into the market behavior of the *family unit.*

A Conceptual Framework

A previous formulation of this framework was on financial decision making within the family—in other words, on such decisions as whether to save or to spend, where to save, and the management of one's assets. These decisions are essentially marketing decisions since, in each of these instances, the family is deciding what action to take in the marketplace, albeit this marketplace may refer to "financial goods" rather than to products and product-related services. Thus the reverse aspect of the decision to save is the decision to spend; the selection of a type of asset in which to save is conceptually identical to the selection of a product on which to make a purchase; the selection of a savings institution is essentially the same as selection of a brand of a particular product; and decisions on management of one's assets are analogous to decisions on management of one's goods and other possessions. Although the variables and alternatives may be different in each case, from a conceptual point of view the factors entering into these decisions are essentially the same.

For these reasons the early conceptual framework can be broadened to cover all family marketing decisions. This framework is shown in Figure 6.1. It differs from the earlier framework in the change of two words, made not to alter any meaning, but to bring out the particular aspects more strongly.[1] Thus as in the earlier diagram, the three rectangular boxes at the top represent the principal exogenous forces influencing the marketing actions of the family and the attitudes of the different family members. Thus reference groups will influence the attitudes of the husband, wife, and any other family members who may be present. The sociodemographic and other characteristics of individual family members obviously influence their attitudes, while some of these characteristics, such as occupation, will influence the financial resources of the family.

The third box, "external events," is essentially in the nature of a catch-all category for the innumerable economic and other events that enter into family decisions, with the most likely avenue for such events being through the financial resources of the family. At the same time, however, from a marketing point of view these events may also affect the attitudes of the different family

---

1. The reference is to Ferber (1973*b*, Chart 2, p. 55). The changes were made to alter the term "family structure" to "family roles," and at the bottom of the diagram, to put "Marketing Decisions" in place of "Financial Decisions."

Figure 6.1

**FACTORS ENTERING INTO MARKETING DECISIONS
WITHIN THE FAMILY**

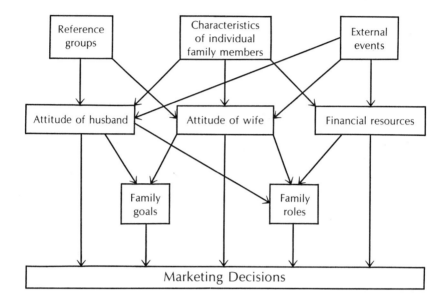

members, and arrows have therefore been added from this box to the attitudinal factors on the second level.

Moving down one level in this diagram, we encounter the key decision-determining variables, "family goals" and "family roles." The goals of a family are determined largely by the attitudes of its members, which in turn have been influenced by their characteristics, the reference groups with which they came in contact, and external events. The family roles, which represent the influence and responsibility that each family member exerts in the family decisions, are influenced by all the variables at the higher levels.

These two key family variables, goals and roles, are major determinants of family marketing decisions. Family member attitudes and financial resources are shown to influence family marketing decisions both directly and through these two key family variables. It is perhaps needless to mention that all of these activities and decisions take place over time, with numerous lag relationships involved at different stages, so that the framework is a highly dynamic one. Conceptually, any particular decision should be representable in the form of a system of equations, though in practice the necessary information and data are not yet likely to be available.

The Use of Behavioral Concepts

Although this framework is a fairly simple one and much more elaborate ones have been developed to represent consumer marketing behavior (see, for example, Howard & Sheth 1969, Burk 1967, and Nicosia 1966) it can serve as a useful medium for indicating how various behavioral concepts may be applied to the study of family marketing behavior. Thus some of the questions that almost immediately come to mind and that involve such concepts are:

1. What are the reference groups that affect the attitudes of different family members from a marketing point of view? How is the effect of these reference groups manifested on family member attitudes? Answers to such questions involve, on the one hand, use of concepts from communication research and, on the other hand, the study of small groups.

2. How are attitudes of the different family members influenced by their characteristics and by the characteristics of other family members? Clearly, an answer to this question involves use of concepts from personality and social psychology, on which there exists an immense literature that has still to be applied to this area of inquiry.

3. How do the characteristics of individual family members influence the financial resources of the family? This question is partly psychological and partly economic and requires simultaneous application of concepts from both of these major disciplines.

4. How do external events influence the attitudes of the different family members? Again, this is clearly a question that involves the use of concepts from social psychology.

5. How do external events influence the financial resources of the family? This is a question of economic analysis and, although much work has been done on this subject at an aggregative level, relatively little has been done at the level of the individual family.

6. How are family goals formed? How are these goals influenced by the attitudes of the different family members? Indeed, from a marketing viewpoint, what is meant by family goals? Much work has been done on this question by home economists, but operational definitions for marketing purposes still have to be developed; very little has been done as yet on the relationship between attitudes of different family members and family goals.

7. How do family member attitudes relate to the roles that different members play in the family from a marketing point of view? Family sociologists, social psychologists, and home economists have developed numerous concepts relating to this question, but virtually nothing seems to have been done as yet to bring these concepts together to describe relationships of this type from a marketing viewpoint.

8. How do financial resources influence family goals and family roles? Some work on this subject has been done by home economists, but again practically nothing exists in terms of marketing applications.

9. Last, but certainly not least, how do all these different variables interact, both directly and indirectly, to influence the marketing decisions of the family? This question involves moving toward the third level of analysis which sees the family as a system of interactions among its members.

To be sure, possible answers to this broader question can still be investigated within a simpler framework—and this is being done—but such an answer can only be a partial one at best. Even so, such an answer is bound to involve applications of concepts from these other disciplines.

What we propose to do in the remainder of this chapter is to focus on three especially promising concepts, the use of which enters into a resolution of some of these individual questions posed earlier as well as into resolution of the basic question on the factors influencing family marketing decisions. For each of these factors, we will indicate how they enter into this framework, review their implications from a theoretical viewpoint, and then illustrate how they have been, or might be, applied to the study of market behavior. The concepts on which we shall focus are: the concept of permanent income, the concepts of attitudes and intentions to buy, and the concepts of family roles.

The Permanent Income Concept

It seems hardly possible that the topic of financial resources as an influencing factor in marketing decisions would have been overlooked in the past. It is a key variable in the conceptual framework presented in Figure 6.1 and is taken into account in any consideration of factors relevant to consumer marketing decisions, at least to the extent that current family income or current resources are introduced as variables in such studies—whether theoretical or empirical. Yet, rather paradoxically, by doing so, marketing analysts seem to be overlooking a major facet of financial resources, a facet that is a well-accepted tool among consumer economists—namely, the concept of permanent income.

This concept derives from the very provocative idea propounded over twenty years ago by Milton Friedman (but which had still earlier origins) to the effect that consumption expenditures are determined not by the current level of income of the family, but by the latter's idea of the average annual income it can expect to receive over its lifetime. Since the theory is explained very well in a number of sources, it need only be mentioned here that, according to this theory, a family's total income, as well as consumption, in a particular period—say, a year—is divided into permanent and transitory components. The hypothesis is that only the permanent components of income and consumption are related to each other, while the transitory components are related neither to each other nor to the permanent components. (For an especially good explanation, see Mayer 1972. Also see the original exposition in Friedman 1955.)

Although later empirical work has placed considerable doubt on the validity of these individual hypotheses (Mayer 1972, Ferber 1973), these studies have also shown that the concept of permanent income is highly meaningful for analytical purposes and for understanding consumer behavior. Thus it is clearly feasible to divide income and consumption expenditures into permanent and transitory components. Also, the propensity to consume out of the permanent component, although not in accord with the original theory, seems to be very different from the propensity to consume out of transitory income, at least with regard to total expenditures and to total expenditures for durable goods. In other words, being able to segregate income into permanent and transitory components seems likely to yield a better understanding of both total expenditures and many of their components.

Moreover, some very interesting work has also been done on the determinants of spending out of transitory income, which suggests that a relatively small amount of such income is likely to be spent, while a larger amount is either likely to be saved or spent later on a major durable good (Landsberger 1966).

In view of these provocative findings, one may well ask how the permanent-income concept has been applied to marketing research. The surprising answer is that, to the best of my knowledge, not a single such application has yet been attempted, even though, as mentioned before, the theory is over twenty years old.

The logical product areas of application would be major durables, financial services, and major services other than financial, such as vacations. Topics for investigation might include the extent to which better explanations and forecasts of such expenditures by individual families can be obtained by the use of this concept and whether particular products and services may not be especially sensitive to fluctuations in transitory rather than in permanent income. Thus products with a highly elastic demand, such as luxuries, may be more likely to be purchased by families that have received transitory income, especially if the amount of such income makes such a purchase possible. If a couple suddenly receives an inheritance of, say, $300, and had hoped to buy an automatic dishwasher at some future time, this unexpected money may well influence the couple to use the funds for that purpose.

In a somewhat similar manner, one may also hypothesize that large amounts of transitory income (several hundred dollars or more) are likely to be either spent for large-ticket items (a high-cost durable, a vacation, etc.) or put into some form of savings. Alternatively, a relatively small amount of transitory income—say, $10 to $20—is more likely to be spent for a number of different things, such as particular items of clothing or better groceries.

Still another hypothesis would be that, other things being equal, a family receiving transitory income is more likely to be receptive to trying a new product. The rationale for this view is that because this income was unexpected, the family is more likely to look on it as something to be spent for purposes out of the ordinary, assuming of course that the family does not need the money for everyday living expenses.

Also worthy of investigation is the question of whether, for the same product, particular brands are perhaps more likely to be purchased out of transitory rather than out of permanent income. Thus one hypothesis that might be tested is that brand loyalty varies in inverse proportion to the relative amount of transitory income received by a family, for might not such a windfall income make the family more receptive to trying different brands of a product that has been of interest, but on which the family did not think it should spend its regular funds?

Means of estimating transitory and permanent income is an area for investigation itself and one to which marketing researchers could undoubtedly make contributions. At the present time the most common means of segregating income into these two components with cross-section data is to begin by estimating permanent or "normal" income on the basis of a regression of observed income on age, occupation, education, and other variables that might be expected to act as long-run determinants of income (for example, see Friend 1966). The estimate computed for a particular family by using this regression is then considered to be permanent income. The difference between observed income and this estimate of permanent income is then transitory income.

Little evidence is available at the present time on the sensitivity of results obtained from use of the permanent-income theory to the particular means of estimating permanent income. Even so, it seems clear from past work that the current estimation procedure is rather crude and needs improvement. A highly promising means of improving these estimates would seem to lie in the use of panel data, which are scarce in economics but with which marketing researchers are relatively well endowed. The estimation of permanent income through the use of panel data should considerably improve the reliability and stability of the results obtained on purchasing behavior from use of the concepts of the permanent-income theory.

Such undertakings, however, require conceptual and methodological development concerning the choice of the unit of analysis, i.e., resolving the difficulties in moving from the application of the concept at the individual level to that of the "relevant" family unit.

Attitudes and Intentions

Many different types of consumer attitudes enter into marketing decisions—attitudes toward life, business conditions, inflation, and product purchases, among others. Our concern here is with the latter, principally because of the very great attention it has received in recent years.

Although economic theory has considered the ability to buy (or income) as the basic determinant of consumer purchases for at least two hundred years, it was only toward the middle of this century that social psychologists and others suggested that the desire to make a purchase should be considered as another key variable, possibly on an equal plane of importance. That this latter development occurred fairly recently may itself be interpreted as an economic phenomenon since it was only recently that this nation and others reached a stage of affluence where most consumers can choose to make purchases as a matter of preference rather than as a matter of necessity.

While economists were not unaware of this trend, the idea has been pushed and developed to a much greater extent by other social sciences. Within the social sciences there are numerous conceptual and empirical approaches to the study of attitude formation and change (to name a few: Hovland, Lazarsfeld, Katz, Festinger, Rosenberg, and Abelson).

The following discussion will be concerned mainly with the contributions of economic psychology. In particular, George Katona (Katona & Mueller 1954) gained wide acceptance of the importance of the concept of desire to buy. This "attitude" makes a net contribution to the explanation of auto and other major durable goods purchases even after fluctuations in income are taken into account.

This concept has proved especially effective in explaining variations in consumer durable goods purchases over time, although it has not been as successful as data on consumer "intentions to buy" for explaining variations in purchases among households at the same point in time.

In effect, these and other attitudes attempt to measure consumer desire for products. From an analytical point of view, these measures may be divided into two types—those that seek to explain the purchase of a product and those that seek to explain the selection of a brand, given that a purchase is made. The attitude approach of Katona focuses on the former problem. The same is true of the field force theory of Kurt Lewin, which was applied to marketing some years ago by Warren Bilkey (1957). By that approach, consumers were asked to indicate on a set of scales the intensity of their desires and off-setting costs (valences) toward purchasing particular products, the idea being that a purchase will be made when the sum of the positive valences sufficiently exceeds the sum of the negative valences.

The prediction of brand choice, given that a purchase has been made, seems to have occupied marketing researchers much more than the prediction of a purchase. Since marketing researchers discovered Morris Fishbein, and vice versa, the journals have been full of attempts to develop attitude indexes to reflect preference for different brands of a product based on weighted sums of product attributes and importance ratings. It is not at all clear that the results are any better, or even as good, as the very simple approach reported some time ago of asking individuals which brand they would buy if they were to make a purchase of that product (Axelrod 1968).

In fact, by any of these approaches, a behavioral-intention measure tends to provide a good indication of the brand that the consumer will actually purchase. Unfortunately, the focus of so many of these studies on the use of these methods for predicting or explaining brand choice has led to the tendency to equate behavioral intention with behavior on a number of types of actions where no such premise is warranted. This oversight, particularly prevalent in the minds of many on product purchases, is a very serious mistake. In fact, the many studies of this question indicate that although intentions data may make a net contribution to the explanation of later purchases, the degree of correlation is very low and not too useful for predictive purposes. This is especially so since such a relationship is statistically significant only for cross-section data and seems to be hardly in evidence on a time-series basis. The fact of the matter is that the presumed equality between behavioral intentions and behavior is likely to be more of an exception than the rule. Indeed, after extensive studies of this question, and primarily for these reasons, the U.S. Bureau of the Census in 1973 ceased the collection of buying-intentions data on a quarterly basis, as it had been doing for a number of years (for a critical review, see Juster 1974).

Considering the variables involved and the current state of forecasting, marketing researchers seem to have been placing too much emphasis on using concepts from attitude theory to explain brand purchases and too little to explain product purchases. The real potential for the use of attitude in marketing research would seem to lie in the development of better models that combine attitudinal variables with other variables to explain and predict the purchases of both a particular product and a brand.

Product-purchase models have already been developed by economists from a broad aggregative point of view, as exemplified by the FBMIT and the Brookings models (such as DeLeeuw & Gramlick 1961). An article by Juster and Wachtel (1972) provides another good example of how behavioral intentions may be combined with other variables. The problem for marketing researchers is to adapt these measures and approaches to focus on individual products, especially in the case of major durables and services.

Notwithstanding the negative results obtained from the use of buying intentions for predicting purchases on a time-series basis, it behooves marketing researchers to investigate further the possibilities of these data, especially by including in a model equations that explain purchases in terms of attitudes, buying intentions, and other variables, and at the same time, to have separate equations to explain attitudes and buying intentions. The possibility of recursive systems of this type has yet to be investigated.

Also badly needing investigation is the differential effect of the attitudes of different family members on marketing decisions. Although such differentials are highlighted by the conceptual framework in Figure 6.1, in practice little attempt has been made to investigate the extent to which attitudes of different family members may differ and, particularly, the effect of such differences on subsequent purchases. In at least one study (Ferber and Lee 1973), differences in intentions to purchase automobiles were frequently found between husbands and wives, and these differences were manifested in the extent to which purchase plans were fulfilled. Other studies with the same data suggest that such differences are not limited to automobiles.

Family Roles

The role of different family members in purchase decisions and the sources from which information for such decisions are obtained is another key box in the conceptual framework of factors influencing purchase decisions. Yet, these influences have been studied primarily by sociologists and home economists rather than by marketing analysts. More recently, some attention has been given to these questions in marketing research but with the impetus still from these other fields. (This discussion is based on Ferber 1973b.)

At least two general hypotheses have been advanced to explain the role of husband and wife in influencing spending in different families. Bott (1955) suggested that the extent to which families do things jointly, such as spending money, depends on the "connectedness" of their social network; that is, whether husband and wife have the same friends and interests. Connectedness is said to be more prevalent if the family has low mobility, lives in a fairly homogeneous neighborhood, and the husband is in the working (blue-collar) class.

Taking a somewhat different approach, Komarovsky (1961) advanced the idea, based on examination of various empirical studies, that "there is greater autonomy with regard to expenditures at the bottom and at the top of the socioeconomic hierarchy than among the middle classes" (p. 260). The studies she examined tend to support the fact that the wife in the lower socioeconomic classes seems to have greater influence in decision making relating to expenditures. In addition, in all social classes she found a higher rate of joint decision making on spending among young couples.

A roughly similar point of view was taken by Barton (1955). He argued that, according to marketing research observations, housewives forty-five years of age and over tend to have accumulated sufficient experience so that they can act essentially as professional purchasing agents for the family, even with regard to men's clothes and furnishings; and they know the needs of their family well enough so that consultation is much less likely to be needed.

The empirical studies of these questions have taken many different forms and, not surprisingly, have yielded results that are not always compatible. In one of the earlier studies of this subject, based on the replies of marketing students in seven universities about their parents' behavior, Converse and Crawford (1949) estimated the percent of purchases influenced by women, men, and children according to category of the products. They found that men make most purchases of their own clothing and toilet articles, hardware, cars, and gas and oil; women, of their own clothing and children's clothing and of home furnishings; while children are important only with regard to their own clothing purchases. They also found that joint purchases are in the majority only for furniture, and that joint shopping and joint influence tend to be lower among low-income families.

Another study based on interviews with parents corroborated some of the Converse and Crawford findings in that purchases of furniture and household equipment were planned on a joint basis approximately 75 percent of the time, and that children usually participated with the parents only in buying their own clothing (Van Syckle 1951). In another study, however, Wolgast (1958) noted that joint decisions on the purchase of household goods were reported only 54 percent of the time, while Sharp and Mott (1956) reported joint decisions on a major item, such as the selection of a house or an apartment, only 58 percent of the time. However, the data in the latter study were obtained only from the wife.

On the basis of these various studies one may infer that a tendency toward increased joint decision making with regard to purchases is likely to characterize younger families, those families in which the husband and wife have been married a short time, middle-class families, and also those purchases where a substantial outlay relative to family income may be involved. In addition, Granbois hypothesized that joint participation in the process of deciding purchases "will vary directly with the degree in which they [family members] directly engage in use of the product" and is more likely "the more nearly equal the contribution of resources such as income, education, and social participation by husbands and wives" (1971, pp. 196–197).

Perhaps the single purchase decision studied most often with regard to husband-wife roles is the auto purchase, and here too the findings are somewhat different. In her study, Wolgast reported that the timing of the car purchase was set by the husband in more than half the families, and jointly in another 28 percent of the cases. Sharp and Mott (1956) reported that in the purchase of the family car, the husband had the greater influence 70 percent of the time and that the decision was made jointly 25 percent of the time, with the dominance of the husband becoming more frequent as income rose.

On the other hand, Davis (1970a), in a study of 211 French-speaking Catholic families in and around Quebec City, found that the relative influence in seven different types of auto-purchase decisions (such as when, where, how much, make, etc.) varied substantially within the family, with the main influence being exerted either by the husband or by the husband and wife together.

A similar finding was reported by Jaffe and Senft (1966). On the basis of a study of ten different products conducted by personal interviews with one or more members of 300 middle-income households in Hartford, Cleveland, and Seattle, they found that husband-wife roles vary substantially depending partly on the product and partly on the stage in the consumption process. The stages in the consumption process used were information gathering, latent (initiator) stage, purchase, use, and consolidation. They also found, as had Converse and Crawford, that the husband is more important than originally thought in the selection and the purchase of many of these products.

Two other very different studies tended to support the hypothesis that husband and wife roles vary substantially with the particular type of decision, and that many different decisions may underlie a particular purchase. In one such case, Cahalan (1961) reported on a study conducted first by interviewing husbands and wives together to obtain facts on purchases and later by interviewing them separately for their opinions. While the wife was more influential in deciding whether to *consider* buying major appliances and in *thinking* about spending money, the husband seemed to be more influential in the purchase *decision* and in whether to *consider* buying a new car. He also found that husbands in high-status families tend to be more frequently dominant in these decisions than husbands in low-status families.

In the other study, which relates to twelve different aspects of car and furniture purchase decisions of 100 families in Chicago suburbs, Davis (1970b) found that the decision roles in the purchase of a car are not related to decision roles in the purchase of furniture. Moreover, for the same family, Davis advanced the rather surprising hypothesis that the relative influence in "product selection" (model, make, color) is unrelated to the relative influence of that member in "allocation" or "scheduling" (how much or when to buy).

This result may not be entirely unexpected in view of the growing literature in the area of consumer marketing to the effect that people who are opinion leaders in one sense are not necessarily opinion leaders in another sense (King & Summers 1970). This is so even though it also seems to be true that opinion leaders in accepting innovations relating to household goods are more likely to be younger people, well educated, married, having children, and with higher incomes (Mueller 1958). The fact remains that people who tend to take the initiative and tend to be innovative with regard to one aspect of purchase behavior may not be equally aggressive in other aspects.

The identity of the decision maker for numerous purchases will vary substantially from one family to another. If so, the very real and significant question for marketing research becomes to investigate whether and how the purchase of a product (or of a particular brand) may vary with the identity of the decision maker.

That purchase patterns and individual purchases may depend on the identity of the decision maker is a very real possibility and receives support from another study by Ferber and Lee (1974) of panel data on young married couples in Peoria and Decatur. As part of this study, the so-called family financial officer was pinpointed in each of the families on the basis of a series of screening questions as being either the wife, the husband, both jointly, or not clear. As it turned out, a family financial officer could be pinpointed on the basis of these questions in 97 percent of the sample families.

Relating this information to financial and purchase behavior, if the husband alone was the family financial officer, the couple was more likely to save a higher proportion of its income and to put more of its assets into the form of real estate and negotiable securities—that is, it was more likely to make speculative investments. At the same time, auto purchases were less frequent when the husband was the family financial officer. These results were supported by multiple regressions in which the identity of the family financial officer was entered as a dummy variable.

With regard to purchase patterns, the foregoing study has only scratched the surface. No concentrated attempt has been made as yet to investigate the extent to which particular types of purchases and, more generally, purchase patterns are affected by the identity of the family financial officer. Even where the purchase patterns are similar, are the decision processes the same? Moreover, apart from the influence of the family financial officer, what is the influence of different family members at different stages of the decision process? What is the nature of decision interrelationships among different family members in the case of families other than the "simple" nuclear couple? And to what extent does the role of people outside the family vary with the type of decision and the identity of the family financial officer?

Indeed, it is not at all clear that when a wide range of expenditure and saving decisions are considered, the family financial officer is always the same person. Duties may well be delegated from one family member to another, something about which we have virtually no information.

In a roughly analogous manner, the relation of brand choice and brand loyalty (including store loyalty) to the identity of the family financial officer seems hardly to have been considered. While relationships of this type may seem unlikely at first thought, further consideration would seem to suggest that such relationships may well exist. To take one example, if the wife is the family financial officer and does most of the grocery shopping, is she not more likely to be brand loyal to grocery products than the husband because her frequent shopping experiences lead her to develop loyalties to certain products? On the other hand, if the husband is the family financial officer, might he not be less committed to particular brands and be more likely to try different kinds?

Another hypothesis is that when two or more members of the family share responsibility of serving as the family financial officer so that decisions are made jointly, brand loyalty will be lower than when either individual alone is the family financial officer.

To date, most consumer and marketing studies concerned with family behavior have focused on the relatively simple husband-wife dyad. The influence of children on purchase behavior has been largely ignored, despite an increasing interest in the effect of advertising on children. Some of the pertinent findings about children's influence on purchase decisions are summarized below.

The Influence of Children

The studies of Converse and Crawford (1949) and of Van Sycle (1951) suggest that children seem to influence only the purchase of their own clothing. The relatively few other studies on the influence of children on family spending decisions yielded similar results. Thus Brown (1961), in his study on automobile buying decisions, reported that parents claim that their children, even the teenagers, have little influence on the make of car purchased. Rayburn (1956) reported that 27 percent of the mothers she interviewed said that their teenagers were consulted on family purchases, but further details were not obtained.

Perhaps even more surprising is a study by Berey and Pollay (1968) in which they ascertained cereal preferences of forty-eight children in an elementary school and compared them with the cereals that their mothers had purchased and were in the house. A negative correlation was found between the assertiveness of the child (based on teacher ratings) and the tendency of the mother to buy the preferred cereal. The explanation advanced by the authors for this odd finding was that the mothers seemed to be more concerned with buying products that would contribute to the health of the child than with satisfying the child's whims. (The sample was from a middle- to upper-middle-income segment.)

On the other hand, an advertising research study by Munn (1968), based on mail questionnaires to parents with small children, stated that nine of ten parents reported they were influenced by their children in the choice of specific branded products. In addition, substantial proportions reported products being used in the home of the type advertised on children's television programs to which their children had apparently been exposed (based on the choice of the sampling frame). However, the nature of the study (a mail questionnaire), the lack of any control group, and the low rate of response (44 percent) cast doubt on the significance of these findings.

Some attention has also been given to decision making by children, especially by teenagers. In one such study, Gibbs (1963) showed that purchases of grooming, clothing, and recreation items by teenagers in a Georgia high school were mostly planned, although many girls' grooming items were still purchased on the basis of impulse. It does not seem necessary to delve into this literature here (see Cateora 1961). Especially pertinent, however, are the findings of one study that spending and savings habits of adolescent siblings show only low correlations with each other as well as with those of the other children and of the mothers (Phelan & Schvaleveldt 1969).

In a very general sense, two things are clear from the foregoing work on family roles. One is that, contrary to the postulates of earlier economic theory, for the purposes of market behavior the family is not a homogeneous unit but is a collection of individuals with different interests and different motivations, sometimes working with each other and, at other times, working against each other. Second, the implications of this finding for the explanation and the prediction of market behavior have hardly begun.

Concluding Comment

This chapter has tried to show how different behavioral concepts may be applied to the study of marketing decisions within the family. Although each of these applications, and others as well, could be carried out independently, a much more desirable approach is to do so within the context of an integrated framework of family behavior, such as that illustrated in Figure 6.1. This is particularly desirable because a frequent characteristic encountered in the study of marketing behavior is the intercorrelation of different sets of variables. Hence, studying any particular variable in isolation is likely to result in distorted inferences of its influence. In effect, what is suggested in the study of marketing decision making is something similar to a partial equilibrium approach in economic analysis, whereby the effects of particular variables are studied in relation to other variables also felt to be relevant to that particular type of decision. Such an approach not only has advantages from a conceptual and a statistical point of view but is also more likely to yield a balanced view of the role of different types of behavioral influences in family marketing decisions.

References

Axelrod, J. N. 1968. "Attitude Measures That Predict Purchase." *Journal of Advertising Research* 8 (March).

Barton, S. G. 1955. "The Life Cycle and Buying Patterns." In *The Life Cycle and Consumer Behavior*, ed. L. H. Clark. New York: New York University Press.

Berey, L. A. and Pollay, R. W. 1968. "The Influencing Role of the Child in Family Decision-Making." *Journal of Marketing Research* 5 (February):70–71.

Bilkey, W. J. 1957. "Consistency Test of Psychic Tension Ratings Involved in Consumer Purchasing Behavior." *Journal of Social Psychology* 45 (February).

Bott, E. 1955. "Urban Families: Conjugal Roles and Social Networks." *Human Relations* 8:345–384.

Brown, G. H. 1961. "The Automobile Buying Decision within the Family." In *Household Decision-Making*, ed. N. N. Foote. New York: New York University Press.

Burk, M. C. 1967. "An Integrated Approach to Consumer Behavior." *Journal of Home Economics* 59 (March):155–162.

Cahalan, D. 1961. "Comments." In *Household Decision-Making,* ed. N. N. Foote. New York: New York University Press.

Cateora, R. R. 1961. *An Analysis of the Teenage Market.* Austin: University of Texas Bureau of Business Research.

Converse, P. D. and Crawford, C. M. 1949. "Family Buying: Who Does It? Who Influences It?" *Current Economic Comment* 11 (November):28–50.

Davis, H. L. 1970a. "Determinants of Marital Roles in Consumer Purchase Decisions." Unpublished working paper, Graduate School of Business, University of Chicago (October).

———. 1970b. "Dimensions of Marital Roles in Consumer Decision-Making." *Journal of Marketing Research* 7 (May):168–177.

DeLeeuw, F. and Gramlick, E. 1961. "The Federal Reserve-MIT Econometric Model." *Federal Reserve Bulletin* 54 (January).

Du Pont de Nemours, E. I. Company. 1945, 1949, 1954, 1959. *Consumer Buying Habits Studies.*

Evans, F. D. 1959 "Psychological and Objective Prediction of Brand Choice." *Journal of Business* 32 (October).

Farber, B. 1964. *Family Organization and Interaction.* San Francisco: Chandler Publishing Co.

Ferber, R. 1955. *Factors Influencing Durable Goods Purchases.* Urbana: University of Illinois Bureau of Economic and Business Research.

———. 1973a. "Consumer Economics: A Survey." *Journal of Economic Literature* (December).

———. 1973b. "Family Decision-Making and Economic Behavior." In *Family Economic Behavior: Problems and Prospects,* ed. Eleanor Sheldon. New York: Lippincott.

Ferber, R. and Lee, L. C. 1973. "Increasing the Effectiveness of Buying Plans Variables in Economic Models." Working Paper 119. University of Illinois College of Commerce and Business Administration.

———. 1974. "Husband-Wife Influence in Family Financial Economic Behavior." *Journal of Consumer Research* 1 (June).

Friedman, M. 1955. *A Theory of the Consumption Function.* New York: National Bureau of Economic Research.

Friend, I. 1966. "The Propensity to Save in India." In *Economic Development: Policy and Issues,* ed. P. S. Lokanathan. Bombay, India: Fora and Co.

Gibbs, M. 1963. "Decision-Making Procedures by Young Consumers." *Journal of Home Economics* 55 (May):359–360.

Granbois, D. H. 1971. "Decision Processes for Major Durable Goods." In *New Essays on Marketing Theory,* ed. G. Fisk. Boston: Allyn & Bacon.

Howard, J. A. and Sheth, J. N. 1969. *The Theory of Buyer Behavior.* New York: John Wiley & Sons.

Jaffe, L. J. and Senft, H. 1966. "The Roles of Husbands and Wives in Purchasing Decisions." In *Attitude Research at Sea,* ed. L. Adler and I. Crespi. Chicago: American Marketing Association.

Juster, F. T. 1974. "Comment on McNeil, 'Federal Programs to Measure Consumer Expectations.'" *Journal of Consumer Research* 1 (December).

Juster, F. T. and Wachtel, P. 1972. "Anticipatory and Objective Models of Durable Goods Demand." *American Economic Review* 62 (September).

Katona, G. and Mueller, E. 1954. "A Study of Purchase Decisions." In *Consumer Behavior: The Dynamics of Consumer Reaction*, ed. L. H. Clark. New York: New York University Press.

Kenkel, W. F. 1957. "Influence Differentiation in Family Decision-Making." *Sociology and Social Research* 42 (September–October):18–25.

King, C. W. and Summers, J. L. 1970. "Overlap of Opinion Leadership across Consumer Product Categories." *Journal of Marketing Research* 7 (February):43–50.

Komarovsky, M. 1961. "Class Differences in Family Decision-Making in Expenditures." In *Household Decision-Making*, ed. N. N. Foote. New York: New York University Press.

Landsberger, M. 1966. "Windfall Income and Consumption: Comment." *American Economic Review* 56 (June).

Mayer, T. 1972. *Permanent Income, Wealth and Consumption*. Berkeley: University of California Press.

Mueller, E. 1958. "Desire for Innovations in Household Goods." In *Consumer Behavior: Research on Consumer Reactions*, ed. L. H. Clark. New York: Harper & Bros.

Munn, M. 1968. "The Effect on Parental Buying Habits of Children Exposed to Children s Television Programs." *Journal of Broadcasting* 2 (Summer):253–258; reprinted in *Consumer Behavior, Contemporary Research in Action*, ed. R. J. Holloway, R. A. Mittelstaedt, and M. Vankatesan. Boston: Houghton Mifflin, 1971.

Nicosia, F. 1966. *Consumer Decision Processes*. Englewood Cliffs, N.J.: Prentice-Hall.

Phelan, G. K. and Schvaneveldt, J. D. 1969. "Spending and Saving Patterns of Adolescent Siblings." *Journal of Home Economics* 61 (February):104–109.

Rayburn, M. B. 1956. "A Study of Money Management Practices of Selected Rural Families in Pontotoc County, Mississippi." Master's thesis, University of Mississippi.

Schomaker, P. K. and Thorpe, A. C. 1963. "Financial Decision-Making as Reported by Farm Families in Michigan." *Quarterly Bulletin* 46. Michigan State University.

Sharp, H. and Mott, P. 1956. "Consumer Decisions in the Metropolitan Family." *Journal of Marketing* 21 (October):149–156.

Van Syckle, C. 1951. *Practices Followed by Consumers in Buying "Large Expenditure" Items of Clothing, Furniture and Equipment*. Michigan State Agricultural Experiment Station Bulletin 222.

Wilkenberg, E. A. 1958. "Joint Decision-Making in Farm Families." *American Sociological Review* 23 (April).

Wolgast, E. O. 1958. "Do Husbands or Wives Make the Purchasing Decisions?" *Journal of Marketing* 20 (October).

Chapter 7

Behavioral Models of Organizational Buying Processes

F. M. Nicosia and *Yoram Wind**

Editors' Note
Compared with the study of the individual and the family buying behavior, the level of complexity in this chapter increases. Following a brief examination of the current literature on organizational buying, the authors propose a new perspective that stresses the need to study both the intra- and interorganizational processes leading to and following a transaction. Much of the chapter discusses the new research directions implied by this new perspective.

The purpose of this chapter is to assess past and current trends in the literature on buying decisions by organizations and to look constructively toward future problems and developments. Until recently, organizational buying behavior has been largely ignored. There are, however, a number of promising developments, and we might be at the threshold of moving from alchemy to the beginning stages of scientific understanding.

*F. M. Nicosia and Yoram Wind are from the University of California, Berkeley, and the University of Pennsylvania, respectively. The authors would like to thank Karlene Roberts for her helpful suggestions.

The chapter starts with a brief discussion of the *methodological* and *substantive* choices that can be made in studying organizational processes that underlie buying behavior. An appreciation of these choices is necessary for the examination of the past and current literature. The major trends in the study of organizational buying behavior are next identified and evaluated. Building upon these trends we sketch the basic dimensions of the organizational buying processes and highlight some of the major problem areas to be faced in future research and model development. Throughout the chapter we assume some familiarity with the professional and academic literature in industrial buying.

A Framework for the Study of Organizational Buying Processes

As indicated in Part One of this book, the study of any event reflects the researcher's view of the event itself. The study of organizational buying behavior is no exception, and the researcher has to make a series of methodological and substantive decisions. These choices ultimately determine the "real numbers" or "facts" and their meaning as they bear upon the problem under study.

To illustrate, if 80 percent of the advertising budget of a disk-pack manufacturer is allocated to media read primarily by purchasing managers, the implicit or explicit hypothesis is that managers of data processing and machine operators have little or no influence on the purchase of disk packs.

Suppose that this allocation choice is explicit; that is, a survey has been made of a past campaign where the firm allocated one-third of its budget to each of the media read most frequently by purchasing managers, data processing directors, and machine operators. The survey data show that "readership" and "comprehension" were in fact much higher among the purchasing managers and much lower among the data processing directors and machine operators, thereby suggesting the above allocation of 80, 10, and 10 percent, respectively, to the three audiences. So far, all this looks "rational."

Yet, several implicit images of, or assumptions about, the event (purchasing of disk packs) may have sneaked into this seemingly rational procedure. To illustrate, suppose that the test ads stressed economic/cost considerations and/or that the survey questionnaire stressed these considerations in its attempt to measure readership and comprehension. Such methodological choices would necessarily lead purchasing managers to be more likely to notice and comprehend the ads. But, to the extent that the other two audiences are more interested in quality, reliability, freedom from error, and other considerations, the data-processing directors and machine operators would be less likely to notice and comprehend the ads. Thus in constructing the questionnaire it was assumed, consciously or not, that all three audiences are interested in, and thus motivated by, the same factors. If this assumption is incorrect, then no matter how statistically significant the facts are, they lead to the wrong budget allocation. Similarly, other assumptions were made in this case—for example, that readership and comprehension are the relevant criteria, that the three managers are the only ones involved, and that their influence on the final choice is equal and linearly additive.

All in all, whether we are concerned with a researcher's or a manager's image of a phenomenon, methodological and substantive choices determine what we know about it and, eventually, what we do about it. It is therefore essential to spell out the nature and range of these choices. For example, scientific method, including its use of statistical inference, does not and cannot tell us whether we should choose one or another level of observation or analysis, which independent variables should be included in our study, or whether simple cross-tabulation of raw data should be preceded by factor analysis or other procedures.

All methodological choices are, in principle, arbitrary. Their objectivity—and their ultimate validity—must be assessed against two criteria: (*a*) the researcher's or manager's question to be answered, as reflected in their image or model of the phenomenon, and (*b*) the cost versus value consideration.

For both researchers and managers, the first and most crucial set of decisions is the identification and formulation of the problem. This, in turn, provides the guidelines for the development of an appropriate model of organizational buying behavior. The operationalization of this model requires the construction and implementation of a research design which implies many choices—e.g., population and sample selection, cross-sectional or longitudinal design, lab versus field work, etc. Below, we shall consider only a few key choices.

The Unit of Analysis

The alternatives range from a focus on the individual purchasing agent, the buying center (i.e., all persons involved in the buying process), the entire organization, to an aggregate analysis at the total market level. The choice of an appropriate unit of analysis affects the subsequent and critical choices of variables, their measurement, and analytical procedures. This choice involves complex procedures which are generally ignored; in fact, most current research focuses on individuals as units rather than higher-order groups and variables *inherent to groups.* Also, current research often chooses only one organizational unit (e.g., the purchasing department), thus ignoring the implications of intra-organizational heterogeneity and multiplicity of influences and conflicts.

The Dependent and Independent Variables

In developing a model of organizational buying processes, it is essential to select the desired dependent variable(s). Should it be the purchase of a given product or service? The amount purchased? The specific brand selected? The brand loyalty pattern? The decision process of an individual or the entire purchasing department? Should it be a purchase activity, such as preparing a requisition, negotiating, conducting a value analysis, or transmitting certain types and amounts of information? Or should it be the buyers' attitudes toward various vendors? Or the criteria they intend to use in selecting vendors?

The selection of any of these or other dependent variables is essentially guided by the nature of the questions asked and one's own view of what an organizational buying process is. It is important to note, however, that many of the variables mentioned as possible dependent variables can, in turn, serve as the independent (explanatory) variables once the specific dependent variable(s) has (have) been selected. It is this arbitrary boundary that suggests the desirability of identifying the total set of relevant data (including both dependent and independent variables). Once such a data matrix has been completed, the researcher can partition it into dependent and independent variables according to his or her specific model and needs and can change the partitioning rule as may be required. All of this applies to the choice of the so-called intervening (endogenous) variables.

The variables that should be considered for inclusion in the data matrix, and which traditionally have been viewed as the components of organizational buying processes, can be grouped into four sets.

1. General organizational characteristics
   a. standard industrial classification
   b. size
   c. economic and financial resources
   d. nature of operations and technology
   e. geographical location
   f. general buying procedures and rules
   g. etc.
2. Situation-specific organizational characteristics
   a. amount and type of purchases
   b. vendors considered acceptable
   c. criteria for vendor selection
   d. composition of the buying center
   e. buying situation: straight rebuy, modified rebuy, or new task
   f. etc.
3. General characteristics of the individual decision maker(s)
   a. age
   b. sex
   c. position and task in the organization
   d. personality
   e. etc.
4. Situation-specific characteristics of the individual decision maker(s)
   a. attitude toward vendors
   b. loyalty to vendors
   c. criteria used in selecting vendors[1]
   d. response to marketing stimuli
   e. etc.

1. The criteria used by an organization in making purchase decisions are a most useful basis for segmentation of organizational buyers in a fashion analogous to benefit segmentation of consumers; see Wind (1973*b*).

The consideration of these and similar components of organizational buying implies that the researcher is interested in developing a behavioral model of organizational processes (as opposed to the use of a simple black box—i.e., "stimulus-response" or "input-output" type of model). Furthermore, behavioral models require information on both controllable (by the firm's managers) and uncontrollable variables. Such models also focus on task-related variables (e.g., desire to obtain the lowest price) and on nontask-related variables (e.g., a buyer's personal values) (Webster & Wind 1972).

Selecting the variables to be included in the data matrix still requires a number of measurement decisions, such as: Which operational definitions must be developed for the selected variables? What scale properties are required? How are the variables to be treated—as single measures or composite indices?

Nature of Association and Type of Model

Once the data matrix is specified, the researcher still has the task of determining the type of model to be developed—a verbal, a logical flow, or a mathematical model (see Chapter 4 of this book). In addition, he has to determine the nature of the association between the dependent and independent variables (linear or nonlinear), the stochastic and dynamic nature of the model, and the desirability of using the model as input or framework for appropriate computer simulation.

Nature of Analysis

Given the data and model, the research task involves data analysis. In planning and conducting this analysis, decisions should be made concerning the focus of analysis—subjects (as in segmentation research), variables (as in product positioning), or a combined analysis of both subjects and variables, as in joint space multidimensional scaling (Wind 1973a), or in the discontinuous models of latent structure analysis (Nicosia 1976). In addition, decisions should be made concerning the specific analytical techniques to be employed. (For a discussion of multivariate techniques, see, e.g., Green & Tull 1974.)

In the following sections we shall rely on this framework to position current and emerging trends and to locate problems in the study of organizational buying.

Past and Current Trends in the Study of Organizational Buying

The literature on organizational buying ranges from academic to professional, from basic to applied, and covers almost the entire spectrum of human endeavors. Numerous disciplines (e.g., economics and the behavioral and management sciences) and especially various professions (e.g., purchasing, material management, and marketing) have all contributed directly or indirectly to the growth and consolidation of the field.

The study of buying by organizations has been approached from several different viewpoints. One classification of these was suggested by Webster and Wind (1972), who distinguished between task, nontask, and complex models. The *task-oriented models* include those such as the minimum price model, the lowest total cost model, the rational buyer model, the material management model, the reciprocal buying model, and the constrained choice model. The *nontask models* introduce behavioral (or, as some call them, nonrational) factors into the buying situation and include the self-aggrandizement model, the ego enhancement model, the perceived risk model, the dyadic interaction model, the lateral relationships model, the buying influence model, and the diffusion process models.

While the task and nontask models capture the spirit of the traditional literature, the third category of *complex models* represents a new, emerging trend. Among the more popular are a number of decision process models, the COMPACT model, the BUYGRID model, and a few computer simulations of the organizational buying process (for a discussion of these, see Webster and Wind 1972).

A more common classification is by discipline. The following subsections highlight some of the major features of the purchasing/marketing models, the economic models, and the emerging interdisciplinary models.

Purchasing/Marketing Models

Both the professional and academic (especially textbook) variants of the industrial selling, marketing, and purchasing literature have been concerned with how to sell to organizations or how an organization should buy. Beginning in the 1940s, we notice a consolidation of perspectives, topics, terms, and other technical items, and especially a consolidation of "dos" and "don'ts"; that is, a substantial agreement on the *marketing principles* that should guide marketing decisions toward a higher probability of making profitable sales, and on the *purchasing principles* that should improve the buying procedures of an organization.

But are these dos and don'ts based on explicit and hard knowledge of the *organizational processes* that eventually evolve into the "decisions" to sell-buy? As we shall see, the answer is largely negative, for we notice in the marketing-selling and purchasing literature a conspicuous lack of explicit assumptions and facts about these buying processes. The principles established in the literature seem essentially sound and intuitively clear—in practice they seem to work. But it appears that the only key to success is the intuitive feelings of marketers and salesmen as to what makes organizations buy. Why do we depend on intuition in applying these principles? Why are such principles not derived from explicit *knowledge* of organizational buying processes?

The established literature in industrial purchasing has achieved a high sophistication in describing the "what" of buying decisions—that is, it lists rather completely the *activities* that are necessary components of a buying process, e.g., preparing a requisition, receiving and inspecting of goods, vendors' evaluation, and value analysis.[2]

These achievements of this traditional literature are certainly fundamental and were not easy to attain. Yet, *activities* are not the only relevant aspect of any individual or organizational decision process. A more complete picture of decision making in an organization includes the observation and understanding of *who* performs which activity, both at the individual and group levels, and eventually the *why*—that is, why are certain activities performed by such individuals or groups in some types of firms but not in others? Is it because of factors internal to the firms (e.g., differences in technological know-how, financial strengths, past history, personality and group traits), and/or because of factors external to the firms (e.g., variations in economic conditions, geographic characteristics involving both the inputs and outputs of markets, the kind of competitive situations in both markets, the laws and regulations applicable to some but not all firms)?

It is understandable why the industrial purchasing literature has emphasized the more immediate needs to systematize procedures and activities—that is, what to do and how to do it—for these are useful means in gaining management acceptance of the idea that buying implies highly skilled operations (i.e., activities). Yet it is surprising that industrial firms have not followed the example of firms selling consumer goods and have not devoted substantial and continuous efforts to understanding more precisely and explicitly the organizational processes that underlie the buying decisions of their prospective customers.

Economic Models

Two branches of economics have and may have some bearing on the study of organizational buying processes: managerial economics and a branch of economics called industrial organization theory.

Managerial Economics

This theory of a firm's decision making has reached a high level of sophistication and sufficient maturity to be encoded into precise mathematical models. Its key contribution is that it allows us to compute "optimal" decisions with respect to what and how much to buy (or sell), given one or more goals and limitations confronting a decision maker.

Since the 1950s, mathematical and computational developments have allowed economists to identify optimal decisions with respect to a utility function that may include several goals (needs) held by any subject—a consumer, a family, or an organization of persons. Such developments have made

---

2. We must stress that both the academic and professional literature in this area has succeeded in standardizing topics and even basic terminology and procedures. This consolidation of perspectives in the study of buying *activities* is already evident in the first edition of Aljian's *Purchasing Handbook* (1958) and in the early editions of classic textbooks (e.g., England 1970, and Heinritz & Farrell 1965).

managerial economics practical in a number of areas of relevance to organizational buying, for instance, inventory control, quality control, warehouse location, scheduling, and so on. Although the operations research departments of some firms deal with such topics, the vast majority of firms' buying departments, as well as textbooks on industrial purchasing, reflect very few of these developments and applications.

Industrial Organization Theory

Another branch of economics has developed a way to think about the organization of an "industry," i.e., the economic relationships among firms. The most frequent and visible attempts to apply this theory are in public policy and especially in antitrust legislation (see Chapter 9 in this book). The established purchasing literature is rather insulated from the developments of this branch of economic theory. Yet, it is extremely useful to understand trends in demand and supply, and intra- and inter-industries' relationships as captured by input/output analysis.

All in all, the incorporation of these theories in organizational buying models can expand our understanding and improve the performance of the buying function. But even when the merging of such theories is accomplished, we still have only a partial view of organizational buying, for economic theories are concerned with optimizing a *decision* and not with describing decision *processes*—i.e., how people interact among themselves through formal and informal ties within an organization *and* across organizations.

Emerging Interdisciplinary Models

Industrial purchasing texts say "the purchasing manager decides. . . ."; the applied economic texts say "the decision maker chooses. . . ."; and so on. But in an organization of two or more persons, things are more complex and it is necessary to study both the individuals or groups involved *and* the way they interact.

Even when *one* person makes the final decision, the information used by this person was prepared and filtered by an organization of persons and departments who, furthermore, will "implement" the decision. Even when only *one* buyer and only *one* seller meet, much of what they bring to the meeting relates back to other persons and departments in their respective organizations, and the consequences of their decision will, in turn, affect other persons and departments.

Organizational buying and selling is a multidimensional process. Our understanding of it must include not only activities of the buying *process*, but also the people who initiate and perform these activities and an evaluation of the results of such activities. The emerging literature recognizes this complexity and can be characterized by the following:

1. Unlike the tradition of viewing a purchase as an act, this literature focuses on the *process* of organizational decisions by people leading to and

following the act of purchasing. This calls for the *description* of a buying process over time in great detail: the interactions of people and activities, i.e., who does what, when, and where, are mapped out by flowcharts (for some pioneering work, see Cyert et al. 1956, Harding 1966, and Robinson et al. 1967).

2. The approach is *descriptive*. The researcher simply asks: "What happens?" instead of using the normative approach, which asks: "What should happen?" A normative approach to the study of any phenomenon must be preceded by a description and understanding of how it does in fact behave. That is, we may have a clear idea of how our car's engine *should* behave, but we cannot make it behave the way we wish unless we know *how* it actually is working. As stated in other chapters, we cannot optimize the performance (behavior) of a process if we do not know *how* the process actually works.

3. Description requires observation and this, in turn, requires the choice of what and how to observe. The models and research methods employed have been primarily those elaborated in the *behavioral sciences*.

4. The emerging literature makes practically no use of, or reference to, the notion of *rationality*. It is necessary here to clarify a subtle but crucial problem that has hindered our understanding of industrial buying. The traditional literature often relies on the notion of rationality as if this notion were that postulated in economics. This is incorrect, for in economics this concept has a very precise but limited meaning—that is, *given* a subject's preferences, the means available to him/her, and the environment, one can compute the choice that is "best" with respect to the decision maker's own preferences. If the subject makes another choice which would not best satisfy his/her preferences, then, and only then, is he/she irrational.

The emerging literature argues that the behavior of a buyer cannot be classified as rational or irrational unless the buyer's preferences are known. It then proposes the distinction between "task" and "nontask" variables as a practical way of overcoming the limitations of the time-honored dichotomy of "rational-irrational" or "economic-emotional" behavior. This distinction is based on the premise that organizational buying behavior is affected by *both* economic, task-related variables and social-psychological, nontask-related variables (Webster and Wind 1972).

5. Organizational buying activities involve many people who occupy a variety of buying roles. Users, influencers, deciders, and buyers can be identified in most buying situations, and there are likely to be a number of people enacting each role—several influencers, decision makers, users, etc. To put it differently, the buying process tends to be *diffused* throughout an organization. Increasing evidence suggests that this "diffuseness" applies to many firms in different industries (for recent evidence concerning all industries in the Chemical Processing Industry SIC group, see Swandby 1973). Furthermore, the persons occupying each role in a given organization are likely to change from one purchase situation to the next.

The emerging research trend, therefore, strongly argues that observation and measurement should not be concerned exclusively with the buyer—the organizational "specialist" for buying who is a member of the purchasing department—but with a *buying center,* i.e., all those individuals and groups who participate in the purchasing decision process and who, although interested in a purchase, may have different goals and bear different risks arising from the decisions.

6. All in all, the new trend stresses that organizational buying behavior is a system of dynamic interactions among individuals within the context of a formal organization, and that such interactions are affected by four interrelated sets of variables: *individual, social, organizational,* and *environmental* characteristics (Webster & Wind 1972 and Wind & Lotshaw 1973).

The above six points cannot do justice to the variety of ideas and approaches reflected in the new emerging trend. They are primarily intended to point out the intellectual ferment in both the professional and academic communities that began in the sixties. An appreciation of these points is a necessary introduction to the material in the next sections.

The following discussion of key perspectives and problems is organized around both *intraorganizational* processes (i.e., buying) and *interorganizational* processes (i.e., how two or more organizations interact before, during, and after a transaction). As strange as it may seem, the interdependence of the two processes has been overlooked. Although putting the two sides together presents problems, we must begin to study reality more closely if we want to gain theoretically and practically sound knowledge. Although this "intra versus inter" distinction mostly concerns substantive issues, we shall also discuss methodological issues whenever appropriate.

Constructing Models of Intraorganizational Buying Processes: Perspectives and Problems

To understand the wide variety of organizational buying processes that exist *and* to design better processes, it is essential to observe both *people* (alone and in groups) *and activities.*

Describing Buying Processes in Terms of Individuals and Groups

This is the area about which we know the least. In our opinion, this is because much of the current and past literature tends to make two simplifications: (*a*) "personification" of the organizational process by postulating that the purchase decision is made by one person—the purchasing manager—and (*b*) collapsing the entire process into an anthropomorphic abstraction—the "purchasing department decides."

These two simplifications have for too long led us to study many relevant aspects of organizational buying at the cost of failing to learn anything concrete about how people and departments interact. However useful, these two simplifications have deprived us of concepts and data that are needed not only for theory and model development, but also for answering pressing and practical management questions.

Two Illustrations. The two following examples explain the current situation. In the first, we look at the organizational buying process from within to illustrate what is hidden from us when we personify a decision by saying: "Mr. X decides. . . ." In the second example, we take the point of view of a selling organization and illustrate how many management questions cannot be answered when we think of our potential customers in anthropomorphic terms: "Department Y decides. . . ."

A car manufacturer is tooling up for introduction of a new model in the medium-price range. One of the items to be purchased is seat covers, and many kinds of materials are available. The engineering department (upon consultation with the R&D office) wants an entirely new synthetic material because lab tests have shown it provides high performance with respect to fading, washability, and wear. The production department has learned, however, that the vendor who supplies the seats would have trouble tailoring and bonding the new material to the seat frame. The production department is concerned with smooth assembly operations and few rejects at the quality control station and, therefore, prefers to stick with the proved synthetic material. The marketing department is mostly concerned with whether consumers will recognize the "brand name" of whatever material is used. The legal department is worried about the "fire-resistant qualities" of the material to be chosen because court decisions are clearly setting a trend: a car manufacturer is responsible for everything! Last but not least, there is one item of interest to all, especially to the financial and corporate management: cost.

Even if we were willing to assume that the final decision would be made by one person, the purchasing manager, his decision would have to be derived from the information and pressures originating from all these people and departments. In fact, a successful purchasing manager will explicitly recognize the different points of view of all those involved and will search for points of consensus—that is, he does not make the decision but helps the organization to make a decision that will reconcile as many of these viewpoints as possible. In this sense the purchasing manager *is* or can be the crucial catalyst of an organizational buying process. This basic catalyst function cannot be appreciated as long as we simplify the organizational process by collapsing its "diffuseness" into "Mr. X decides. . . ."

The second simplification prevailing in the literature—the purchasing department decides—is almost a mirror image of that just discussed. To illustrate, suppose that a medium-sized firm wants to introduce a new mechanism for taking the body temperature and pulse of hospital patients. Armed with a prototype of the apparatus and common sense, one can guess that three departments (persons) may be involved in the decision to buy or not to buy: the administration, the chief physicians, and the nurses. That is, a marketing professional intuitively feels that the financial, scientific, and user points of view (and perhaps that of the patients) may affect the decision to buy, or at least try, the new gadget.

But this intuition is not enough for planning a marketing program or at least a market pretest. For example, even if our manufacturer had the time and money to run a pretest, which hospitals should be sampled? Does the weight of the physicians', nurses', and administration's views vary by type of hospital? What do we mean by type of hospital? Large versus small, profit versus nonprofit, urban versus suburban versus rural? In which type of hospital does the viewpoint of the administration or that of the physicians prevail? And in those hospitals where the physicians' role in the buying process is stronger, which types of doctors are more likely to go for mechanical gadgets: those with new or old degrees, trained in which schools, and in what medical traditions?

Can our manufacturer afford the time and cost of finding out whether any of these characteristics of the hospital population are relevant to his/her marketing problem? And if they are relevant, what are their proportions in the population (for, if they are not known, a representative sample cannot be drawn)?

If our manufacturer cannot afford such investments in time and money, can he turn to current "knowledge" for strong and practical theories and models? In our opinion, the answer to these and many other industrial marketing questions is no. Many limitations of current knowledge are due to the two prevailing simplifications—collapsing an organizational process into a decision by a person or a department.

In sum, the development of useful models of organizational buying requires a concentrated effort in observing and describing how people—individually and in groups—share in the processes leading to purchase decisions and follow-up. This need had been perceived by a small but increasing number of researchers (e.g., Cyert et al. 1956, Weigand 1968, Webster & Wind 1972) and managers (Harding 1966, Swandby 1973). Some of the critical research areas are: (1) the number and types of people and departments involved, (2) the individual versus the group issue, and (3) the discrepancy between intended and enacted organizational roles.

1. *The number and types of people and departments involved.* Future studies should carefully trace and record how many and what kinds of people and departments are involved in buying processes. Present experience suggests that both the number and kinds of people involved vary by size of firm, degree of geographical centralization, type of industry and product line, and a few other characteristics. But this experience is still intuitive and must be strengthened by *systematic* research attempting to identify the number and types of persons (roles) involved in the buying process and to observe whether there are *systematic variations* by organizational characteristics and purchase situations.

2. *The individual versus the group.* Just as the job title of an individual may not be informative as to the role played in the buying process, so may the label of a department be uninformative and possibly misleading in our attempts to

understand the buying processes. In some companies, for example, the purchasing department may be involved in practically *all phases* that precede and
follow a purchase decision for *all inputs* (from raw materials to equipment and
operating supplies); in other companies, it may be responsible for *only materials
and supplies;* or it may be responsible for those phases of a buying process that
only lead to delivery of the inputs; and so on with other *combinations.* All such
possible variations may exist in firms that are classified in the "same" SIC
industry.

It is, therefore, useful to trace each individual involved prior to, or at least
concurrent with, tracing of the departments involved in a buying process. This
is essential since the way formal groups interact is observable only by focusing
on individuals and observing their use of *formal and informal* channels in
implementing organizational tasks and the satisfying of other, non–task-oriented goals.

The study of individuals rather than formal groups allows the observation
of the extent to which buying decisions are sufficiently described by the
formally prescribed interactions among formal groups and by informal interactions among informal groups.

In observing the qualities of one or more groups, we make, explicitly or
implicitly, some "measurement" decision concerning the qualities of interest. A
common approach to the measurement of groups' qualities has relied on
"aggregating" the values that any given quality—age, education, years of
service, etc.—has for each member of a group.

Consider age. This quality is "inherent" to each individual member of the
group. We can easily derive from the age of each group member an average age
and then think of this mean value as the age of the group itself. This allows us
to study group behavior; for example, whether the performance of different
buyers' groups varies by their groups' ages.

Such aggregate group properties are not inherent to each group but are
derived by some procedure from qualities inherent to each member. The ease
with which we can make these measurements has probably been one reason
why we have consistently overlooked another approach to the measurement of
groups' qualities, such as cohesiveness, friendship, or centralization. Such
qualities are not inherent to one individual, but rather imply a kind of *relationship* among two or more persons; thus such qualities are *inherent to* a group.[3]

Basic and applied literature on organizational processes has made verbal
use of such group qualities, but it has rarely proceeded to their proper and
direct measurement. Yet we must learn how to measure such qualities, for they
provide additional insights into our understanding of group processes.

3. *Organizational roles.* In principle, an organization assigns a set of rights
and responsibilities—i.e., a role—to an individual, a group (say, a task force), a

---

3. To illustrate, one person may be friendly, but friendship implies at least two persons
and a kind of relationship between these two persons. For a methodological discussion of
the measurement of "aggregate" and "inherent" group qualities, see Nicosia et al.
(forthcoming). For an example of how aggregate group properties may not be appropriate
for modeling industrial adoption processes, see Ozane and Churchill (1968).

department, a division, or whatever. Definitionally, rights and responsibilities imply doing something—i.e., activities—and thus a role is a set of activities that a "unit" can or may perform.

Individuals, however, tend to perceive their role in ways that may differ from those intended by the organization. Thus the "enacting" of a role may lead to unintended results.

A considerable amount of organizational literature has searched for ways to lessen the discrepancies between intended roles and how they are enacted by studying the determinants of role perceptions (e.g., personality traits, social needs, education, aspirations, etc.). This approach has not been applied to the study of organizational buying, and it may be useful in explaining why purchasing departments vary widely in what they do—from simple order taking to a wide range of tasks, including those of a long-range planning (e.g., forecasting) and/or financial nature.

Another important aspect of purchasing roles is the distinction between routinizable (programmed) and unprogrammed roles. There are certainly subsets of activities in organizational buying that can be spelled out precisely and in enough detail to be translated into a computer program (e.g., routine, reorder decisions). But it is also clear that there are many tasks that require "interpretation" of general company policies, market conditions, and so on. That is, there will always be some parts of the buying process that are intrinsically open-ended problems. Here, people must "perceive," be "creative," and use individual judgment. In these cases, a firm cannot avoid the risk of individuals and groups enacting their roles in unintended ways with some likelihood of undesired consequences, but it can provide conditions that facilitate the enacting of intended roles and timely feedbacks when deviations occur.

Describing Buying Processes in Terms of Activities

As noted, much of the established literature on organizational buying has stressed activities—what people as individuals or as members of formal and informal groups do; it has identified essential activities and recorded the many ways in which such activities interact with those performed by other organizational processes. The knowledge gained thus far suggests a few conclusions and some basic directions for future research on organizational buying.

1. *From elemental to higher-order activities.* A purchase is a response to a need; thus the first elemental activity in a buying process is the identification of a need. The next elemental activity implies search for an appropriate means—a tangible or intangible good—to satisfy such a need. Concurrently, another elemental activity is the identification of the source(s) that can provide the appropriate good(s). And so on with other elemental activities, each corresponding to key "chapters" in established textbooks, for example, in industrial procurement.

Each of these elemental activities is, in fact, a problem area to be studied and solved by a decision. Solving a problem implies further activities, gradually more specific in content and less ambiguous in terms of the detailed and varied subset of activities that are necessary for its solution.

This bewildering variety of activities raises the question of whether one can move from the "elemental" descriptions toward the identification of a higher-order set of properties which may explain the variation in the elemental activities. Attempts at developing higher-order properties include the type of inputs purchased and the different kinds of purchase situations—essentially the nature of the decision and especially the informational requirements and uncertainties faced.

Three such buying situations were identified in the BUYGRID model as new buy, modified rebuy, and straight rebuy. Each of these situations activate different kinds and amounts of activities (and persons). The "new buy" process, on the one hand, activates practically all the elemental activities, whereas the "straight rebuy," on the other hand, requires only a minimum number of activities. Concurrently, the former implies a maximum amount of information gathering and uncertainty, while the latter implies a minimum of both activities and uncertainty (Robinson et al. 1967).

2. *Activities, problem solving, and decisions.* Although not explicitly, the established literature sees each elemental activity as a set of activities performed to solve a problem. The conceptualization of a decision as the result of a set of activities searching for a solution of a problem is certainly not new in several branches of organizational theory (see, e.g., Simon 1945). In our field, this point of view must be recognized explicitly for an appreciation of its potential.

To begin with, let us consider the standard organizational chart, which is a description of a cascade of problems (i.e., the progressive specification of a general problem into more concrete and solvable subproblems) and a cascade of activities that specify what must be done to solve a given problem. Basically, an organization chart articulates, in some "organized" manner, the nature of a firm's decision process. Such charts divide the firm's decision making into a set of organized activities.

Viewing problem-solving activities as a series of nested trees, hierarchically ordered, may make sense for the so-called line functions. For example, the sales manager and the advertising manager report to the higher "box," the marketing vice president; the district sales managers report to the higher "box," the sales manager, etc.

But how can we describe the so-called staff functions? Staff activities often imply support to boxes nested in different trees. The usual way to graphically portray these activities that do not relate to other activities in the chart's sequential ordering is as "horizontal" lines. Yet, organizational charts do not describe the nature of the "lateral" relations among marketing research and sales and brand managers, for example. This is one of the difficulties in studying organizational buying.

The question is very basic: Where should one depict the set of activities concerned with buying in an organizational chart? In principle, there are a few possible answers. If we agree that practically all the activities in an organizational chart imply the purchase of some tangible or intangible good, then the "purchasing" box should be shown as a staff function reporting to the "highest" box in the chart.

Note that some of the boxes in the chart imply buying. The personnel department "buys" personal services, the finance department buys financial means, the "president" buys other firms, and so on. Even if we were to exclude the acquisition of real estate from purchasing, we are still left with an enormous amount of goods needed everywhere in an organization—from electricity and stationery to materials, equipment of all kinds, and operating supplies.

From this point of view, purchasing serves all other activities and units and, therefore, it should not be portrayed—as it is so frequently done—as reporting to the plant superintendent, the material management department, or other production (and engineering) related activities.

It follows that, from the diffusion of buying activities, we cannot develop an understanding of organizational buying processes if we limit ourselves to the study of the activities grouped under the heading of purchasing department or purchasing manager. Although some purchasing departments may include more activities than others, and some purchasing managers may participate formally or informally in more decisions than others, reality says that we must work toward observing the wide domain of an entire organization to develop realistic and strong theories and models of buying processes.

In essence, as in other areas of organizational studies, we must avoid interviewing only "heads" of departments bearing the purchasing or some similar label. Understanding buying activities must be based on identifying these activities *wherever* they are performed. It is an incredibly difficult task, but it must be faced by those interested in developing theories and models.

Toward Complete Descriptions of Organizational Buying Processes

An organizational decision process consists of two main components: subjects and activities. The literature unfortunately has stressed either one or the other. The real payoff is to find operational ways to merge the two approaches, for neither one alone can give us a complete and useful description of organizational buying, and thus provide the basis for designing optimal buying processes and evaluating their performance.

An organizational chart is a design that says that such and such an organization of activities is the "best" way to go about solving problems and ultimately reaching optimal decisions. But who is to perform such activities?

A most popular answer is the assumption commonly made in reading organizational charts—namely, if the chart is the best organization of decision-making activities, then all we have to do is to find the person(s) who should be placed in each box to perform the activities indicated in the box. From this perspective—which emphasizes the activity component—the construction of an organizational decision process is completed by assigning persons or groups of persons to subsets of activities. That is, we assign people to roles and each role is thus a pair of person(s)-activities.

This seems a "rational" way to *construct* an "ideal" buying process. As noted previously, however, it does not usually work that way, for people tend to perceive their assigned roles in somewhat different ways, in degree and often in kind, from those intended by the social engineer who constructed the chart.

Further complications arise when, as time goes by, organizational and individual reasons lead to gradual changes in the activities assigned to a given role, either formally or informally. In particular, any person, especially an enterprising one, may tend to acquire new activities and/or relinquish others. These and other dynamic considerations are particularly applicable to organizational processes such as purchasing where activities tend to be diffused throughout the organization and over time.

As we attempt to bring activities and people together to obtain better descriptions and understanding of organizational buying processes, we must find devices that allow us to do so. The concept of role seems to be a most promising "accounting" device for searching, observing, and eventually conceptualizing fundamental properties of organizational buying.

The notion of "role" has received some attention in organizational theories, especially in some branches of sociology and social psychology. However, little progress has materialized for a variety of reasons, mostly because the various definitions of role have been too vague and difficult to operationalize. Recent developments in the study of group behavior in laboratory settings (Mackenzie 1976) suggest that our current ignorance regarding organizational or group behavior stems from our inability to observe the interactions, always in a state of flux, among the four major components of group processes:

1. The task, i.e., recalling that in German the term also means problem solving, the goal assigned to a person or a group.
2. The activities, i.e., both the activities formally assigned to the group and/or its members and the activities the group members somehow assign to themselves.
3. The subject, i.e., the persons who formally or informally perform these activities and those who directly or indirectly affect their performance.
4. The structures and changes in the structure of activities (e.g., the organizational chart, the job manual), and the structure of subjects—i.e., which individual *or* group is performing what activity *and* which individual or group is interacting about what with whom.

There is no doubt that most academicians and professionals agree on what is meant by "task" in our area. The task of an organizational buying process is that of acquiring the right economic good, at the right price, of the right quality, in the right quantity, delivered at the right time and place to the right users. This is a neat definition but is rather weak in providing criteria to guide our study of the other points. The weakness of this definition is that, as we have noted, there are literally millions of activities that make up the process, usually a large number of people who may be involved one way or another, many plausible and workable ways to organize the activities, and many plausible and workable ways to organize people—i.e., assign them to different subsets of activities *and* determine which persons should relate to whom (that is, formation of formal groups or departments).

We see (or, better, we feel) the enormous variety of different organizational buying processes in business; we sense that this variety is most likely smaller than the almost infinite number of ways in which "subjects-groups-activities" can be ordered in an organizational design. And yet we feel at a loss to cope with the variety of organizational buying processes we see at work. It is here that we should be modest and willing to go back to one of the basics: observation.[4]

But what shall we observe, and how? The notion of role we propose should help in finding an answer. To begin with, a role should always be a unit of observation on two dimensions: the subject and activity dimensions. Thus a role is a pair of observed subject-activity values. One may, therefore, develop a matrix of all buying activities by subjects.

Each observational study could terminate with the compilation of such a matrix. Each cell in this matrix arrangement is a "molar" role in the specific sense that each pair of observed subject-activity values is a unique point of the observed organizational buying process. Thus a molar role is a "unit"—the unit that allows us to count and thus search for properties of the observed buying processes in many and different firms. Such a count is an essential operational step toward building theories and models of any organizational process (e.g., consider the description of an assembly-line process or any use of critical path method).

Summarizing our argument, we propose that the first task is the careful identification of all atomistic activities and all subjects (individuals) involved in the process. These raw observations can be reproduced into a matrix form. Each cell thus represents a unique pair of observed "subject-activity" values, and it becomes the molar role or unit for describing the process under consideration.

Juxtaposing this molar description against the traditional units—departments, for instance—we shall begin to observe, at the very least, deviations of the observed reality from the current abstractions so entrenched in organizational charts. We shall thus learn how to get rid of these abstractions whenever they tend to be misleading and shall begin to observe "natural," higher-order units—that is, "fields" of molar roles—and thus be on our way toward understanding organizational life and formulating theories (and eventually models of it) that may be useful for administrative action.

In this section we have sketched an approach to the study of only one major aspect of organizational buying—its *intraorganizational* dimensions. But, more importantly, we have outlined the key areas where research must be stressed. Such research will be difficult no matter what approach is used.

A major reason for such difficulty is that whatever goes on within the intraorganizational process is partly due to the many interactions of this process with the firm's environment, especially the selling processes in the vendors'

---

4. Most of the new literature has relied on observation in real life (e.g., via survey research methodology), but we must also learn how to study group buying processes in laboratory settings (see, e.g., the pioneering efforts in Cardozo and Cagley 1971).

organizations. Accordingly, we now turn our attention to the other major aspect of organizational buying, i.e., interorganizational processes. Our examination will be speculative, for it is concerned with extremely uncharted problem areas—but a start must be made.

Constructing Models of Interorganizational Processes: Some Basic Challenges

The purpose of this section is programmatic in the sense that we cannot report much research on interorganizational processes. But we can assert the existence of certain fundamental problems and the urgent need to conceptualize them so as to guide future empirical research.

The transaction between a "buyer" and a "seller" is obviously a very visible moment in an often complex interaction between two or more organizations. This transaction—especially the resulting price and quantities exchanged—is the focal point of interest of much microeconomic theory and empirical research. As long as economists are interested in the formation of value (i.e., price), they can legitimately pay no attention to the intraorganizational processes (the selling and buying processes) that lead to the meeting of a supply and a demand (see top part of Figure 7.1).

The professional literature naturally poses additional questions. Thus sales management and personal selling (and, to some extent, marketing management) focus on the activities that lead to the formation of a supply and eventually to sales. Similarly, industrial procurement examines the activities that lead to the formation of a demand and eventually to purchases.

The direction of the arrows in the lower panel of Figure 7.1 captures the development of the buying and selling literature: each focuses on one *or* the other side of a transaction. Although the "other side" is obviously implicit, the treatment, to a large extent, is one-sided. In fact, there are practically no textbooks on the transaction per se[5] nor studies of the complex interactions between the selling and buying processes that precede and follow the conclusion of a transaction.

There are several implications for future research that follow from this prevailing one-sidedness in past and current research. We shall point out a few of them, for they affect the development of more useful theories and models.

To begin with, the "dos" and "don'ts" presented in the buying literature are not clearly related to the dos and don'ts presented in the marketing/selling literature. Perhaps the lack of an explicit correspondence between the two sets of prescriptions is due to different vocabularies. But we believe that there are more substantive reasons for this—many differences stem from the partial analysis of the buying (or selling) side.

---

5. A practitioner and scholar was the first to call our attention to the existing dichotomy in the literature and the ensuing one-sidedness of our research (Alderson 1957 and 1965).

Figure 7.1

THE TRADITIONAL APPROACH TO THE STUDY OF INTERORGANIZATIONAL PROCESSES

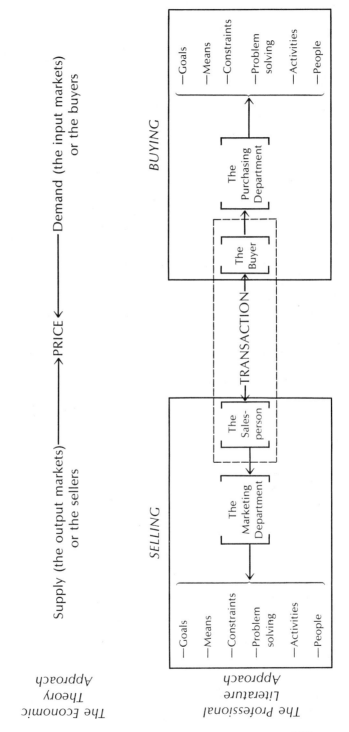

The selling literature sees a sale as the result of an organizational process culminating with a salesperson agreeing with a buyer on a contract. Similarly, the purchasing literature sees a purchase as the result of a process culminating with a purchasing manager agreeing with a salesperson on a contract. At most, the interaction between the buying and selling organizational processes is thus reduced to an interaction between two persons, and some research has been addressed to the study of such a dyad (Silk and Davis 1974). The study of the salesperson-buyer dyad is a person approach. It may be appropriate *if* all the persons/activities in the buying process are, so to speak, eventually funneled through the purchasing manager and, similarly, *if* all the persons/activities in the selling process are also funneled through the salesperson. That is, a dyad approach may enable us to construct theories and models of transactions for those instances where, in fact, the two organizational processes (buying and selling) interact only through two persons and there is homogeneity of values within each of the two organizations.

Although the focus on the buyer-salesperson dyad to gain an understanding of a transaction is welcome, much organizational selling and buying implies the interaction between firms through more than two persons and the presence of intraorganizational heterogeneity. Purchases of high-value or high-risk items call for interactions among several dyads and even among teams across the selling and buying organizations (Robinson et al. 1967). Changing technologies constantly lead to new materials and equipment and tend to "activate" contacts among several people in the selling and buying organizations. In these cases, observing only the "final" dyad—buyer and salesperson—is as misleading as the attempt to understand the meeting of two icebergs by observing only the behavior of their tips.

The established professional literature tells us, for example, that the R&D people in the selling organization may interact with the production people in the buying organization; that the buyer may visit the seller's plant and, by spotting production problems, may expedite the situation by asking his own engineering people to come into the seller's plant and help; that several phases of logistics and materials management (from transportation to receiving and inspection) often call for activities requiring direct contacts among people across the selling and buying organizations; that direct contacts across the two organizations are often involved in maintenance; and that financial and accounting activities also necessitate contacts across the two firms, both before and after a transaction.

All in all, then, not only is buying a multidimensional organizational process, but it also interacts with the selling process at different times through different subsets of people and activities. Thus we must conceptualize the "buyer-seller" interaction as an interorganizational process: a multipeople, multiactivities process over time.

Research on the multidimensionality of the buying process alone is not enough. Careful descriptions of the interorganizational buying-selling processes are needed to build useful theories and models. Such undertakings will not only enrich our understanding of purchasing and selling management, but will provide new perspectives to the study of significant problems at both the micro (firm) and macro (public policy) levels. Consider, for example, the following three cases.

How Can Management Best Organize the Set of People/Activities Performing the Buying (or Selling) Function? The organization of buying processes implicitly reflects the quality and variety of its environment—namely, the input markets. That is, many of the internal characteristics of an organizational buying process (e.g., buyers' specialization by types of goods) reflect this dependency on the environment. This point has been recognized as almost a philosophical truism applying to any organization (from biological to social), but even basic research on how the environmental variety bears upon the internal structure of a social organization is very recent.

The study of organizational buying is no exception. Following the interorganizational orientation of this chapter, we believe that future research should study how best to organize the structure of the buying process (persons/activities): (*a*) in response to the variety of selling processes bearing on it, and (*b*) in stimulating the selling processes to respond to the current and future requirements of the buying firm.

The same considerations apply also to the structuring of the selling process (persons/activities). Most of the marketing literature has ignored this interorganizational orientation. Some initial efforts, however, have been made by Nonaka (1972).

How Do Channel Interdependencies Affect the Organization of the Buying (or Selling) Function? We know, for example, that it is increasingly common for a selling organization to be concerned not only with the needs and problems of its immediate customers, but also with the needs and problems of the customers of its immediate customers, including distributors, agents, and brokers. Similarly, the need to assure supplies (quantity, quality, delivery, etc.) leads buyers to worry not only about their own immediate suppliers, but also about the suppliers of their own suppliers. In formulating, implementing, and evaluating plans, the managerial horizon extends beyond the single transaction—the result of interactions among only two firms—to include and assess interdependencies among several organizational decision processes (Bucklin 1972).

The preceding examples illustrate the potential contributions of the study of interorganizational processes to the management of the buying (and selling) function. This interorganizational orientation may also be relevant to macro (public policy) issues. Recall that most economic theory is concerned with formation of value (price) as it emerges from the meeting of a supply and a demand. Progress was made in the 1930s when it was realized that this meeting may occur in different "market structures" (competition, monopolistic competition, oligopolies/oligopsonies of different kinds, and monopoly/monopsony).

But little has been done since then to bring about an understanding that value ultimately emerges through a series of transactions across several market levels (see, e.g., Balderston 1955, Balderston & Hoggatt 1962, and Baligh & Richartz 1967). Only appropriate coordination among the several organizations linking the original points of supply with the points of final demand can create satisfactory value for both society and each of its economic agents (Alderson 1957 and Nicosia 1962).

Concluding Remarks

The study of interorganizational interactions can eventually lead to more useful theories and models of the entire marketing system and the economy. The road to this goal begins with the realization that we must conceptualize and study interorganizational processes more carefully.

As we plan for such study, we must strongly help the new developments in studying intraorganizational processes. We have discussed some specific direction for research on buying processes and have argued that understanding organizational buying will have at least two immediate effects: (*a*) the buying firm can structure itself more efficiently, and (*b*) the selling firm will be able to cater more efficiently to the needs of its potential customers.

Research on buying as an intraorganizational process already has relevance for at least one crucial professional issue: What is the *professional status* of purchasing managers? The major professional associations (National Association of Purchasing Managers and the American Purchasing Society) and all the textbooks in industrial procurement are very concerned with the public image of buyers. The argument is that the buyer *is* a manager.

During the 1960s, empirical evidence increasingly showed that buying is a process very diffused throughout the organization. That is, much information, many activities, and many people are crucial parts of the buying process and yet are not parts of the "purchasing department." The more diffuse a process is, in this sense, the less appropriate it may be to think of the "buyer" only as a decision maker in a narrow sense.

This evidence is not "against" the future of the buyer as a basic member of corporate management. To the contrary, it suggests where his or her future is, as well as that of the department. From an organizational theory point of view, it is increasingly evident that the more diffused the information-activities-persons process is, the more necessary it is to find a structural way to plan and coordinate such a process. The structural answer to the need for a planning and ongoing coordination is the creating of the "purchasing" department/manager.

But what is the nature of the coordinating task assigned to this unit? Basically, the task is to understand the different points of view and needs within the organization. These views and needs tend to be not only different, but necessarily conflicting. And usually, none of these views and needs can be met directly by the potential suppliers. Thus the purchasing task is to understand and resolve two sets of conflicts.

One conflict is that between the firm's environment and the firm itself—this has been reasonably stressed by the traditional literature. But the emerging literature suggests that resolving conflicts within the organization is an even more crucial task.

Solving this internal conflict is a prerequisite for the solution of the conflict between the firm and its environment. To solve these internal stresses necessitates acquiring information and understanding. It also means "to bargain" across the internal needs and points of views and to search for common grounds, i.e., for an internal consensus of what is a suboptimal, feasible (and thus best) solution. From this organizational perspective, the purchasing manager and department are *catalysts*, not just decision makers.

If our understanding of the empirical evidence is correct, the continuing struggle by purchasing managers to be recognized as "decision makers" is too narrow. If a main role of the purchasing manager/department is that of a catalyst—i.e., *to manage organizational conflict* within the buying process—then the road to professional recognition by corporate management is to stress also this role.

The controller/accounting department does not derive its strength and recognition from an organizational chart and title or from attempting to be a "profit center." It derives its power by acquiring and processing data relevant to financial and other activities. Similarly, the buyer/department will achieve its recognition if it aggressively acquires and manages the information, points of view, and needs bearing on the purchase of some entity, on input markets trends, on technological developments impinging on suppliers, and on the firm itself.

Much current discussion concerns the organizational position of the buyer/department—should it report to the plant superintendent, or to the materials management department, etc.? The underlying view of these discussions is that the buyer/department is a "line" function, for it makes decisions. But the emerging empirical evidence seems to suggest that the buyer/department has also the fundamental task of being a "staff" function—i.e., of serving as a catalyst across the entire firm's organization. He/it is the friend who knows the rigor of the input environments and can lead the diverging internal interests to an efficient and effective solution for all.

References

Alderson, W. 1957. *Marketing Behavior and Executive Action.* Homewood, Ill.: Richard D. Irwin.

———. 1965. *Dynamic Marketing Behavior.* Homewood, Ill.: Richard D. Irwin.

Aljian, G. 1958. *Purchasing Handbook.* 3rd ed. New York: McGraw-Hill.

Balderston, F. 1955. "Communication Networks in Intermediate Markets." *Management Science* (January).

Balderston, F. and Hoggatt, A. 1962. *Simulation of Market Processes.* Berkeley: Institute of Business and Economic Research, University of California.

Baligh, H. and Richartz, L. 1967. *Vertical Market Structures.* Boston: Allyn and Bacon.

Bucklin, L. P. 1972. *Competition and Evolution in the Distributive Trades.* Englewood Cliffs, N.J.: Prentice-Hall.

Cardozo, R. N. and Cagley, J. W. 1971. "An Experimental Study of Industrial Buyer Behavior." *Journal of Marketing Research* 8 (August).

Cyert, R. M., Simon, H. A., and Trow, D. B. 1956. "Observations of a Business Decision." *Journal of Business* (October).

England, W. 1970. *Procurement: Principles and Cases.* 5th ed. Homewood, Ill.: Richard D. Irwin.

Green, P. and Tull, D. 1974. *Research for Marketing Decisions.* 3rd ed. Englewood Cliffs, N.J.: Prentice-Hall.

Harding, M. 1966. "Who Really Makes the Purchase Decision?" *Industrial Marketing* (September).

Heinritz, S. and Farrell, P. 1965. *Purchasing: Principles and Applications.* 4th ed. Englewood Cliffs, N.J.: Prentice-Hall.

Mackenzie, K. D. 1976. *A Theory of Group Structures: Vol. I, Basic Theory; Vol. II, Empirical Tests.* New York: Gordon and Breach.

Nicosia, F. M. 1962. "Marketing and Alderson's Functionalism." *Journal of Business* (October).

———. 1976. "Latent Structure Analysis: The Measurement of Brand Images, and of Audience or Market Types." In *Multivariate Analysis in Marketing,* ed. J. Sheth. Chicago: American Marketing Association.

Nicosia, F. M., MacLachlan, D., and Schreier, F. (Forthcoming.) *Marketing Research: A Behavioral Approach.* Belmont, Calif.: Wadsworth.

Nonaka, I. 1972. "Organization and Market: Exploratory Study of Centralization versus Decentralization." Ph.D. dissertation, University of California.

Ozane U. and Churchill, G. 1968. "Adoption Research: Information Sources in the Industrial Purchasing Decision." In *Marketing and the New Science of Planning,* ed. R. L. King. Chicago: American Marketing Association.

Robinson, P., Faris, C., and Wind, Y. 1967. *Industrial Buying and Creative Marketing.* Boston: Allyn and Bacon.

Silk, A. and Davis, H. 1974. "Small Group Theory." In *Handbook of Marketing Research,* ed. R. Ferber. New York: McGraw-Hill.

Simon, H. 1945. *Administrative Behavior.* New York: The Macmillan Company.

Swandby, R. K. 1973. "Chim Show Study Reveals Nine Job Functions as CPI Buying Influences." *Industrial Marketing* (July).

Webster, F. and Wind, Y. 1972. *Organizational Buying Behavior.* Englewood Cliffs, N.J.: Prentice-Hall.

Weigand, R. E. 1968. "Why Studying the Purchasing Agent Is Not Enough." *Journal of Marketing* (January).

Wind, Y. 1973a. "A New Procedure for Concept Evaluation." *Journal of Marketing* 37 (October).

———. 1973b. "Recent Approaches to the Study of Organizational Buying Behavior." In *Increasing Marketing Productivity. Proceedings of the American Marketing Association Conference,* April.

Wind, Y. and Lotshaw, E. 1973. "The Industrial Customer." In *Marketing Handbook,* ed. S. H. Britt. New York: The Dartnell Corporation.

Chapter 8

A Normative Theory of Market Segmentation

William F. Massy and *Barton A. Weitz**

Editors' Note

The preceding three chapters were concerned with the observation of how individuals, families, and organizations go about making purchase decisions. One of the generalizations of current knowledge is the high heterogeneity of buying processes. Faced with this heterogeneity, management has increasingly felt the need to identify and reach homogeneous market or audience segments. In this chapter the authors focus on market segmentation and how management should use it for the optimization of marketing policies.

Suppose that the market research department for a consumer goods company develops a segmentation scheme that classifies customers with different product usage levels by a personality trait, gregariousness. The relationship was developed using a regression model. With a sample of 500, the R^2 of regression was .08, significant at the .01 level. The company's advertising agency has concurrently completed a survey indicating that product consumption is related to the consumer's income. The agency also used regression to develop the relationship. The R^2 was .10, significant at the .005 level using a sample of 2,000.

*William F. Massy and Barton A. Weitz are from Stanford University and the University of California, Los Angeles, respectively.

Are these variables useful for developing a marketing program or should further research be undertaken? If the variables are useful, which variable should be used for segmenting the market?

The company decided to adopt the segmentation scheme based on income. Through additional market research, the following relationships between consumption and advertising were estimated:
Segment 1 (high usage, low income)

$$\text{Sales } (S_1) = 100 \times (1 - .7e^{-.65 \times Adv(A_1)})$$

Segment 2 (high usage, high income)

$$\text{Sales } (S_2) = 70 \times (1 - .9e^{-.30 \times Adv(A_2)}).$$

What should be the level of advertising directed toward each segment?

The above are segmentation questions that might face a marketing manager. They illustrate the types of problems addressed by a normative theory of segmentation. This chapter contrasts the role of normative and descriptive theory with respect to market segmentation, presents a framework for developing a normative segmentation theory, and reviews elements of a normative theory emphasizing the managerial implications.

The Role of Normative and Prescriptive Theory

In Zaltman's chapter (Chapter 3), a classification scheme for marketing models or theories is presented. Our chapter concentrates on one dimension of this scheme—the use of theory. Zaltman presents two uses of theories—descriptive and normative. Descriptive theories or models are used to understand problems, while normative theories are used to solve problems.

Differences between descriptive and normative theory can be directly related to the two major schools of market segmentation research—a behaviorally oriented school and a decision-oriented school. Behaviorally oriented or descriptive research focuses on uncovering differences in consumers. These differences are important because they can lead to understanding the basic process of consumer behavior. Much research concentrates on relating consumption variables like usage rates and brand loyalty to individual characteristics like demographics, socioeconomic status, and attitude-interest-opinion inventories. By carefully identifying these relationships, the causes of differences in consumption can be inferred. The benefits of behaviorally oriented market segmentation research are substantial. Not only can this research shed light on what relationships exist in consumer behavior, but also the reasons why these relationships exist can be investigated. Individual findings can eventually be incorporated into a comprehensive theory of consumer behavior.

Decision-oriented or normative segmentation research or theory builds on the findings of behaviorally oriented work. Starting with the assumption that individual differences among consumers exist and that these differences can be used to predict variations in consumption, decision-oriented research concentrates on how these differences can be used to increase the effectiveness of a company's marketing effort. More specifically, normative segmentation research attempts to provide solutions for the following two managerial problems.

1. How should heterogeneous consumers be analyzed to form meaningfully homogeneous groupings or segments?
2. How should marketing effort be allocated among the segments?

The two examples at the beginning of the chapter reflect the different objectives of descriptive and normative segmentation research. In the first example, descriptive research uncovered two variables, gregariousness and income, that have statistically significant relationships to product consumption. (Perhaps a causal relationship was also developed to explain why these relationships could be used to develop a marketing strategy.) In the second example, descriptive research determined that the effectiveness of advertising in the two segments, and the differences between them, are statistically significant. Normative research, on the other hand, is concerned with how these relationships can be used to allocate marketing effort.

The practical importance of market segmentation is recognized in academic circles as well as by business firms. Considerable descriptive research has been done. Numerous sophisticated, multivariant techniques have been directed at empirically determining what segmentation variables are relevant in different marketing situations. Recently thought has been given to how this empirical research can be used to make better management decisions. This normative research has raised some interesting questions about the objectives of segmentation research (Claycamp & Massy 1968 and Guiltinan & Sawyer 1974).

A Framework for Normative Segmentation Theory

With the plethora of empirical segmentation findings, there is a need for a powerful and parsimonious normative segmentation theory against which these findings can be assessed. By powerful and parsimonious, we mean a theory that can be applied to most market segmentation situations—one that can offer simple, basic principles upon which extensions can be built to incorporate elements of specific situations. This type of normative theory can be contrasted to microanalytic simulations designed to solve specific problems or highly complex models incorporating many variables and relationships from which simple decision rules can only be developed through extensive analysis.

Since the objective of a normative theory is to provide solutions for managerial problems, a normative theory should be evaluated in terms of its relevance to managerial decision making and the directions presented for improving such decision making. Thus a useful normative theory should provide solutions under typical information conditions encountered in actual decision-making environments. These solutions should be compared to solutions under ideal information conditions to indicate the benefits that might be realized from additional market research to reduce uncertainty.

A normative theory of segmentation must provide solutions or insights into the following two market segmentation problems: *defining segments* and *allocating resources to segments.* These insights are the outputs from the theory or model. The inputs are data concerning differences in individual or group responses to marketing tools, and the degree to which these marketing tools can be directed toward individuals or groups of individuals.

Under ideal information conditions, a multivariant response function relating consumption to the levels of the marketing variables would be known, without error, for each individual. In addition, all marketing variables could be targeted to each individual in any predetermined amount. While these ideal conditions rarely exist in real-world situations, some industrial marketing situations closely parallel the perfect information model. As an example, Lodish's CALLPLAN model allocates sales effort to each company in a territory using judgmentally derived response functions, relating sales to sales effort, for each customer (Lodish 1971). In this situation each customer can be considered as a market segment. While only one marketing variable is considered (sales effort), this variable can be directed in any amount to any segment with "known" response.

However, a comprehensive normative theory must consider the manager's actual environment. First, individuals usually cannot be treated as unit segments. Various *levels of aggregation* of both responses to and targetability of marketing efforts must be considered. Groups of individuals must be used when statistical techniques are directed toward developing response functions relating sales or consumption to marketing variables. Similarly, marketing efforts can rarely be aimed precisely at specific individuals. There are legal constraints on discriminatory pricing, and standard communication methods, such as advertising in particular media, have relatively inflexible coverage patterns.

The fixed distribution of most marketing tools has led to two strategies for reaching potential customers: *customer self-selection* and *controlled coverage.* The concept of product positioning is directed toward customer self-selection. The product is made available to the general public; however, through product design features or promotional appeals, the product is differentially attractive to the target segment. On the other hand the controlled coverage strategy makes the product or communication available only to members of the target segment by using specialized distribution channels or media. While mass-marketing tools used in the customer self-selection strategy waste money by presenting the product to customers outside the target segment who have a low probability of consumption, the controlled coverage strategy does not take advantage of economies of scale and can miss parts of the target market.

A second real-world consideration is *uncertainty* associated with aggregated response characteristics and targetability of marketing efforts. Even when homogeneous individuals are grouped to estimate response functions, there will be some individual differences plus measurement error that lead to uncertainty

124

in response estimates. Also, the audience characteristics for most marketing tools cannot be described with certainty.

Thus a normative segmentation theory must consider the typical situation in which less than perfect information is available only for groups of individuals and marketing effort can be targeted only imperfectly to these preselected groups of individuals.

A final consideration is the special role of *descriptor variables* in market segmentation strategy. In order to implement a market segmentation strategy, information relating the effect of each type of marketing effort devoted to each segment is needed. Generally, these relationships or information links are known only through intermediate or "descriptor" variables: consumer descriptor variables are variables that, on the one hand, can be related to the consumption characteristics of segments and, on the other hand, can be related to the effectivenes of a marketing tool, such as advertising media. This concept is shown in Figure 8.1. As an example, product consumption can be related to age (a demographic descriptor variable), and age can also be related to media coverage or channels of distribution. These two relationships can be represented mathematically as follows:

$$\text{consumption} = f_1 \text{ (descriptor categories)}$$

$$\begin{array}{l}\text{descriptor categories reached}\\ \text{by an advertising campaign} = f_2 \text{ (media used).}\end{array}$$

Figure 8.1

INFORMATION LINKS WITH DESCRIPTORS

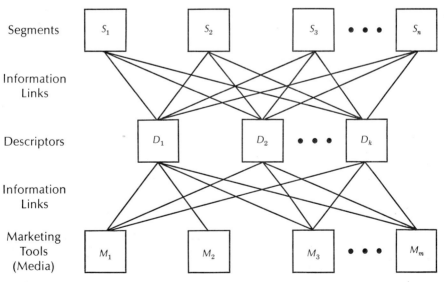

Number of information links $= k\,(n + m)$

SOURCE: *Frank et al. 1972, p. 18.*

If both relationships are established empirically, then by substituting the second relationship into the first, the following relationship can be developed:

$$consumption = f \text{ (media used)}.$$

By using the descriptor variables to split the relationship in two, the task of developing the relationship for specific products is greatly simplified. With a common set of descriptor variables, advertising agencies and media organizations can relate the descriptor variables to the media used for many products, while market research departments can develop specific relationships between consumption of their product and the descriptor variables. Although descriptor variables are often not important as a marketing objective or segmentation criterion, they assist in implementing segmentation strategies. A normative theory of segmentation must include this two-stage process involving descriptor variables.

Normative Theory under Perfect Information

Extension of Price Theory

While the concept of market segmentation was elucidated in the mid-1950s, contributions to a normative theory of segmentation can be traced to the literature on price theory in microeconomics (Smith 1956). Price theory concepts relevant to market segmentation appear in the treatment of price setting by monopolists, referred to as price discrimination (see Robinson 1954 for example). The price discrimination model is as follows:

1. A monopolist sells product into different markets.
2. Buyers in the markets have different demand functions.
3. Different prices can be charged in each market.
4. The markets are isolated—a buyer in the low-price market cannot resell the product to a potential buyer in a higher priced market.

Under these assumptions, the optimal pricing strategy for the monopolist is realized when the marginal revenue in each market is equal to the marginal production cost:

$$MR_1 = MR_2 = MR_3 = \cdots = MR_i = MC.$$

The marginal revenue in each market is a function of the demand curve in each market and can be altered by varying the price in the market. The marginal production cost is a function of the total quantity produced for all markets. Unless the marginal production cost is constant for all production quantities, the optimal pricing strategy cannot be established by looking at each market separately. The entire system of "i" market demand curves and the production cost-volume curve must be examined together.

The normative conclusions from the simple price theory model have been applied in situations when one group of customers has a higher perceived need than another and the groups are insulated from each other. While price discrimination can increase the profitability of the firm, there are adverse social consequences when price discrimination is practiced, and there is no actual difference in the marginal costs of supplying these different markets. Thus legal constraints have been applied to prohibit the practice of price discrimination.

The simple price theory model can be easily extended to include more than one market segment and additional marketing variables. The profit maximizing solution for a number of marketing variables (which may include price) across several market segments given a homogeneous product is as follows:[1]

$$\frac{\Delta \text{ Contribution}_{11}}{\Delta \text{ Cost}_{11}} = \frac{\Delta \text{ Contribution}_{12}}{\Delta \text{ Cost}_{12}} = \frac{\Delta \text{ Contribution}_{ij}}{\Delta \text{ Cost}_{ij}} = k \tag{1}$$

where

$\Delta \text{ Contribution}_{ij}$ = the incremental contribution to profits resulting from an increase of the ith marketing variable in the jth segment

$\Delta \text{ Cost}_{ij}$ = the incremental cost of the ith marketing variable direct toward the jth segment.

Thus under the optimal marketing policy, the ratio of the incremental response to increment marketing expenditure is equal for all marketing variables and all market segments. This ratio, k, is equal to the marginal return (as measured in contribution to profits) of the last dollar of marketing expenditure. If the value of k is greater than one, additional marketing expenditures will result in a positive contribution to profits—the additional contribution minus the marketing expenses will be greater than zero. The optimum level of marketing effort is realized when k is equal to one. If k is less than one, the level of marketing expenditures should be reduced.

As an example, the decision rule in equation (1) can be applied to the second example at the beginning of the paper. Assuming that the manufacturing cost is 50 percent of sales, independent of the volume level, then the contribution to profit from each segment as a function of the advertising effort directed toward the segment can be expressed as follows:

Contribution from segment 1 (C_1) = .5 × Sales from segment 1 (S_1) = $50(1 - .7e^{-.65 \times Adv \text{ in segment 1}})$ (A_1) $\tag{2}$

Contribution from segment 2 (C_2) = .5 × Sales from segment 2 (S_2) = $35(1 - .9e^{-.30 \times Adv \text{ in segment 2}})$. (A_2) $\tag{3}$

The incremental contribution per incremental advertising expense (Δ contribution/Δ cost) in each segment is simply the slope or derivative of these

1. A complete derivation of this relationship is in Frank et al. 1972, pp. 185–189.

Table 8.1

A_1	C_1	k_1	A_2	C_2	k_2
Adv Directed toward Segment 1 ($M)	Contribution from Segment 1 ($M)	Incremental Contribution per Incremental Adv Expenditure $d(C_1)/d(A_1)$	Adv Directed toward Segment 2 ($M)	Contribution from Segment 2 ($M)	Incremental Contribution per Incremental Adv Expenditure $d(C_2)/d(A_2)$
3.0	45.02	3.2	3.0	22.19	3.8
3.2	45.63	2.8	3.2	22.94	3.6
3.4	46.16	2.5	3.4	23.64	3.4
3.6	46.63	2.2	3.6	24.30	3.2
3.8	47.04	1.9	3.8	24.93	3.0
4.0	47.40	1.7	4.0	25.51	2.9
4.2	47.72	1.5	4.2	26.06	2.7
4.4	48.00	1.3	4.4	26.59	2.5
4.6	48.24	1.1	4.6	27.07	2.4
4.8	48.45	1.0	4.8	27.54	2.2
5.0	48.64	.9	5.0	27.97	2.1
5.2	48.81	.8	5.2	28.38	2.0
5.4	48.95	.7	5.4	28.77	1.9
5.6	49.08	.6	5.6	29.13	1.8
5.8	49.19	.5	5.8	29.47	1.7
6.0	49.29	.5	6.0	29.79	1.6
6.2	49.38	.4	6.2	30.10	1.5
6.4	49.45	.4	6.4	38.38	1.4
6.6	49.52	.3	6.6	30.65	1.3
6.8	49.58	.3	6.8	30.90	1.2
7.0	49.63	.2	7.0	31.14	1.2
7.2	49.68	.2	7.2	31.37	1.1
7.4	49.71	.2	7.4	31.58	1.0
7.6	49.75	.2	7.6	31.78	.9

functions. Table 8.1 summarizes this information. When the marketing budget is not constrained, the optimal allocation to the two segments occurs when the ratio of the incremental contribution to incremental expenditure is equal to one ($k_1 = k_2 = 1$). In this example, $4.8M in advertising should be directed to segment 1 and $7.4M of advertising should be directed to segment 2. This optimal allocation results in a total contribution to the firm of $80M ($C_1 = $48.4M, $C_2 = $31.6M). The total net contribution (equal to the contribution less advertising expenses) is $67.8M.

The effects of a budget constraint can be demonstrated using this example. Consider this situation in which the advertising budget is limited to $7M. An examination of Table 8.1 indicates that optimal allocation occurs when $k_1 = k_2 = 3$. (Since k is greater than 1, the contribution in this constrained situation should be less than the contribution in the unconstrained situation.) With this advertising constraint, $3.6M in advertising is directed toward segment 1 and $3.8M toward segment 2. The total net contribution is $63.3M—more than $4M less than the unconstrained situation examined above.

In this example, the optimal allocation can be determined by examining the slope of the response function of each market segment separately, because the marginal cost of production and marketing effort is constant for all quantities. Due to economies of scale, production and marketing costs usually are not linear functions of quantity. In this more general situation, a series of $N(M + 1) + 1$ equations must be solved using nonlinear programming techniques (N segments, M marketing tools that can be directed to each segment plus one cost/volume production function).

Managerial Implications

In most situations, complete information—response functions for each market segment and marketing variable—is not available and thus the optimal amount of marketing effort to be directed toward each segment cannot be determined exactly. However, the normative theory, as presented in the previous section, can still assist in managerial decisions relating to the direction of change from the present allocation scheme. In other words, should efforts directed toward a segment be increased or decreased?

An example of such a strategy is the *high assay principle* (Moran 1963). The segment with the highest ratio of incremental response to incremental marketing effort is the *high assay segment*. Resources are directed toward this segment until the ratio reduces to a point at which another segment has a higher ratio, a budget constraint develops, or the ratio for all segments drops below one. Thus the high assay principle provides a simple method for applying the optimal allocation presented in equation (1) in a wider range of practical situations.

The high assay principle is essentially a mathematical programming algorithm. In some situations, the application of this rule can lead to less than optimal allocation of resources because the underlying assumption associated with this rule is that all response functions exhibit decreasing returns to scale—the next dollar of marketing expenditures is less effective than the last dollar spent. While this is a reasonable assumption in most situations, it is not appropriate when new marketing tools are used or when marketing efforts are directed toward new segments. In these situations there is often an initial period of increasing returns to scale, attributed to "developing a critical mass," threshold effect, or some buildup of word-of-mouth communication. The response function for segment A in Figure 8.2 reflects such an initial increasing return to scale at low levels of advertising. In the situation depicted, an equality of slopes exists when $MR_B = MR_{A1}$. Using the high assay principle, advertising effort should be increased in the new segment, A, until a level of A_2 indicates the marginal responses of the two segments are equivalent. In effect, strict application of the high assay principle would introduce a bias against entering new markets or using new marketing tools and produce dramatic departures from the optimal allocation in these situations.

Using the high assay principle requires considerable information about the marginal response, i.e., the slope of the response function for each segment and marketing tool. Realistically, it is difficult to obtain information on the marginal response for one marketing variable in the market as a whole, let alone the marginal response over a wide range of levels for each segment. Due to this lack of information, various managerial decision rules are used to estimate the

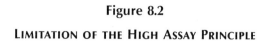

Figure 8.2

LIMITATION OF THE HIGH ASSAY PRINCIPLE

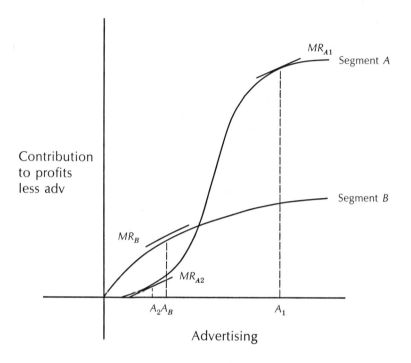

incremental or marginal response. The two most common estimates are the segment's present consumption level and the segment's sales potential.

Perhaps the most common allocation rule is based on demand. For example, if the high-income segment of the market consumes twice as much of a product as the low-income segment, twice as much marketing effort is directed to the high-income segment. This decision rule is based on the assumption that the average response is proportional to the marginal response.

Although the average response rule can lead to acceptable results, it is not without pitfalls. In Figure 8.3 the two response functions from the example at the beginning of the paper are shown. The optimum allocation developed using the marginal response in the previous section is shown by O_1 and O_2. Assume that the present policy directed the same amount of advertising effort to both segments, thus, a $12M budget is split with $6M dollars spent in each segment $(A_1 = A_2 = \$6M)$. This advertising allocation leads to a contribution of $49.3M in segment 1 (C_1) and $29.8M in segment 2 (C_2).

The average response (contribution divided by advertising expense) is greater for segment 1 than for segment 2 ($49M/$6M versus $29M/$6M). Using the average response as a surrogate for the incremental response and employing the high assay principle, advertising effort should be shifted from segment 2 to segment 1 since AR_1 is greater than AR_2. But this adjustment is just the opposite of what should be done! Since the optimum allocation lies at O_1 and

O_2, effort should be shifted from segment 1 to segment 2. If the true incremental responses were available, this shift would be indicated, since MR_2 is greater than MR_1.

The problem with using the average response, as demonstrated in this example, is that segment 1 is much closer to saturation than segment 2. This indicates that sales potential should be considered when estimating the incremental response. The sales potential is defined as the maximum level of sales that could be realized with unlimited marketing effort. In this example, we assume that market analysis has determined the sales potentials to be $100M for segment 1 ($P_1$) and $70M for segment 2 ($P_2$).

A common procedure for incorporating potential into an allocation rule is called *profile matching* (Moran 1963). Profile matching means that marketing efforts are allocated in proportion to the potential, P_1 and P_2 in this example. In this example profile matching also indicates an incorrect reallocation of resources. Profile matching would indicate 40 percent more advertising should be

Figure 8.3

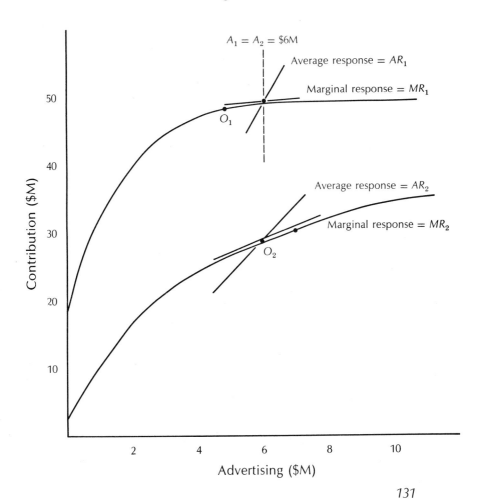

directed to segment 1 than segment 2 because the sales potential in segment 1 is 1.4 times greater than the sales potential in segment 2.

The problem with profile matching is that the levels of sales and marketing effort currently in effect are not considered. By ignoring existing circumstances, the degree to which the company faces decreasing returns to scale does not enter into the allocation decision. Thus profile matching is misleading when applied to mature segments.

A more reasonable way in which sales potential can be incorporated in estimating incremental response to marketing effort is by assuming that the incremental response is proportional to the difference between sales potential and actual sales divided by level of marketing effort. This can be expressed as follows:

$$\begin{pmatrix} \text{Incremental response} \\ \text{of segment } i \text{ to} \\ \text{marketing variable } j \end{pmatrix} \propto \begin{pmatrix} \dfrac{\text{Sales potential} \;-\; \text{Current sales}}{\text{in segment } i \qquad \text{in segment } i} \\ \dfrac{}{\text{Level of marketing variable } j} \\ \text{Expenditure in segment } i \end{pmatrix} \qquad (4)$$

In this example, the estimate of incremental response for segment 1 is .67 and for segment 2 is 4.3; thus this estimate would lead to a reallocation in the proper direction. The estimate of incremental response as presented above represents a refinement in the profile matching approach based on sales potential. Equation (4) indicates that marketers should focus on measurements of untapped potential and heavy users not loyal to their brand, rather than on potential and heavy users per se.

While the surrogate for incremental response suggested in equation (4) is generally superior to estimates based simply on the average response or the sales potential, this surrogate has the same limitations found in all single-parameter characterizations of a more complex response function. At best the estimated incremental response is only proportional to the true incremental response; thus a decision rule based on this estimate can only suggest the direction for a reallocation of efforts between segments. The estimate cannot be used to determine whether the total effort should be increased or decreased.

While the reallocation of resources should be directed toward equalizing the estimated incremental responses for all segments, the allocation producing equal estimated responses may not be the optimal allocation that could have been obtained if the true incremental responses were known. In general, the approximation to optimality is better if the response curves for the various segments are roughly similar. In particular, if the response curves approach saturation at roughly the same rate, the allocation indicated by the estimated parameters will be close to the optimal allocation.

When segments have substantially different response patterns, a better allocation decision can be made by estimating the response curves for each segment directly. An example of how a model might be structured to elicit managerial judgments about sales potential and the incremental effects of promotion is presented by Little (1970). These judgmentally derived response curves can be incorporated into an allocation model using equation (1) as an objective function.

In summation, the normative theory presented in equation (1) requires information about the incremental responses to marketing tools over the entire range of application for each segment. With this information, the amount of effort directed toward each segment can be determined. Since such detailed information is usually not available, considerable emphasis has been placed on estimating the incremental response under existing allocations. These estimates can then be used to indicate the direction of change that might lead to a more optimal allocation. Measurement problems generally limit the applications of a normative theory to offering guidelines for direction, increasing or decreasing expenditures in a segment, rather than the specific amount of change.

Incorporating Real-World Constraints

Formation of Microsegments and Macrosegments

Although the optimal allocation rule presented in the preceding section is simple and appealing, two real-world conditions make it difficult to utilize this concept. First, there is an informational constraint. Response information is only available for groups of individuals. Second, institutional constraints limit the marketer's ability to direct efforts towards specific individuals. In effect these informational and institutional constraints restrict segmentation strategies by aggregating individuals. On the one hand, information on response to marketing variables usually is available only for individuals aggregated by descriptor variables like demographics and socioeconomic status. On the other hand, some marketing tools like advertising media have fixed patterns of distribution to specified groups of individuals.

In this section the implications of these real-world constraints on the decision rule presented for perfect information will be considered. (For detailed treatment of these constraints, see Frank et al. 1972, pp. 193–202.) The fact that marketing tools like advertising media have fixed patterns of distribution, limits the marketer's ability to achieve optimal profits through segmentation. The nature of this profit reduction can be shown in a simple example in which two customers are reached by the same advertising medium but have different responses to various exposure levels. This situation is shown in Figures 8.4 and 8.5. The solid curves in Figure 8.5 give the incremental contribution per incremental advertising expenses. These curves are the derivatives of the response functions in Figure 8.4. Applying the decision rule in equation (1), the optimal strategy is to establish an advertising level of O_1 toward customer 1 and O_2 toward customer 2. Now consider the situation in which the same medium reaches both customers; thus, the same advertising level must be established for both customers. The response for the two customers is the sum of the two response functions in Figure 8.4. The incremental contribution is shown by the dotted line in Figure 8.5. The optimum in this situation, O^*, directs more exposures to customer 1 than should be received. Thus an opportunity loss exists due to this institutional constraint.

Even though an opportunity loss can occur from institutional constraints on coverage, this constraint is rarely binding. Realistically, a manager could not consider directing marketing effort to each individual. Since the number of available media is much less than the number of individuals, the manager's allocation problem is simplified. To further simplify the allocation problem, only a limited subset of media is usually considered in most situations.

Generally, media coverage data are broken down by demographic and socioeconomic descriptor variables. This media coverage information is only available for groups like "high-income, college educated, single people under 34," but not for specific individuals in this group. These groupings by descriptor variables can be referred to as *microsegments* which represent the smallest unit for which audience data are available and which are, therefore, the smallest unit around which a segment can be formed. By imposing this minimum level of aggregation, individual responses to media levels are not needed. No further opportunity loss occurs when the incremental response of a microsegment as a whole is used, rather than the responses of each individual in the microsegment. The example in Figures 8.4 and 8.5 demonstrates that an opportunity loss does not occur if response information is aggregated at the same level as coverage information. When the medium that covers both customers in Figures 8.4 and 8.5 is used, the optimum advertising level can be established using the com- bined response of the two customers rather than each individual response.

After developing the exposure patterns for microsegments, the problem of estimating the incremental sales response to promotion efforts remains. Em- pirical analysis of sales response to promotional variables is an expensive proposition. While such an analysis can be performed at any level of aggrega- tion, institutional constraints on media coverage information indicate that the lowest level of aggregation should be the microsegment. Due to sample size requirements and data collection costs, most empirical estimates of response are

Figure 8.4

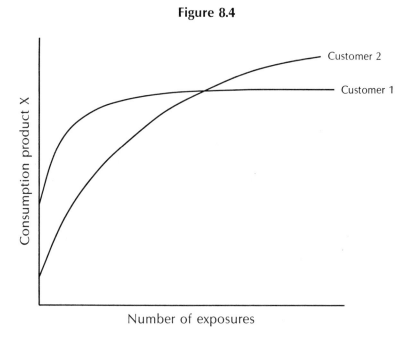

Figure 8.5

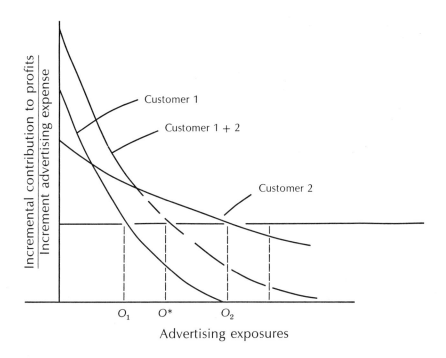

performed by aggregating several descriptor classes. The grouping of micro-segments for which response information is available can be referred to as *macrosegments.*

Managerial Implications

This discussion of institutional and information constraints indicates that segmentation should be viewed as a process of *aggregation* rather than disaggre-gation. If consumers have different incremental responses to marketing varia-bles and there are no diseconomies of scale present in developing programs directed toward each individual, segmentation at the individual level yields the highest profits. Even if this shaky assumption of no economies of scale in developing marketing programs exists, segmentation at the individual level usually is not possible. The lack of information on coverage limits segmentation to the microsegment level at least, and the difficulties in assessing difference in incremental response may even require aggregation to one macrosegment—the mass market.

Successive constraints and higher levels of aggregation lead to reductions in profit levels. This fact is a direct result of the mathematical properties of constrained versus unconstrained optimization as demonstrated in Figures 8.4 and 8.5. Thus the fundamental managerial problem related to market segmen-tation is finding the point at which the marginal reduction in profits due to further aggregation is balanced by the marginal reduction in administrative and research costs. Due to the high cost of assessing incremental response to marketing variables, the optimum level of aggregation will usually occur at the macrosegment level.

Thus a crucial segmentation decision is how microsegments or media descriptor cells should be allocated to macrosegments. It can be shown that the optimal decision rule assigns microsegments to macrosegments in such a way that the variance in incremental response between microsegments in a macrosegment is as small as possible and the variance between macrosegments is as large as possible. With incremental response measures for each microsegment, optimal grouping of microsegments into macrosegments must be established. Methods of optimal taxonomy and multidimensional mapping can be used to form macrosegments with large within-group homogeneity and between-group heterogeneity of response (see Lessig & Tollefson 1971 and Johnson 1971).

Considering Uncertainty

How much uncertainty is acceptable in a segmentation strategy? Is R^2 an appropriate measure to determine acceptability? What level of R^2 is adequate for defining segments? How much effort should be devoted to developing segmentation schemes with higher R^2? These questions can be approached by considering the role of uncertainty in market segmentation theory.

Sources of Uncertainty

While the preceding section dealt with some limitations in the implementation of segmentation strategies, the information, although aggregated, was known with certainty. But perfect information is rarely available. After defining segments using descriptor variables, it is usually necessary to predict media exposure patterns. The incremental response to marketing tools is even more illusive. Rather than predicting the incremental response directly, it is often necessary to estimate a surrogate like sales potential or the ratio of current sales to sales potential, and then estimate the relationship between the surrogate measure and the true incremental response.

Figure 8.6 illustrates the process of forming a segmentation strategy. These elements can also be represented in functional form. The following variables are defined for each segment:

SD = segment descriptor values
ME = media exposure level
RS = incremental response surrogate
RV = incremental response values

Denoting a prediction by "$\hat{}$", the marketer must estimate the following relationships:

$$\widehat{ME} = f(SD)$$
$$\widehat{RS} = g(SD)$$
$$\widehat{RV} = h(RS) \quad \text{or} \quad \widehat{RV} = g'(SD),$$

Figure 8.6
INFORMATION FLOW IN SEGMENTATION DECISIONS
BASED ON DESCRIPTOR VARIABLES

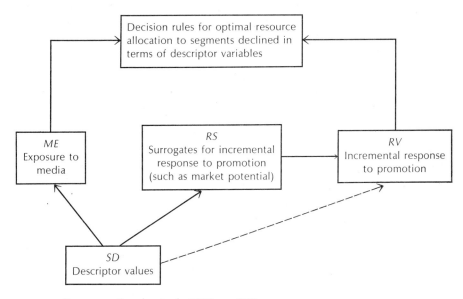

SOURCE: *Frank et al. 1972, p. 208.*

and then the optimal strategy is based on:

$$\text{contribution to profits} = r(\widehat{RV}, \widehat{ME}).$$

Notice that establishing the SD-RS-RV function is associated with the concept of forming macrosegments mentioned in the previous section.

In this process of forming a segmentation strategy, two types of uncertainty arise—uncertainty about response of customers with a given set of descriptor values and uncertainty about the targeting of marketing efforts to customers with a given set of descriptor variables.

In Figure 8.7, examples of situations involving these types of uncertainty are shown. In these situations, potential is used as a surrogate for incremental response, and the level of marketing effort in some cases is discrete (e.g., "send or do not send direct mail"). Although these examples are related to direct mail and advertising marketing tools, the same typology could be used to accommodate other types of promotion as well as selling effort and distribution policy.

The taxonomy presented in Figure 8.7 closely parallels the limitations in segmentation strategy that should be considered by a normative theory as discussed above under "A Framework for Normative Segmentation Theory." The vertical dimensions in the chart represent limitations due to uncertainty in the targeting of and response to marketing efforts. The horizontal dimension represents limitations due to the aggregation of individuals. While the aggre-

Figure 8.7

A TAXONOMY OF SEGMENTATION SITUATIONS

Aggregation of coverage and response information

			Freely targetable	Fixed coverage profits
Uncertainty about targeting of marketing effort	Little	Uncertainty about response — Little	1. Selection of individual direct mail prospects from a list in which each prospect has a rating that accurately reflects his response potential.	2. Selection of discrete direct mail lists from a master list, where the sublists are rated to reflect the average potential of prospects on the list.
		Uncertainty about response — Much	3. As in cell 1, except that only general descriptor variables are known for each prospect.	4. Direct mail: the combination of conditions in cells 2 and 3. Media advertising where coverage of descriptor categories is known accurately, but the potential of descriptor categories is uncertain.
	Much	Uncertainty about response — Little	5. Direct-mail advertising where the potential of customers with given descriptor values can be accurately rated, but where the list does not include all the relevant descriptors.	6. Advertising media selection where the potential of descriptor classes is known accurately, but the coverage profiles of the media are not.
		Uncertainty about response — Much	7. Direct-mail advertising where customer ratings by descriptor value are difficult to obtain and where lists do not include many descriptors.	8. Advertising media selection where neither potentials nor coverage by descriptor value are accurately known.

SOURCE: *Frank et al. 1972, p. 210.*

gation considered is that of the institutional constraint in targeting marketing effort, the response information constraint is also aggregated to the same level as the targeting constraint.

Cell 1 is an ideal situation in which response information is known for each individual and marketing effort can be directed toward each individual. This ideal situation was discussed above under "Normative Theory under Perfect Information." Cell 3 represents a situation in which information is known with certainty; however, a level of aggregation has been imposed. We considered this type of situation above under "Incorporating Real-World Constraints." In the present section, the implications of uncertainty included in the remaining cells will be examined.

Opportunity Loss Due to Uncertainty

Consider the situation presented in Cell 3 as compared to Cell 1. Since the response potentials are known with certainty in Cell 1, direct mail would be sent to all individuals with an expected contribution from response, as indicated by their descriptor variables, greater than the cost of the direct mail. Since each set of descriptors can be related to response with certainty, individuals can be selected for direct mail with knowledge that each individual will make a positive contribution to profit. The expected contribution from all individuals can be determined with certainty, thus the variance on the expected contribution is zero.

When there is uncertainty in the response potential, as in the situation in Cell 3, it can be shown that the same decision rule should be used to select candidates for direct mail. All individuals with an expected contribution greater than the marketing cost should be included in the direct mail program. Since the response potential is not known with certainty, some individuals will be included who should not be included, and some will be excluded who should have been included; thus the expected profit will be less than the profit under the perfect information case. In addition, there will be some uncertainty in the expected profit and a variance associated with the distribution of expected profits.

The existence of uncertainty leads to the possibility of reducing uncertainty. How much would the astute marketer be willing to pay to improve the general set of descriptors in Cell 3 to more closely approximate the specific descriptors in Cell 1 so that individual response could be predicted with greater accuracy? This is essentially asking the Bayesian question, "What is the opportunity loss due to imperfect information?"

The concept of opportunity loss due to imperfect information can be illustrated in a simplified example of a more general situation described in Cell 3. Assume individuals can be divided into two groups by the descriptor variable age: "under 35 and over 35." The distribution of responses for the over 35 group is shown in Figure 8.8. Since the expected contribution of this group is greater than the cost of direct mail, direct mail would be sent to all members of the group. However, a portion of the individuals in the group (represented by the shaded area) are bad prospects because their response is less than the cost of the direct mail. In a similar manner, the distribution of responses for individuals in the under-35 age group is shown in Figure 8.9. Since this group has an expected response less than the cost of direct mail, the group is not included in the direct mail program. However, some individuals in this group would have been good prospects (represented again by the shaded area) since their response is greater than the cost of direct mail. If these individuals had been included, they would have made a positive contribution to profit.

The increased contribution that would have occurred if the individuals in the shaded area of Figure 8.8 had been excluded from the direct mail program and the individuals in the shaded area in Figure 8.9 had been included represents the opportunity loss due to uncertainty. This also represents the amount the astute marketer would pay to have perfect information. This expected

Figure 8.8

EXAMPLE OF OPPORTUNITY LOSS

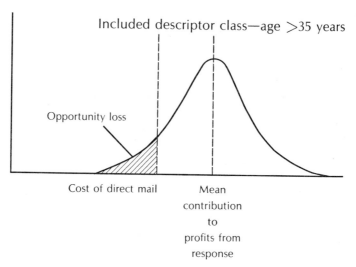

Included descriptor class—age >35 years

Opportunity loss

Cost of direct mail

Mean
contribution
to
profits from
response

Figure 8.9

EXAMPLES OF OPPORTUNITY LOSS

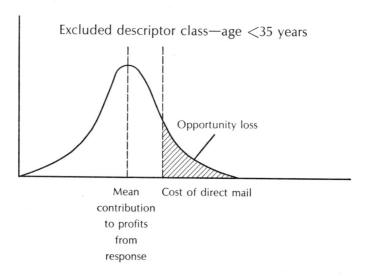

Excluded descriptor class—age <35 years

Opportunity loss

Mean
contribution
to profits
from
response

Cost of direct mail

opportunity loss is directly related to the means and variances of the two distributions. Lower within-group variance and greater differences in the means or between-group variance leads to a smaller opportunity loss. With knowledge of the means for each descriptor class, a decision can be made on whether to include the class in the program or not. With knowledge of the variance of each descriptor class, the expected opportunity loss can be calculated. As indicated in this example, there is an expected opportunity loss associated with each descriptor class whether it is included in the program or not. (See Frank et al. 1972, chap. 8, for a complete treatment of uncertainty, including uncertainty in media coverage.)

Managerial Implications

Differences in mean consumption between groups is a frequently used criterion for evaluating potential descriptor variables. The "alpha level" of the relationship described in the first example at the beginning of the paper indicates a significant difference in means. Although group means permit an optimal determination of which segments should receive promotion, this information is not sufficient for assessing the efficiency of the segmentation scheme.

This argument can be illustrated by the following hypothetical example of segmentation by a marriage counselor. A new personality test has been developed to determine whether two individuals will have a happy marriage. The test was administered to couples who have happy marriages and couples who have or have had unhappy marriages. The distribution of scores is shown in Figure 8.10. The mean score of the unhappily married pairs of individuals, $\bar{U}$, is significantly different statistically from the mean score of the happily married couples, $\bar{H}$. A client couple takes the test, scores X, and then asks you for advice on whether they should get married or not. Even though the test discriminates between unhappily married couples in terms of classical statistics, you would probably draw upon a Bayesian type inference to offer advice. Given the test score X, what is the probability of a happy marriage, and then what is the cost associated with giving the wrong advice? Since the within-group variance is so high on the two distributions of test scores, you might conclude that the test is really not that good an indicator. In light of the importance of this decision, you might attempt to look for other information that would lead to a prediction in which you might have more confidence. In these terms, a superior indicator

Figure 8.10

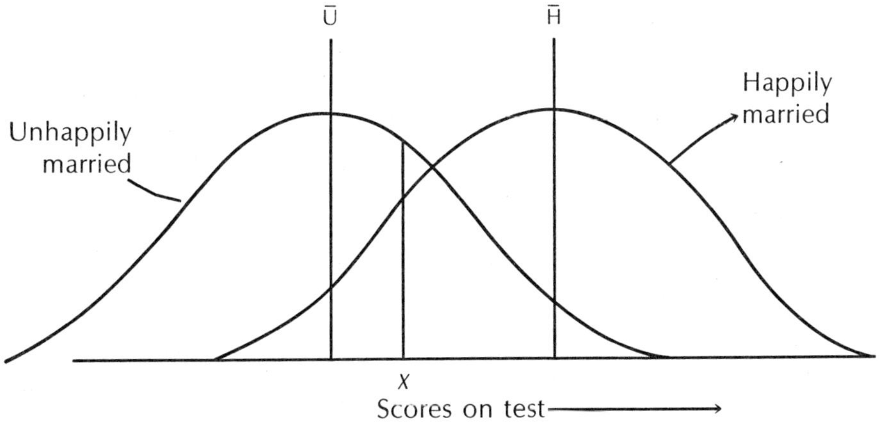

X

Scores on test———→

Figure 8.11

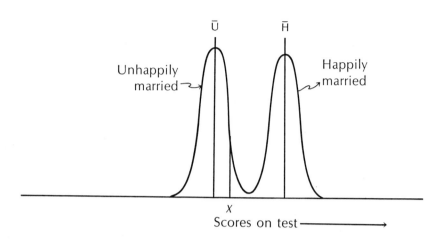

would be a measure that has a distribution of scores like that in Figure 8.11. Even though the means are closer, the smaller within-group variance leads to fewer errors in giving advice.

As the marriage counselor example illustrates, difference in means has only limited usefulness. Empirically the variance of the estimated mean is inversely proportional to the square root of the sample size; thus any difference in means is statistically significant with large enough sample size. However, the variance of the individuals in the underlying population is more relevant for decision making than the variance of the estimated means in this case.

How useful is R^2 as a measure of the usefulness of descriptor variables for segmenting markets? Bass et al. (1968) have argued that low values of R^2 do not necessarily imply that descriptor variables cannot serve as an effective basis for segmentation. Their argument against the use of R^2 as a criterion for assessing the efficacy of a segmentation scheme rests on the following three points:

1. Market segmentation is a management strategy. Hence the proper criterion for assessing the effectiveness of descriptor variables is whether they lead to efficient resource allocation decisions, not whether they explain individual behavior.
2. Linear correlation analysis may well understate the true degree of relationship between descriptors and product usage, for example, by ignoring important threshold, saturation, or interaction effects.
3. Evaluation of segment differences due to descriptor variables should depend exclusively on between-group variance, whereas R^2 is affected by between-group and within-group variance (Frank et al. 1972, p. 230)

The concepts presented in this chapter are in full accord with the first two points. Segmentation as a management strategy must be the basic tenet of any normative segmentation theory. Nonlinearities, if appropriate, should be included in any segmentation strategies; however, R^2, as a measure of variance relations, is not restricted to linear models.

The concept of opportunity loss due to uncertainty as presented in this chapter is in conflict with point 3; that is, it supports the use of R^2. Concentration on between-group variance provides useful hints to a viable segmentation strategy, but it does not consider potential increases in profit due to additional information.

Placing Figure 8.10 in a segmentation context, it could represent the distribution in consumption for two market segments. If no other segmentation scheme were available, then the marketer should probably accept this scheme as viable since the difference in means is statistically significant. However, due to the high within-group variance compared to the difference in means, there will be a high opportunity loss associated with this scheme. Therefore, the marketer should be strongly motivated to allocate effort to market research directed toward finding a better set of descriptor variables with which to form segments. Since R^2 is a convenient measure of the relationship of within-group variance to between-group variance, a low value for this statistic would signal the possibility of reducing opportunity loss through an improvement in the set of descriptor variables or the segmentation model.

Conclusion

In this chapter a framework for, and some aspects of, a normative segmentation theory have been presented. This normative theory emphasizes the importance of managerial relevance when evaluating segmentation research. Hopefully, this treatment will stimulate additional research to extend the normative theory of segmentation and provide direction for descriptive segmentation research, so that findings can be applied more directly to managerial decisions.

References

Bass, F. M., Tigert, D. J., and Lonsdale, R. T. 1968. "Market Segmentation: Group versus Individual Behavior." *Journal of Marketing Research* 5 (August):264–270.

Claycamp, H. J. and Massy, W. F. 1968. "A Theory of Market Segmentation." *Journal of Marketing Research* 5 (November):388–394.

Frank, R. E., Massy, W. F., and Wind, Y. 1972. *Market Segmentation*. Englewood Cliffs, N.J.: Prentice-Hall.

Guiltinan, J. P. and Sawyer, A. G. 1974. "Managerial Considerations for Market Segmentation Research." In *1974 Combined Proceedings*, ed. R. C. Curhan. Chicago: American Marketing Association, pp. 25–30.

Johnson, R. M. 1971. "Market Segmentation: A Strategic Management Tool." *Journal of Marketing Research* 8 (February):13–18.

Lessig, V. P. and Tollefson, J. O. 1971. "Market Segmentation through Numerical Taxonomy." *Journal of Marketing Research* 8 (November):480–487.

Little, J. D. C. 1970. "Models and Managers: The Concept of a Decision Calculus." *Management Science* 16 (April):B466–B485.

Lodish, L. M. 1971. "Callplan: An Interactive Salesman's Call Planning System." *Management Science* 18, pt. 2 (December):25–40.

Moran, W. T. 1963. "Practical Media Selection and the Computer." *Journal of Marketing* (July):28–29.

Robinson, J. 1954. *The Economics of Imperfect Competition.* London: McMillan and Co., pp. 179–188.

Smith, W. R. 1956. "Product Differentiation and Market Segmentation as Alternative Strategies." *Journal of Marketing* (July):3–8.

Part Three

Models of
Market Analysis:
The Competitive Setting

Chapter 9

Theories to Describe Some Competitive Conditions in Which the Firm Operates

*James M. Carman**

Editors' Note

The previous part focused on models of how buyers behave in the marketplace in which firms compete by offering alternative goods. In making decisions, a marketing manager requires information about the nature and intensity of the competition facing his or her firm. Similarly, public policy-makers require information not only about buyers' behavior, but also about the market and its competitive structure.

In this chapter, Carman discusses how a branch of economic theory—industrial organization—describes competitive market structures. In addition, he considers some of the limitations and modifications of this approach.

When we speak of the environment in which a system or an organization within that system operates, we mean the set of conditions or variables in the host system that affect or constrain the organization and, to some extent, are

*James M. Carman is from the School of Business Administration, University of California, Berkeley.

affected by the organization but are not under the control of the organization per se. When we speak of an organization within the marketing system, the environmental conditions are frequently subdivided into six subsets: culture, economic conditions, legal constraints, technology, competition within the system, and the structure of the vertical channel system within which the organization operates. To discuss all of these conditions in this chapter is clearly not feasible. Therefore, I will concentrate on theories that concern only the last two environmental subsets: competition and vertical channel structure.

Marketing teachers and scholars today have a tendency to ignore theoretical developments in these areas. Many contributions come from the agricultural and industrial organization branches of economics. The lack of interest in the theory in this area stems from a dissatisfaction with the extent to which the classical theory either reflects real-world marketing systems or is useful to the marketing decision maker in improving his decision-making skills. A number of well-known scholars in marketing, John A. Howard and Hans B. Thorelli, for example, have tested the theoretical water in this stream and found it too cold for their continued interest. The theory of classical industrial organization was static, too partial, employed incomplete models of market structure, and settled for unrealistic treatment of buyer, seller, and organizational behavior.

The chapters by Zaltman and by Dominguez and Nicosia in this book have developed some of the problems and criteria for success in building models that bridge theory and reality. One purpose of this chapter is to define some specific problems we face in building operational models of competitive and vertical channel relationships in marketing systems. A second purpose is to review some more recent work in this area—a neoclassical industrial organization theory—that I hope may suggest that this is an area deserving attention.

Classic Industrial Organization

By way of introducing some of the problems of the industrial organization framework, it may be well to briefly review that framework. The analysis of how the marketing system operates to produce consumer benefits is analyzed through the study of three sets of variables: (1) competitive structure, which influences both the others; (2) competitive conduct, which feeds back to influence structure; and (3) performance (see Figure 9.1).

The characteristics of competitive structure are the number of buyers and sellers in a market, the relative size of these organizations, the extent of product differentiation, the shape of the function describing the economies of scale, the barriers to entry of new firms into the market, and the merger activity which alters structure. Industrial organization today does concern itself with vertical market structure, but the classifications of structure are more complex than they are in Chamberlain. The analysis of conduct also is much more involved since vertical channel structure also influences the amount and kind of rivalry. There will be greater competitive rivalry (1) the larger the number of levels in the vertical system, (2) the more channel members at each level, and (3) the greater the geographic complexity of the channel system (see Figure 9.2).

Figure 9.1

A MODEL OF INDUSTRIAL ORGANIZATION ANALYSIS

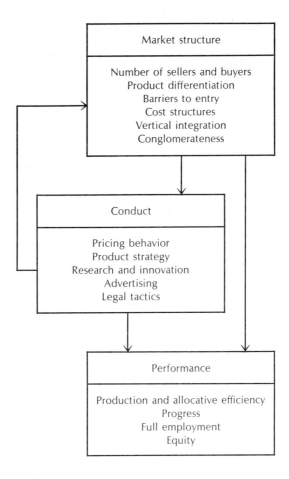

While market structure encompasses the number of players and constraints on their movement, competitive conduct refers to the alternatives,
strategies, and actions of the competitors. We are aware that much trade-regu-
lation public policy centers around pricing, marketing, and collusive behavior,
which is believed to lead to unsatisfactory performance or is patently undesir-
able in itself.

The payoff for the players, including society, in the competitive games in
the marketing system is the performance of the system. Elsewhere, I have
suggested over twenty dimensions on which to measure the performance of a
marketing system (Carman & Uhl 1973, pp. 608–609). These dimensions can be
grouped into three sets: (1) static efficiency, (2) dynamic efficiency, and
(3) quality of life.

Figure 9.2

CLASSIFICATION OF VERTICAL MARKET STRUCTURES

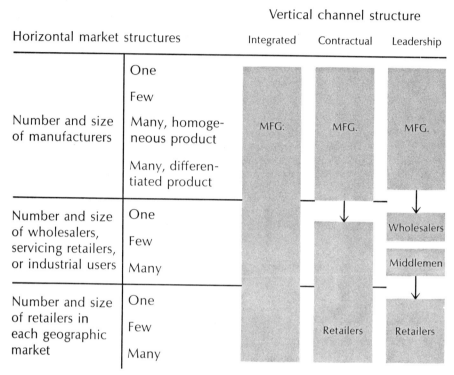

Horizontal market structures		Vertical channel structure		
		Integrated	Contractual	Leadership
Number and size of manufacturers	One	MFG.	MFG.	MFG.
	Few			
	Many, homogeneous product			
	Many, differentiated product			
Number and size of wholesalers, servicing retailers, or industrial users	One			Wholesalers
	Few			
	Many			Middlemen
Number and size of retailers in each geographic market	One			
	Few		Retailers	Retailers
	Many			

SOURCE: *Carman and Uhl 1973, p. 593.*

Some Problems

Specifically, what are the problems with the classical industrial-organization theory which have led us to neglect it in marketing? While there are many, I will briefly mention four. The student should go back to the chapter by Dominguez and Nicosia and classify each of these as a problem in substantive modeling.

First, there are serious measurement problems which are sufficient to discourage all but the strongest of scholars. Here are some of the ways in which measurement has been a great handicap.

1. We have not seen fit in this country to develop and systematically collect data on the many dimensions of performance. Rather, there has been a preoccupation with measures of structure at a single channel level. The result is that it is difficult to determine how particular markets are performing even when there is agreement on the dimension of performance that is of interest.

2. Without adequate measures and data on the dimensions of perfor-

mance, it has been difficult to study the way (i.e., functional form) performance changes as a result of changes in various structural and conduct variables.

3. Even if one sticks to fairly traditional economic notions of the output of a marketing system, marketers know that finding aggregate measures of the output of a marketing system is like sailing through an uncharted sea with many shoals. Unless the price system is operating perfectly, the concepts of high revenues or high value added can mean either great buyer satisfaction or great inefficiency.

4. Similarly, the problems of measuring inputs to a marketing system present some measurement problems. Since ultimate consumers perform some marketing functions, their costs must be added to the total costs within the system. These costs are frequently not imputed.

The second problem with the theory which is encountered in every anti-trust case is the difficulty of isolating the particular marketing channel system to study. This problem, more usually known as the problem of defining the relevant market, is a classic one for the systems analyst and one that is not likely to go away soon. However, marketing has been responsible for some major improvement in recent years. One historic source of confusion on this point stems from the reliance on SIC industries as the main organizing device for statistics on outputs and inputs. The Standard Industrial Classifications are based on raw materials or manufacturing processes and were never intended to define all or part of particular channel systems. Then, too, the collection efforts for these statistics make major separations between manufacturing, finance, agriculture, wholesaling, and retailing, so that it is very difficult to draw together the data for one vertical system.

Marketers have chipped away at these difficulties slowly over the years, but one major contribution has come more recently in the form of multidimensional scaling. The extent to which two products are substitutes is a question of buyer perceptions of substitutability, not the similarity of raw materials or manufacturing process. While economists have long worked with the concept of cross-elasticity of demand, the concept has severe empirical limitations when used to define the relevant market or system. Multidimensional scaling now permits us to define relevant market using consumer perceptions—a major contribution.

The third problem with the theory is really a combination of the first two, for it relates to the problem of defining and isolating the relevant channel system and is a reason for poor data. I call it the *multi problem* (see Exhibit 9.1). The multi problem is of at least four types. (1) Marketing systems may be operationally independent in space, but the firms in the system may be operating in multiple geographic markets domestically and globally. (2) Conglomerate firms may be operating in multiple industries which are clearly not parts of a single marketing system. (3) A firm may have a multiple product line which includes complements to the product of interest. (4) A firm may be selling multiple brands of the same product and these brands are substitutes for one another in a single marketing system (Revzan 1971). Analysis of a single

Exhibit 9.1

AREAS OF INSTITUTIONAL OVERLAP ACROSS MULTIPLE MARKETING CHANNEL SYSTEMS

1. Multiple geographic markets

2. Multiple product lines sold to independent demanders

3. Multiple product lines which are complements

4. Multiple products or brands which are substitutes

marketing system which contains such "multi" firms causes serious problems in both data collection and analysis. How does one handle joint costs in marketing as well as production? How does one get data on costs and revenues for that portion of the firm which is of interest? The latter problem has been reduced during the past two years by the new product line sales and earnings reporting requirements of the SEC 10-k reports, but serious research is still difficult without confidential data.

The fourth problem with the theory is one which is more fundamental to the cause and effect relationships explicit in Figure 9.1. The figure suggests that poor structure causes poor conduct which, in turn, causes poor performance and feeds back to worsen structure still more. This model is simply too naive for serious analysis. First, structure has a direct influence on performance as well as working through conduct. Second, as in any system, some exogenous, environmental variables must be explicitly brought into the analysis in order to understand differences in the effect of structural and conduct variables on performance. Third, the structure of the components of the system must concern not only firms (i.e., institutions), but also the physical establishments, resources, and facilities of those firms (Bucklin & Carman 1974). Fourth, conduct does indeed feed back to structure and to environment. Fifth, these conduct or behavior variables need to be more carefully described.

Statistical methodologies exist for beginning to test alternative models which are richer than that of classical industrial organization. Behavioral as well as economic theories have been advanced which suggest just how such alternative models might be structured and tested. Marketers are at the forefront of much of this work. Therefore, the balance of this chapter will be devoted to reviewing some of these newer contributions which combine to form a much richer neoclassical industrial organization theory. Note that each either sharpens the theory or improves our ability to test these models.

The Structure of Vertical Marketing Systems

The first set of new contributions I want to review concerns the expansion of the model of the structure of the system to include vertical as well as horizontal structure and to include other characteristics of structure beyond number and size of firms. By no means is there complete agreement among marketing scholars as to the dimensions to be used or the names to be given to these

Exhibit 9.2

THE DIMENSIONS OF A VERTICAL MARKETING SYSTEM

1. The institutions (firms)
2. The goals of each institution
3. The establishments which compose the institutions
4. The marketing functions performed by each establishment
5. The level in the channel of each establishment
6. The nature of the coordination among establishments
7. The good involved

dimensions in describing vertical marketing systems. I do observe, however, that with the development of general systems theory, the jargon and list of dimensions have stabilized somewhat. My suggested list of dimensions of component structure of a marketing system includes: (1) the institutions or firms; (2) the goals of each institution; (3) the establishments which compose these firms; (4) the marketing functions performed by these establishments; (5) the level in the channel of each establishment; (6) the nature of the linkage, i.e., market, contract, or vertical integration; and (7) the product or service involved (see Exhibit 9.2). (For some recent thinking on this problem, see Bucklin 1970, pp. 9–24; Carman and Uhl 1973, pp. 19, 56–59; and MacKenzie & Nicosia 1968, pp. 19–22.)

It is Bucklin who has emphasized the importance of including establishment structure as well as firm structure in the analysis of vertical marketing systems and has been the most productive worker in this field in recent years. While he has not made the case for establishment structure in this way, it aids our understanding to see why this dimension does not appear in classical industrial organization. The reason stems from the assumption in classical economics that the firm is allocating its resources optimally. Bucklin seems to argue (1) that this optimum allocation is not going to come about unless those of us concerned with firm management study just what organization of establishments is optimum for the firm; (2) that an optimum structure is difficult for the firm to design since it often includes buying functions and use of resources from other institutions in the channel; and (3) that optimum establishment structure for the firm will not necessarily result in maximum efficiency for the total vertical system. It requires external study of the total system to reach decisions as to the establishment structure which will maximize the efficiency of the total channel system. Vertical marketing systems theory should include these considerations.

Bucklin's approach to the study of efficiency of alternative establishment structures is contained in his COPE (*cost-performance*) model. This model employs static microeconomic theory and the total cost approach of logistics to provide a basic analytic approach (Bucklin 1966, and 1970, pp. 158–174). The analysis must concern itself not only with the number and location in space of establishments, but with the functions they perform and the flow of goods, title, and information through them.

The model usually restricts itself to total commercial costs which result from a specified level of performance. By comparing alternative structures over a range of output levels, it is possible to select the establishment design which minimizes total commercial cost at each output performance level. The use of only commercial costs makes the model more operational because they are easier to measure and we can avoid the problem of differences in cost between individual consumers. However, the model recognizes that if the commercial sector does not perform the tasks, the consumer must. At a given level of product flow, high levels of commercial service reduce consumer costs but increase price and commercial costs. An optimal structure is one which minimizes the total costs of the system, including final users, by the appropriate adjustment of the level of service outputs in each establishment.

By consideration of a range of output levels of marketing services, the model can consider a great variety in final buyers' demands for both quantity of product and marketing services associated with the delivery of that product. Total equilibrium (remember this is static analysis) for a channel is derived from the partial equilibria associated with the optimum channel system design for the level of output required by each market segment of final buyers.

To date, Bucklin has developed his normative analysis so as to suggest the optimal design for consideration of four kinds of system outputs: (1) the size or physical quantity of the good desired by the final buyer in a single order; (2) the time period desired by the final buyer between order placement and delivery of the good ready for consumption in the place desired; (3) decentralization of final markets, i.e., the proximity of sellers and model assortments to buyers; (4) the assortment of quality, size, and minor variations of the goods which are offered to final buyers by individual establishments.

Bucklin's analysis is far less complete when one shifts the focus from optimum establishment structure to optimum institutional structure. When service outputs require small lot sizes, extensive decentralization, and broad assortments, the communication needs within the channel increase greatly. Evidence suggests that price alone is not efficient as the sole type of information used to communicate information on the supply and demand by type, quality, and location. Even when the types of information are expanded, it is not clear when communication is superior in markets or in vertically integrated institutions. Chain organizations have historically been more concerned with simplifying communications via standardization than have small firms dealing at a single level in the channel (Bucklin & Carman 1974, pp. 23–24).

Vertical institutional structure has been considered in neoclassical industrial organization theory because of the demand for an evaluation of the social consequences of the large number of vertical mergers which took place during the past two decades. The usual reasons given for such moves are market foreclosure, cost savings resulting from coordination of production and marketing activities at two levels of the channel, the heightening of barriers to entry, the potential for price discrimination, and the existence of excess profits at another level in the channel. The public policy debate in recent years has brought these arguments—if one assumes maximum firm efficiency and profit maximization—rather clearly into focus (Bork 1969; Needham 1969, pp. 113–

126; Crandall 1968; and Vernon & Graham 1971). We will not review the analysis here.

Improving the theory of industrial organization requires relaxing another assumption of much classical economics—that of perfect resource allocation in markets. Many economists have been active in the analysis of behavior in imperfect markets since the 1930s. What follows is only a very selective review of some recent advances.

The Behavior of Actors in Small Group Markets and Vertically Integrated Channels

Oliver Williamson has long worried over whether the assumption of profit maximization in economic theory is acceptable for gaining operational insights (Williamson 1970). In the analysis of resource allocation in integrated firms versus imperfect markets, however, he concludes that we can move forward without relaxing the assumption of profit maximization (Williamson 1971). The traditional preference for market allocation stems from doubts about bounded alternatives and biased decisions within bureaucratic, integrated institutions. However, as most marketers would agree, if intermediate markets fail in their tasks, the integrated firm may indeed have greater transactional efficiency.

The research on transaction efficiency in marketing has largely been static (Balderston 1968). The important issue, though, is how the system returns to an acceptable equilibrium after some exogenous shock. Four rather different foci have been used to analyze the behavior within and among firms that might be used to predict the relative dynamic efficiency of marketing transactions: organizational considerations, bargaining considerations, psychological considerations, and power considerations (see Exhibit 9.3).

Organizational Considerations

Williamson's focus is on organizational considerations. He identifies three characteristics of the firms which may make internal organization superior to a market (Williamson 1971, p. 113). First, the similarity of goals within an institution is the antithesis of most bargaining between independent channel members. Second, institutions possess control instruments for their own resources and employee actions that are far more direct than market control. Third, information flow and message precision within an institution may be superior to that in a market. These three types of advantage are well developed in the literature of both organizational behavior and marketing (Howard 1973, pp. 124–134; Carman & Uhl 1973, pp. 63–67; Mallen 1965; and Stern 1967).

The failures of intermediate markets stem principally from the bilateral

Exhibit 9.3

NONCLASSIC APPROACHES TO THE ANALYSIS OF
COMPETITIVE RIVALRY

1. Organization behavior emphasis
2. Bargaining emphasis
3. Psychological emphasis
4. Power emphasis

monopoly or bilateral oligopoly structure of a vast majority of intermediate markets. Price and quantity determination in such markets involves bargaining, and the results of that bargaining need not yield a socially desirable bargain, a complete contract which provides a procedure for handling every contingency in an efficient manner or a desirable distribution of risk within the channel.

We will return to bargaining considerations in a moment, but first another word about the goal of profit maximization within the firm. If firms do not make decisions designed to maximize the present value of future earnings, then how different would be our analysis or conclusions regarding competition or vertical market structure? In answering this question, I mention the work of only two men whom I believe are on a track which is fruitful and which should be followed by more marketing scholars. This is the work of Almerin Phillips and Oliver Williamson (Phillips 1967, 1970; and Williamson 1970). For a more complete recent review, see Cyert and Hedrick (1972). Our treatment is in no way intended to minimize the contribution of Cyert and March (1963) to this subject. Phillips and Williamson attempt to explain organizational behavior under the assumption that firms attempt to maximize an objective function which has been enriched by the addition of variables other than profit; i.e., profit is not abandoned but merely supplemented. While empirical tests are weak, these models do seem to increase the explanatory power of models which are in other respects neo-classical maximization models. The models of Phillips and Williamson analyze the implications of a firm's utility function considering terms such as: minimum acceptable profit rate; aspired profit rate; the difference between actual and minimum profit; the difference between actual and aspired profit; total taxes in the current year; staff size; the friendliness of competitive, customer, dealer, and regulatory environments; and the techniques of competitive conduct employed.

Bargaining Considerations

Models of the type just discussed are useful in analyzing the effect of environmental variables on a large number of decisions of a firm, including those concerning both horizontal and vertical relationships. The work on bargaining is much more narrowly focused and the theory more rigidly structured.

Within classical economic theory, there are well-known static equilibrium solutions for bilateral monopoly of the Cournot type (Bowley 1928 and McKie 1959, pp. 10–34). The result shows that an equilibrium at competitive output levels is not impossible and that countervailing power of strong buyers helps in achieving this result. But when one extends this analysis to bilateral oligopoly, adds a vertical market structure, the potential for vertical integration, the possibility for coalition, and an unequal distribution of power among channel levels, almost any solution is possible.

One task of game theory is to attempt to derive theorems which will specify just what set of coalitions, allocations, and equilibria are possible. (For some recent developments, see Friedman 1968, Shakun 1972, and Manas 1972.) The set of possible results is called the *core* of the game. Given the appropriate conditions and assumptions, the classic competitive equilibrium is in the core. With other assumptions and fewer players, the classic equilibrium may not be in the core. Game theory is concerned with bargaining. While most of the advances to date have dealt with small numbers of players, usually two, Telser (1972) has recently tied these results into a continuum up to a large number of players as in the classic competitive case. The work is of significance not only because of its theoretical contribution, but because it brings together into a single theory environments of competition and environments of conflict. In both economics and sociology, there has been the distinction between competition and conflict which has divided classical economic theory from other approaches to the study of competitive activity (Cyert & March 1963 and Stern 1971). Competition is indirect, impersonal, and object-centered in that actors do not consider the actions of their competitors as they vie for the payoff held by a third party—the demanders. Conflict (or bargaining) is direct, personal, and opponent-centered in that actors react to one another's moves, form coalitions, and in other ways attempt to control the competitive environment rather than treat it as exogenous. Also, the payoff is usually held by one of the competitors rather than by a third party.

Beyond the focus on a small number of players, game theory does not require a vertical channel system. The application to vertial marketing systems has been made by Baligh and Richartz (1967) and Richartz (in Bucklin 1970, pp. 177–204). The theory can also treat bargaining where, as in real markets, the information available is incomplete and not the same for all players (Harsanyi 1967–1968, and Harsanyi & Selten 1972).

One way to overcome the restrictions of formal game theory and a large number of possible solutions in bilateral oligopoly is to use simulation. Simulation allows the model builder to include environmental considerations, complex vertical relationships, and even the decision-making process. A number of simulations of vertical channel systems have been constructed (Dutton & Starbuck 1971, Claycamp & Amstutz 1968, and Preston & Collins 1966). Amstutz has constructed another simulation in which a government sector monitors intercompany communications with response functions sensitized to covariance in behavior that might be construed as manifestations of collusion or conspiracy in restraint of trade (Amstutz 1967, pp. 370–375). However, beyond the insights that are inevitably obtained from the process of model construction, it is not clear just how much we can learn from complex simulations of vertical marketing systems. Validity and sensitivity are serious problems.

Psychological Considerations

What appears to be a far more fruitful way to break out of the restrictions of game theory is to test game theory solutions and empirically add behavioral variables through behavioral gaming in a laboratory environment. Although the laboratory may seem to eliminate most environmental variables, very exciting results are beginning to emerge. Competitive gaming can be described as a controlled, simplified business game where the objective is to test empirically theories of small-group competitive behavior with statistical experimental design models under laboratory-controlled conditions. Until very recently, these experiments have been restricted to duopoly situations, where the personal characteristics of both actors strongly influenced the results. Although such experiments are interesting, they are of little value in predicting behavior in real market environments. The Cournot solutions of classical economics will do as well.

However, employment of special-purpose computers has greatly increased the value of such experiments. Hoggatt (1969) has reported on experiments in which human players compete against robots in the computer that have programmed responses to each move. The decision variables still concern only price and quantity in each decision period, but the increased control permits rather detailed analysis of the effect of individual characteristics on the equilibrium solutions achieved. For example, it has been possible to develop a measure of differential cooperativeness in which it is postulated that cooperative robot behavior evokes cooperative human behavior, and noncooperative robot behavior evokes noncooperative human behavior. Human subjects were administered the California Psychological Inventory (CPI) to see what effect personality characteristics have upon the cooperativeness of subjects and their ability to reach the equilibrium predicted by classic economic theory. Personality and other personal characteristics do have a predictable influence on the outcome of the games.

Hoggatt has recently extended his experiments to an empirical test of some parts of the Harsanyi-Selten theory mentioned earlier. Hughes has extended competitive gaming to consider real products and more traditional marketing variables, such as promotion and past purchase behavior (Hughes & Guerrero 1971a and 1971b, Hughes & Naert 1970). Stern and his associates have recently begun laboratory experimentation centered on the bargaining between a manufacturer and a wholesaler (Stern et al. 1973).

Such experiments add a very different dimension to traditional economic analysis because economists have traditionally been interested in propositions that are true for large groups of actors or for an "economic man." This point of view eliminates any interest on the part of the researcher in making observations on individual actor behavior. But only by studying the variance in individual behavior can we hope to really bring about a marriage of economics and psychology, which is so vital to the development of a science of marketing.

Power Considerations

Another group of researchers has attacked the problem of enriching economic theory by considering another set of actor or institutional variables. These are concerned with the power of an actor to influence the bargain in small-group competition by inclusion of variables measuring the power one actor has over another. Much of this work has its roots in the discipline of sociology. The Hoggatt experiments do include the influence of low (or high) production costs and personality on the dynamics of the bargaining, but one actor may exert other types of power over his competitor to achieve a favorable bargain.

One research tradition of this type is that of the industrial organization economists who have studied this use of power in vertical, small-group competitive situations through the vehicle of descriptive industry studies. (McKie 1959 is just one example.) Such analysis provides one way to avoid the two-person limitations and the other constraints imposed by price theory and game theory. In those situations where collusion among sellers is minimum and large retail buyers have significant market power, there is considerable evidence that excess profits need not get locked into intermediate markets. However, the large buyers must possess at least the potential power to integrate backward so as to compete with their suppliers. If the powerful buyers do indeed integrate backward, however, the argument is often made (as in the current debate over integrated gasoline marketers) that the potential for innovative and efficient entrants will be foreclosed and monopoly profits will result (Comanor 1967). This argument regarding external market power takes us back, then, to the Williamson interest in studying the transactional efficiency of the vertically integrated organizations as compared with the transactional efficiency of bilateral oligopolistic markets.

Another fledgling research tradition for the study of power in vertical market systems is that which has developed in marketing principally by Louis W. Stern and his students. While much more validation remains to be done, they have moved far down the road from definitions and conceptualization of power, to identification of the dimensions of power, to construction of measures of these dimensions, and to empirical testing of the measures (Heskett et al. in Bucklin 1970, pp. 75–91). The dimension of power, the bases of power, and the measurement of potential and exercised power in vertical marketing systems are clearly different from those in other social systems such as domestic politics or international relations (Carman & Uhl 1973, pp. 67–69). Rosenberg has attempted to empirically measure the extent of conflict and coalition in a vertical channel system as a precondition to describing the power relationships (Rosenberg & Stern 1971). El-Ansary has attempted to measure power perceived and attributed to middlemen in a channel in the U.S. (El-Ansary & Stern 1972). Using a slightly different conceptual framework and different measures, Wilkinson (1974) has done similar empirical work in Australia.

In both cases, the work represents the application of sociological concepts to marketing systems. With additional field validation, it should be possible shortly to link this work to the laboratory gaming of vertical systems, which

159

itself is close to a marriage with some of the mathematical results of game theory. It should then be possible to apply the resulting structures and theory to design richer descriptive industry studies than have been possible to date.

Concluding Note

This chapter has attempted to provide the foundations of those theories and marketing models concerned with the competitive environment within vertical marketing systems. We have seen that these foundations are found in a number of different academic disciplines. As Blankenship suggests in his chapter in this book, the nonclassical approaches do draw "other points of view into the process of inquiry . . . and redefine categories of thought." Therefore, an attempt has been made not only to report on the research progress in each discipline, but to suggest where the models of one discipline have been or can be linked to the models of another. Principal attention has been focused on classic microeconomic theory of the firm, industrial organization economics, game theory, vertical market structure theory, organization theory, social psychology, and sociology.

Our review suggests that the researchers on competitive behavior in each of these disciplines are not on divergent tracks. In fact, I believe that while progress is slow, these tracks are on a course clearly headed for intersection—an intersection which can be a neoclassical industrial organization theory.

Marketing scholars are playing an important role in bringing us closer to intersection. We need to do a better job in bringing those different foundations together and pointing out the relationships between them.

References

Allen, B. T. 1971. "Vertical Integration and Market Foreclosure: The Case of Cement and Concrete." *Journal of Law Economics* 14 (April):251–274. See also comments in October 1972 issue.

Amstutz, A. E. 1967. *Computer Simulation of Competitive Market Response.* Cambridge, Mass.: MIT Press.

Balderston, F. E. 1968. "Communication Networks in Intermediate Markets." *Management Science* 4 (January):154–171.

Baligh, H. H. and Richartz, L. E. 1967. *Vertical Market Structure.* Boston: Allyn and Bacon.

Bork, R. H. 1969. "Vertical Integration and Competitive Processes." In *Public Policy toward Mergers,* ed. J. F. Weston and S. Peltzman. Pacific Palisades, Calif.: Goodyear Publishing Company.

Bowley, A. L. 1928. "Bilateral Monopoly." *Economic Journal* (December):651–659.

Bucklin, L. P. 1966. *A Theory of Distribution Channel Structure.* Berkeley: Institute of Business and Economic Research, University of California.

———, ed. 1970. *Vertical Marketing Systems.* Glenview, Ill.: Scott, Foresman.

Bucklin, L. P., and Carman, J. M. 1974. "Vertical Market Structure Theory and the Health Care Delivery System: An Analysis." In *Marketing Analysis for Societal Problems*, ed. J. N. Sheth and P. L. Wright. Urbana: University of Illinois.

Carman, J. M. and Uhl, K. P. 1973. *Marketing: Principles and Methods*. Homewood, Ill.: Richard D. Irwin.

Claycamp, H. J. and Amstutz, A. E. 1968. "Simulation Techniques in the Analysis of Marketing Strategy." In *Applications of the Sciences in Marketing Management*, ed. F. M. Bass, C. W. King, and E. A. Pessemier. New York: John Wiley & Sons.

Comanor, W. S. 1967. "Vertical Mergers, Market Power, and the Antitrust Laws." *American Economic Review* 57 (May):254–265.

Crandall, R. W. 1968. "Vertical Integration and the Market for Repair Parts in the United States Automobile Industry." *Journal of Industrial Economics* 16 (July):212–234.

Cyert, R. M. and Hedrick, C. L. 1972. "Theory of the Firm: Past, Present, and Future: An Interpretation." *Journal of Economic Literature* 10 (June):398–412.

Cyert, R. M. and March, J. G. 1963. *A Behavioral Theory of the Firm*. Englewood Cliffs, N.J.: Prentice-Hall.

Dixon, D. F. 1972. "Some Competitive Effects of Vertical Relationships in Australian Petrol Distribution." *The Antitrust Bulletin* 17 (Fall):791–809.

Dutton, J. M. and Starbuck, W. H., eds. 1971. *Computer Simulation of Human Behavior*. New York: John Wiley & Sons.

El-Ansary, A. I. and Stern, L. W. 1972. "Power Measurement in the Distribution Channel." *Journal of Marketing Research* 9 (February):47–52.

Friedman, J. W. 1968. "Reaction Functions and the Theory of Duopoly." *The Review of Economic Studies* 35 (July):257–272.

Harsanyi, J. C. 1967–1968. "Games with Incomplete Information Played by 'Bayesian' Players." Part I, *Management Science* 14 (November 1967):159–182; Part II, *ibid.* (January 1968):320–334; Part III, *ibid.* (March 1968):486–502.

Harsanyi, J. C. and Selten, R. 1972. "A Generalized Nash Solution for Two-Person Bargaining Games with Incomplete Information." *Management Science* 18 (January):80–106.

Hoggatt, A. C. 1969. "Response of Paid Student Subjects to Differential Behavior of Robots in Bifurcated Duopoly Games." *The Review of Economic Studies* 36 (October):417–432.

Howard, J. A. 1973. *Marketing Management: Operating, Strategic, and Administrative*. Homewood, Ill.: Richard D. Irwin.

Hughes, G. D. and Guerrero, J. L. 1971a. "Simultaneous Concept Testing with Computer-Controlled Experiments." *Journal of Marketing* 25 (January):28–33.

———. 1971b. "Testing Models through Computer-Controlled Experiments." *Journal of Marketing Research* 8 (August):291–297.

Hughes, G. D. and Naert, P. A. 1970. "A Computer-Controlled Experiment in Consumer Behavior." *Journal of Business* 43 (July):354–372.

MacKenzie, K. D. and Nicosia, F. M. 1968. "Marketing Systems: Toward Formal

Descriptions and Structural Properties." *Proceedings.* Chicago: American Marketing Association, pp. 14–23.

McKie, J. 1959. *Tin Cans and Tin Plate.* Cambridge, Mass.: Harvard University Press.

Mallen, B. 1965. "Conflict and Cooperation in Marketing Channels." *Proceedings.* Chicago: American Marketing Association, pp. 65–85.

Manas, M. 1972. "A Linear Oligopoly Game." *Econometrica* 40 (September):917–922.

Needham, D. 1969. *Economic Analysis and Industrial Structure.* New York: Holt, Rinehart and Winston.

Phillips, A. 1967. "An Attempt to Synthesize Some Theories of the Firm." In *Prices: Issues in Theory, Practice, and Public Policy,* ed. A. Phillips and O. W. Williamson. Philadelphia: University of Pennsylvania Press.

————. 1970. "Structure, Conduct, and Performance—and Performance, Conduct, and Structure?" In *Industrial Organization and Economic Development,* ed. J. W. Markham and G. F. Papanek. Boston: Houghton Mifflin.

Plessner, Y. 1971. "Computing Equilibrium Solutions for Imperfectly Competitive Markets." *American Journal of Agricultural Economics* 53 (May):191–196.

Preston, L. E. and Collins, N. R. 1966. *Studies in a Simulated Market.* Berkeley: Institute of Business and Economic Research, University of California.

Revzan, D. A. 1971. *A Marketing View of Spatial Competition.* Berkeley: Published by the author.

Rosenberg, L. J. and Stern, L. W. 1971. "Conflict Measurement in the Distribution Channel." *Journal of Marketing Research* 8 (November):437–442.

Shakun, M. F., ed. 1972. "Game Theory and Gaming." *Management Science,* Part II, 18 (January).

Stern, L. W. 1967. "The Concept of Channel Control." *Journal of Retailing* 43 (Summer):14–20, 67.

————. 1971. "Antitrust Implications of a Sociological Interpretation of Competition, Conflict, and Cooperation in the Marketplace." *The Antitrust Bulletin* 16 (Fall):509–530.

Stern, L. W., Sternthal, B., and Craig, C. S. 1973. "Managing Conflict in Distribution Channels: A Laboratory Study." *Journal of Marketing Research* 10 (May):169–179.

Telser, L. G. 1972. *Competition, Collusion, and Game Theory.* Chicago: Aldine-Atherton.

Vernon, J. M. and Graham, D. A. 1971. "Profitability of Monopolization by Vertical Integration." *Journal of Political Economy* 79 (July-August):924–925.

Wilkinson, I. F. 1974. "Researching the Distribution Channel for Consumer and Industrial Goods: The Power Dimension." *Journal of the Market Research Society* 16 (January):12–32.

Williamson, O. W. 1970. *Corporate Control and Business Behavior.* Englewood Cliffs, N.J.: Prentice-Hall.

————. 1971. "The Vertical Integration of Production: Market Failure Considerations." *American Economic Review* 61 (May):112–123.

Chapter 10

The Perception of a Firm's Competitive Position

*Yoram Wind**

Editors' Note
Consumers' preferences have always been the foundation of basic economic theory in the explanation of value. However, most applications do not explicitly consider these preferences. Advances in mathematical psychology today enable the measurement of consumers' preferences for, and perceptions of, products and services available in the market.

In contrast to the previous chapter, which was based on "objective" measures of competition, in this chapter the focus is on "subjective" measures of competitive market relationships, as perceived by the relevant publics.

In the previous chapter, Carman discussed the economic theories related to competition and vertical channel structure. The focal point of the model of industrial organization analysis which he presents is the market (competitive) structure. Following the industrial organization aproach, Carman defines the competitive structure in terms of the number of buyers and sellers in a market, the relative size of these organizations, the extent of product differentiation, the

*Yoram Wind is from the University of Pennsylvania.

shape of the function describing the economies of scale, the barriers to entry of new firms into the market, and the merger activity that alters structure.

As recognized by Carman, the major limitations of the industrial organization model is the approach it takes in measuring the competitive structure—i.e., the reliance, whenever hard numbers are available (such as number of firms), on "objective" measures, or the analyst's subjective judgment, as in the case of trying to determine the degree of product differentiation. Carman mentions, as one of the ways to overcome this limitation, the utilization of multidimensional scaling to define the market structure using consumer perceptions. It is the purpose of this chapter to expand on this notion, to explore the relationship between positioning and the commonly advocated classification-of-goods schemes, and to highlight how one can approach the determination of market and channel structure via an analysis of buyers' perceptions of a firm's competitive position.

Positioning as a Guide to Product Differentiation, Market and Channel Structure

The basic premise of this chapter is that the degree and nature of product differentiation and the characteristics of the market and channel structure can best be determined by measuring consumers' and other relevant publics' perceptions and evaluations ("positioning") of the products and firms.

The term "product (brand) positioning" refers to customers' perceptions of the "place" a product occupies in a given market. In this context, the word "positioning" encompasses most of the common meanings of the word "position"—position as a place (what place does the specific product occupy in its relevant market?), a rank (how does the given product fare against its competitors on various evaluative dimensions?), and a mental attitude (customer attitudes—the cognitive, affective, and action tendencies) toward the given product.

Product differentiation on the basis of some physical, functional, or structural characteristic (such as those in the Standard Industrial Classification [SIC] system, which also applies to consumer goods) is not very useful unless it is consistent with consumers' perceptions of the products. Chemically, for example, two brands of aspirin might be identical; yet they might be perceived differently by various consumer segments. Conversely, two brands that are quite dissimilar in some physical characteristics might be perceived as quite similar if their differentiating characteristics are viewed by the consumers as unimportant ones. Product differentiation is, therefore, a meaningful concept only to the extent to which it is based on consumers' perception of the differences among competing products or brands.

Market structure can be defined as the position (strength and weakness)—as perceived by buyers—of a firm versus its competitors in a given market. The complexity of determining market structure via positioning arises when a firm has multiple brands in multiple product lines in more than one strategic business. In this case, one can conduct the market-structure (positioning) analysis at three levels: the brand level, the product-class level, or the firm level. At each level, the positioning of the brands, products, and firms will be determined in the context of their natural "competitive" set, providing insight into the competitive structure of the market and the features of the brands, products, and firms that lead them to be positioned as they are in the given market structure.

If all three positioning studies are conducted, it might be useful to compare the results and see to what extent the firm's positioning is consistent in all levels of analysis. Further extension of the positioning analysis of market structure can be achieved by collecting (and subsequently analyzing) the perceptual and evaluative data not only from buyers, but from other relevant publics, such as the firm's own employees, its suppliers, and even government agencies, if any of those are concerned with the market structure of the given industry and the competitive position of the firm in question.

Channel-structure analysis can be conducted in a way similar to the market-structure analysis. The major difference is in the characteristics of the relevant publics, which in this case should include the relevant channel members.

Positioning and Classification-of-Goods "Theories"

Whereas product/brand positioning is based on actual consumers' perceptions and evaluations of products and brands, the classification-of-goods theories are based on a priori criteria assumed to be relevant. Since both the classification-of-goods theories and positioning are aimed at classifying products to provide guidelines for the design of appropriate marketing strategy, it might be useful to discuss the similarities and differences between the two approaches.

All classification-of-goods theories stem from the original trichotomy into convenience, shopping, and specialty goods proposed as early as 1924 by Copeland. The various classification-of-goods "theories" vary, however, with respect to the criteria they use to classify products and the number of categories. Copeland, for example, used three implicit criteria—the travel effort involved in getting to a store; the effort in comparing brands on prices, quality, and style at the time of purchase; and the amount of brand attraction (which, in the case of specialty goods, "induced the consumer to put forth special effort to visit the store in which they are sold and to make the purchase without shopping") (Copeland 1925, p. 14).

Whereas Copeland did not provide an operational definition for these criteria, Holton (1958) attempted to provide an operational definition for the classification of consumer goods (as to convenience, shopping, and specialty) based on the ratio of cost of search to gain from search, and the volume of demand for, and supply of, a certain good. Aspinwall (1962) suggested a trichotomy of goods into red, orange, and yellow according to the products' marketing characteristics—length of distribution channel and nature of the promotion media. Miracle (1965) extended Aspinwall's marketing characteristics and developed five product categories based on a number of characteristics, such as unit of value, significance of each individual purchase to the consumer, rate of technological change, technical complexity, consumer need for service, frequency of purchase, rapidity of consumption, and extent of usage.

Bucklin (1963), while maintaining the traditional distinction of convenience, shopping, and specialty goods, redefined it based on the degree to which a consumer, before his need arises, possesses a preference map that (1) indicates willingness to purchase any of a number of known substitutes (convenience goods), (2) requires a search to construct such a map (shopping), or (3) indicates a willingness to expand the effort required to purchase the most preferred item rather than a more readily accessible substitute (specialty goods). Using the criteria of preference formation, Bucklin extends the same definition to cover all stores, resulting in a nine-cell classification (three product types times three store types).

More recently, Holbrook and Howard (1976), after a critical review of these and other approaches to the classification-of-goods theories, suggested the addition of a "preference goods" category. They base this fourfold classification on three sets of criteria: (1) product characteristics (magnitude of purchase and clarity of characteristics), (2) consumer characteristics (ego involvement and specific self-confidence), and (3) consumer responses (physical shopping and mental effort). Accepting these underlying considerations, they develop a 2 × 2 matrix based on two complex dimensions: (1) magnitude of purchase, ego involvement, and physical shopping effort (when all three are low, it can result in either convenience or preference goods—when they are high, it suggests shopping or specialty goods); and (2) clarity, self-confidence, and mental effort during or prior to shopping (high clarity and self-confidence and mental effort during shopping result in either convenience or shopping goods, while the opposite condition results in preference and specialty goods).

These and other classification-of-goods "theories," despite their intuitive appeal, cannot provide useful guidelines for marketing strategy since it is unlikely that all consumers will view a brand as belonging to one and only one of these categories. The perception and evaluation of a brand can differ across consumers, and even for a given consumer, it may vary over time or across consumption and purchase occasions.

Given this limitation, useful input for marketing strategy requires detailed information on how various market segments perceive the firm's brands—i.e., the brand positioning.

Positioning thus provides an empirically based product/brand classification which can provide useful guidelines for marketing strategy. The "objective" classification-of-goods theories, and primarily the criteria underlying the various classification systems, may be helpful as inputs to the design of positioning studies and interpretation of their results but cannot by themselves provide useful managerial guidelines.

Alternative Approaches to the Measurement of a Product's and Firm's Competitive Positioning

The traditional approach to the measurement of the perceived positioning of a firm's products and services had been a profile chart of brands by attributes.

The major change in this practice came in the late sixties with developments in multidimensional scaling (MDS). (For an excellent review of these approaches, their assumptions, applications, and limitations, see Green & Carmone 1970, Green & Tull 1975, Green 1975, and Shepard 1974. This set of techniques, developed by mathematical psychologists, provides a spatial (geometric) representation of relationships among brands, products, firms, or other objects of interest, based on data on consumers' perceptions of, and preference for, these objects.

Applications of multidimensional scaling and hierarchial clustering procedures to product positioning have been reported earlier. Wind and Robinson (1972), in discussing the concept and measurement of positioning, described a number of studies in which multidimensional scaling procedures were used to determine the product's market positioning. Some additional studies were described in a more recent review by Green and McMennamin (1973).

Today the utilization of multidimensional scaling in product-positioning studies is quite widespread. It has entered the introductory marketing textbooks (Kotler 1972), and it is frequently used in commercial studies. Clustering procedures, despite their appropriateness for the identification of a product positioning, are less frequently used. Yet, consumers' perceptions of product positioning, as assessed by multidimensional scaling and clustering procedures, have not been accepted by the regulatory agencies as appropriate to the identification of market and competitive structure.

Another more recent tool that can be utilized in product positioning is *conjoint measurement* analysis. This more recent development in mathematical psychology is concerned with measuring the joint effect of two or more independent variables (product attributes) on the ordering of a dependent variable (overall liking, preference, appropriateness for various usage occasions, or some other evaluative measure). The output of this procedure consists of the simultaneous measurement of the joint effect and separate independent variable contributions to that joint effect, all at the level of interval scale with common unit. (For a discussion of this approach, see Green & Wind 1973).

From the standpoint of product positioning, conjoint measurement can provide insight into the value of the brand name (when brands are treated as independent variables) as well as the appropriateness of various brands for providing certain types of features and benefits (when brands are the dependent variables and various combinations of product features are sorted according to their similarity to various brands). This latter case utilizes the categorical conjoint measurement procedure.

Given that both multidimensional scaling and conjoint measurement procedures have been discussed in detail elsewhere, the focus of this section will be on describing a number of different, although related, ways of determining a product positioning by the use of these two analytical procedures.

MDS Positioning Based on Similarity of Brands

The simplest and most common approach to determining positioning is based on the similarity of brand I to other brands. Two types of data can be collected from the respondents: overall similarity of brands (e.g., rank or rate all brands according to their similarity to an anchor brand and rotate the brands until all brands have served as an anchor), or evaluation of brands (rating or ranking) on a set of relevant attributes. In the first approach—the direct measure of similarity—the $k \times k$ matrix of interbrand distance is submitted to any of a number of multidimensional scaling programs (e.g., TORSCA), resulting in a simple n dimensional space.

The second type of data can also be transferred into a $k \times k$ matrix of brand similarities (across attributes) and submitted to some multidimensional program. (For a discussion of the technical details involved, see Green & Rao 1972.)

This procedure would result in the familiar perceptual space presented in Figure 10.1, in which the position of any brand can be determined by calculating its distance from all other brands.

To gain better insight into the finer structure of relations among the brands, the data can also be submitted to a hierarchical cluster analysis, such as the one presented in Figure 10.2.

MDS Positioning Based on the Brand's Position on the Relevant Dimensions

Further insight into the positioning of a brand can be gained by identifying the position of each brand on the major dimensions (frame of reference along which brands are compared perceptually) identified in the multidimensional space. In Figure 10.1, for example, the two dimensions can be interpreted as economy/prestige versus sportiness/nonsportiness, and the position of each car on these dimensions can be determined.

In conducting such analysis, the researcher can choose the desired level of analysis based on his assumption as to the homogeneity of perceptual configuration. Assuming such homogeneity (Stefflre 1968), the researcher can conduct the analysis at the aggregate level. If, on the other hand, he assumes that individuals may differ in their perceptions, he can follow one of two approaches: cluster the respondents based on their commonality of perceptions, and conduct a separate analysis for each segment, or, alternatively, assume that respondents have a common perceptual dimension, but that they do differ with respect to the weights they attach to the various dimensions. This latter approach seems the most attractive one and can utilize the Carroll and Chang INDSCAL model and algorithm.

Figure 10.1

TWO-DIMENSION CONFIGURATION OF BRANDS OF AUTOMOBILES

Illustrative output

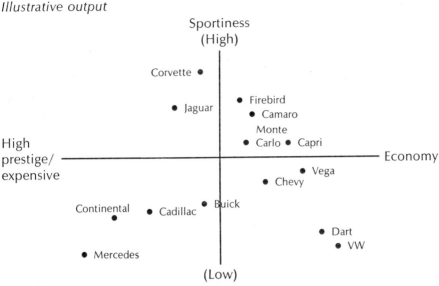

INTERPRETATION: The positioning of any brand is determined by (a) its distance from other brands. The closer two brands (e.g., VW and Dart) are, the more similar they are perceived to be. The further apart two brands are (e.g., VW and Mercedes), the less similar they are. Distance (i.e., similarity) may also connote competition. In this case, Capri, for example, competes with Vega, Monte Carlo, Chevy, and Camaro, but less so with Buick or Dart; (b) the projection of each brand on the two dimensions. In this example, Corvette is viewed as the most "sporty" car, whereas Mercedes is the least sporty. Mercedes, however, is perceived as the most prestigious and expensive car.

MDS Positioning Based on the Brand's Position on the Various Product Attributes

One of the common ways to assess consumers' evaluations of brands is to ask them to rate or rank the brands on a set of attributes. Such data (whether generated by anchoring on brands or attributes) can be submitted to a joint space analysis (e.g., MDPREF), resulting in a space in which the brands are the points (the same ones generated from the overall similarity data), and the attributes are vectors. In this case, the positioning of a brand can be further determined by its projections on the various attributes. Another important feature of this approach is that the cosine of the angle between any two vectors measures the correlation between the vectors. The output from this approach is illustrated in Figure 10.3.

Figure 10.2

A Hierarchical Clustering Analysis
of the Fourteen Automobiles

Illustrative output

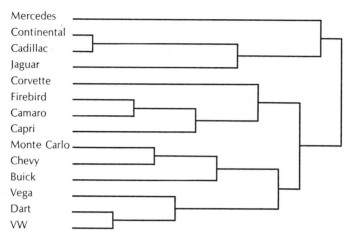

INTERPRETATION: Further insight into the finer structure of positioning can be obtained from a hierarchical clustering of the various brands. For example, Mercedes, which in the two-dimension perceptual space was viewed as quite similar to Continental and Cadillac, is perceived as a unique car with only slight competition with the two other luxury cars. Similarly, Corvette is also viewed as a unique car, but it does compete to some extent with Firebird and Camaro. Interestingly, Capri is viewed as a sport car competing with Firebird and Camaro more than with the Vega or other compact car, etc.

To further facilitate the positing analysis, the results of the hierarchical cluster can be superimposed on the two-dimensional map. This, for example, will result in the following visual output.

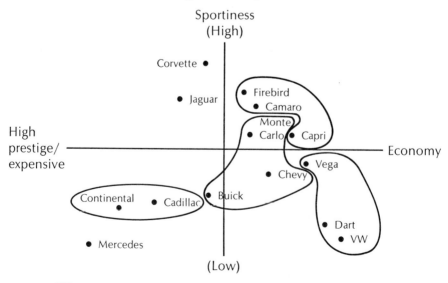

Figure 10.3

JOINT SPACE CONFIGURATION OF AUTOMOBILE BRANDS AND VECTORS

Illustrative output

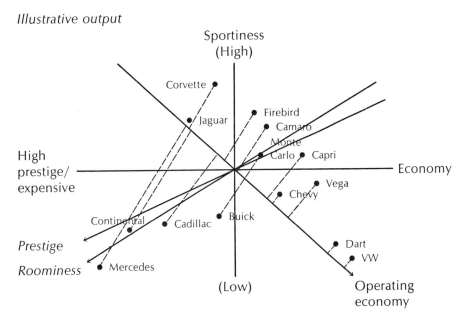

INTERPRETATION: The joint space configuration provides information on the way the respondents evaluate the various cars (the points in the space) on a set of attributes (the vectors). In this example, consumers view VW as the most economical car, followed by Dart, Vega, Chevy, etc. The projection of the cars on the vectors recovers the original rank order given by the respondents (if this were the nature of the task) and provides a metric scale of the position of each car on each of the attributes (vectors). For example, whereas Mercedes and Jaguar are viewed as the worst cars on operating economy, Chevy is positioned midway between them and VW, which is evaluated as the best on operating economy.

Examining the relationship between the vectors (the cosine of the angle between the vectors) suggests, in this specific case, that roominess and prestige are not related positively to operating economy, and that roominess is highly correlated with prestige.

MDS Positioning Based on Both Perceptions and Preferences

The three previous approaches were based only on consumers' perceptions and evaluations of a set of products; ignored were consumers' preferences for these products.

One may gain further insight into a (brand) positioning by measuring both consumers' perceptions *and* preferences for the given product in relation to its realistic competitors (both branded and generic). The necessity to determine product positioning not only on the basis of its similarity to other products, but also on consumers' preferences for it—overall preference as well as preference under various conditions (scenarios)—is a key premise of the *ideal-point* approach to product positioning. This is based on the premise that customers'

Figure 10.4

JOINT SPACE CONFIGURATION OF TWELVE BRANDS OF AUTOMOBILES AND PREFERENCE PATTERN OF THREE CONSUMERS (SEGMENTS)

Illustrative output

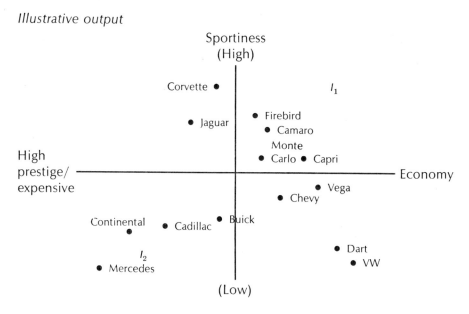

INTERPRETATION: Given that consumers may vary in their preference for the various automobiles, it is useful to present in the same space both the perceptual configuration of the stimuli (points in the space) *and* the respondents' preference for the cars (ideal points). The ideal point *I* represents the point in space which, without distorting the original perceptual configuration, satisfies the condition that the distance of all brands from it will correspond, as closely as possible, to the respondents' rank order of the brands (from most to least preferred). In this specific illustrative map, respondent 1 prefers the sporty type cars, Camaro, followed by Firebird and Capri. Respondent 2 on the other hand, prefers primarily the luxury type cars, Mercedes, followed by Continental and Cadillac.

Such analysis can be done at the individual level, enabling the researcher to segment the market based on similarities in the respondents' ideal points. Alternatively, the respondents can be clustered according to their similarity with respect to the original preference ranking and the ideal points established for each segment.

behavior is a function of *both* their perceptions and preferences and the recognition that buyers may differ with respect to both their perception of, and preference for, a product.

The data for this approach can be a simple rank order of the brands according to consumers' preferences. Joint space program (e.g., PREFMAP) can be utilized, resulting in a joint space of the original similarity space and ideal points, each representing the locus of preference of each respondent in this space. The closer a brand is to the "ideal," the more he prefers this brand. Urban (1975), for example, utilized the squared distance between the ideal point and a brand as a measure of the probability of purchase of the given brand. The output of this approach is illustrated in Figure 10.4.

Conjoint Measurement Positioning

Given the novelty of positioning via conjoint measurement, it might be useful to illustrate it by describing a study that followed such an approach.

The study in question was concerned with the positioning of a large finance company (associated with one of the automotive manufacturers) among automotive dealers. The management of the finance company wanted to get a better understanding of their competitive position as perceived by their dealers. In

Figure 10.5

**ILLUSTRATIVE CARD (1 OUT OF 16)
FOR THE CONJOINT MEASUREMENT STUDY**

Type of Product Bought
NEW TRUCK/AGRICULTURAL EQUIPMENT

The Customer's Credit Rating
POOR

Length of Term
18–36 MONTHS

Your Familiarity with the Customer
UNFAMILIAR CUSTOMER

Percent Downpayment (Including Value of Trade-in)
UNDER 10 PERCENT (i.e., 90–100 PERCENT FINANCING)

Amount to Finance
UNDER 5,000

Figure 10.6

DEALERS' EVALUATION OF THE POSITIONING OF FIVE FINANCE COMPANIES
(RESULTS OF CONJOINT MEASUREMENT ANALYSIS)

Illustrative output

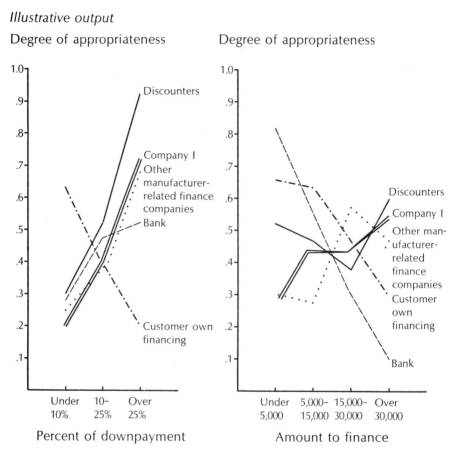

INTERPRETATION: The utility functions suggest the degree of appropriateness of each source of financing on the given factors and levels. For example, if a paper involves less than 10 percent downpayment, the dealers are most likely to suggest to the customer that he get his own financing (too high a risk). On the other hand, as the percentage of downpayment increases, the more likely they are to give it to the discounters, followed by company I (if more than 25 percent), and by a bank if 10-25%.

With respect to "amount to finance," banks are most appropriate for the less than $5,000 paper, whereas company I is least appropriate for such a paper. For high amounts (more than $30,000), the major competitors of company I are the discounters and other manufacturer-related finance companies, but not the banks.

The results of the analysis suggest, therefore, who the company is competing with as well as the fact that the nature of competition differs by the amount to be financed.

particular, they were concerned with their competitive position against local banks. Six factors were identified by management as constituting the major determinants of the assignment of a paper to a finance company. These included the type of product bought (new or used car), the customer's credit rating (poor or good), the length of term (18–36 months or more than 36 months), the dealer's familiarity with the customer (familiar or unfamiliar), the percent of downpayment (less than 10 percent, 10–25 percent, or more than 25 percent), and the amount to be financed (under $5,000, $5,000–$15,000, $15,000–$30,000, and more than $30,000).

A fractional factorial design (Winer 1971 and Green 1974) was developed resulting in 16 combinations (instead of the full set of 192 combinations). Each combination represented a hypothetical customer and his characteristics. Figure 10.5 presents one of the 16 combination cards. Each respondent was presented with all 16 cards, asked to examine them carefully, and to assign each one to one of the five possible finance companies.

The data from this task were submitted to the categorical conjoint measurement program, which resulted in the type of output presented in Figure 10.6. (For illustrative purposes, the exhibit includes only two of the six factors, whereas the actual output included all six factors, of course.)

Examination of this output provided explicit answers to such questions as:

1. For what type of paper is the company viewed as most appropriate?
2. For what type of paper is each of the competitors viewed as most appropriate?
3. What is the competitive position of the company on each of the various factors?
4. What is the relative importance of each of the factors (this is calculated as the range of utility for a given factor as a percentage of the total ranges for all factors)?

Positioning by Comparing the Objective and Subjective Positioning

Up to this point, the various approaches to determine a brand's positioning were based on consumers' evaluation of a set of brands. In some instances management does have information on the actual performance characteristics of the various brands in the product class. For example, the actual caloric content of a food item, its level of protein, and the types and amounts of vitamins are frequently available. Such "objective" data can be submitted to a joint space program, resulting in vectors for each of the objective attributes. When these objective vectors are compared to the ones obtained from consumers' evaluations of the brands on the same attributes, the cosine of the angle between each pair of objective and subjective vectors measures the degree of correlation between the perceived and objective positioning.

Such analysis provides further insights into the brand's positioning in the market. A study illustrating this approach in the context of food items was reported in Wind and Robinson (1972), and another study concerned with the positioning of computers was referred to in Green and McMennamin (1973).

This later study also illustrated the importance of obtaining positioning information by segment. The firm's and competitors' computer models were first positioned in a performance space based on manufacturer data on performance characteristics of the various computers. This objective performance space was then compared to the perceptual positioning obtained from data gathered from the firm's customers, matched companies which did not use the firm's computers, and the firm's sales personnel. The three perceptual positionings, when compared among themselves and with the objective space, revealed little congruence, suggesting a number of significant implications for the firm's marketing strategy.

Extension of the Concept of Positioning and Its Measurement Approaches

Positioning as a concept provides a conceptual framework for the guidance and evaluation of marketing strategies. As such, it allows the manager to develop a number of relevant marketing propositions, such as:

1. The closer the positioning of two brands, the more likely they are to compete with each other.
2. The closer a brand is to the ideal point of a segment and the farther other brands are from this ideal point, the higher the probability of purchase of the given brand.
3. The more isolated a brand is on some relevant dimension, the more unique it is considered to be, etc.

Such propositions, even in this general form, are essential for the development of relevant substantive market models (Dominguez and Nicosia, Chapter 4 in this book). It is hoped that further conceptual and empirical work in this area will lead to more specific and rigorous propositions.

Up to this point, the discussion of positioning suggests that the concept in its current formulation and measurement approaches can provide management with answers to such key marketing questions as:

1. Where am I (as perceived by relevant publics)?
2. Where am I going to be if I initiate changes in my marketing strategies, or if my competitors initiate some changes in their marketing strategies? (The answer to this question requires the utilization of appropriate experimental designs of the "before-after" nature or the incorporation of positioning in a computerized market situation.)
3. How effective are my marketing strategies? (The answer requires the collection and analysis of positioning information over time.)

The concept (and its measurement) provide further flexibility since the analysis of positioning can encompass:

1. Positioning at the individual or segment level (using any desired bases for segmentation)
2. Brands, products, product attributes (benefits), or firms

3. Existing brands as well as new-product concepts (Wind 1973)
4. Brands within or across product categories—this is especially important, given the problem of determining the "relevant" competitive setting that establishes the boundaries of the market (Wind 1975)
5. Comparison of the perceived positioning with the objective positioning of a brand
6. Positioning over time and in response to various marketing stimuli (of the firm and its competitors), including the introduction of new products

A number of the basic approaches to the measurement and study of positioning were presented in this chapter. These approaches were restricted, however, to the following four conditions:

1. The basic market space is a *brand* (product or firm) space, not an attribute (or feature) space.
2. Evaluation of brands on specific attributes requires presenting the respondent with a set of preselected attributes and asking him (her) to rank or rate the brands on the attributes (anchoring on either the attributes *or* brands).
3. The brand space is based on the perception of individual brands, not addressing the question of an *inventory* (or portfolio) of brands. (The mere closeness of two brands in some relevant dimensions does not indicate whether both will be bought or just one of them, and in what combinations of other brands).
4. The unit of analysis is, in most cases, the individual consumer (or some segment of individual consumers), ignoring the issue of buying units composed of the entire family or of subset(s) of persons within it.

Recent methodological developments enable us to relax the first two conditions. These extensions to the measurement of positioning are discussed next, followed by brief speculations on how one might approach the task of relaxing the last two conditions.

A feature (benefit) space, as opposed to a brand space, can be of interest to management when current brands do not cover or emphasize all the relevant product features desired by consumers. A feature (benefit) space can be developed from consumers' data on which features are likely to be associated with others. Such a space in which the attributes are promoted as points was developed in a study of ice cream (Green et al. 1975), which went one step further and incorporated in the same space the positioning of existing brands also presented as points (based on consumers' evaluations of the brands on the various features) *and* the ideal points of each segment (defined as regular users of each brand) in the same space. Following this approach, one can make statements concerning:

1. The feature space and the relationships among the various features
2. The positioning of the various brands based on a brand's relationship to:
   a. other brands
   b. all the product features and their major dimensions
   c. preference of the relevant segment

Since most positioning studies present the respondents with a list of brands and a list of attributes, one may be concerned about the relevance and exhaustiveness of the attribute list. In this case, a procedure suggested by Green et al. (1973) for the analysis of free-response data can be employed.

Following this approach, consumers are presented with a list of brands—one at a time—and asked to say the first things that come to their minds when they hear the name of the given brand. These free-response data provide the basis for a stimulus (brands) by evoked words (attributes) matrix, which is submitted to a multidimensional scaling analysis. The results of this analysis are submitted to a hierarchical clustering program, resulting in a tree structure of *both* the brands and the attributes they evoke. Similarly, one may present consumers with situations or needs and ask them to suggest the brands most appropriate for each. This approach would result in an occasion (stimuli) by brand (evoked words) matrix that can be subjected to the same analytical approach.

The use of free response can also be extended to the establishment of a direct brand perceptual space (not one derived from the analysis of similarities of brands across attributes). In this case, respondents can be presented with various brands and asked to free-associate the names of similar (substitute) brands. Such data can either be treated as frequency of mention (across people) and analyzed in a similar way to the data generated from the previous task, or alternatively, the pattern of response may be analyzed, treating the order of mention as rank-order data.

Whereas the attribute space and free-response approaches to positioning have been well defined and tested, the other two conditions have not been studied in any rigorous way. Yet progress in positioning research requires the development of conceptual and operational ways of determining a brand's position in the context of consumers' brand inventory and multiperson (e.g., family or any subset of it) unit of analysis.

The conceptual issues involved and some of the possible research approaches to the study of multiperson, multibrand situations are suggested elsewhere (Wind 1975). Both of these problems can be analyzed by the use of multidimensional scaling. The inventory problem is similar in its structure to the problem of item collection that was analyzed by Green et al. (1972). The change of the unit of analysis in positioning studies (from an individual to multiperson) is somewhat more complex and can be approached in a number of ways. These may include separate positioning analysis for each individual and examination of the *congruence* of the positioning among the relevant members of the unit of analysis. This can be done, for example, by matching the perceptual maps of husband and wife. (For a discussion of matching procedures, see Cliff 1966 and Green & Rao 1972.) Alternatively, households may be segmented based on the similarities of the perceptions of the members of the unit of analysis. In this case, brand positioning can be determined separately for each of these segments. These and other approaches, however, require further development and testing.

Concluding Remarks

"The Positioning Era Cometh" was the title of a three-part feature article in *Advertising Age* (Trout & Ries 1972). From both the academic interest in the topic and the large number of commercial positioning studies conducted, it seems that positioning is here to stay and is not just a marketing fad.

The understanding of consumers' (and other relevant publics') perceptions and evaluation of the firm's products and services is an essential ingredient of the design of the firm's marketing strategy. It provides management with a clear understanding as to *where they are* versus their competitors (by segment); it further provides some insights into *why* the company is where it is; and can even suggest directions as to *where they may consider going*—via repositioning (i.e., product modification or change in marketing strategy), product deletion, or introduction of new products. Each of these possible strategies has its associated pros and cons, and management should carefully examine the costs, risks, and benefits associated with repositioning attempts (loss of position without ever capturing the desired new position, "cannibalization," etc.), given the company's unique objectives, resources, and market position (the considerations of a dominant firm may be different from those of a marginal firm in a market). Changes in positioning over time, which can easily be noticed as shifts of the brand's position in a multidimensional space, provide management with a tool to use in monitoring, over time, the success of their and their competitors' marketing strategy (Wind & Robinson 1972).

As such, positioning—and especially positioning via multidimensional scaling—can provide a needed conceptual framework for the evaluation of the various marketing strategies of the firm. Further research is needed, however, in this regard. It should focus on two sets of relationships: (*a*) the link between changes in marketing strategy (product formulation, pricing, promotion, and distribution) of the firm and its competitors and changes in the firm's positioning (by segment), and (*b*) the link between changes in positioning and changes in sales, market share, and profitability (or any other dependent variable of interest to management).

Having better insight into these two questions is essential for a better determination of the firm's desired positioning (given alternative competitive action) and the actions necessary to achieve such a positioning.

References

Aspinwall, L. V. 1962. "The Characteristics of Goods Theory," In *Managerial Marketing*, ed. W. Lazer and E. J. Kelley. Homewood, Ill: Richard D. Irwin.

Bucklin, L. P. 1963. "Retail Strategy and the Classification of Consumer Goods." *Journal of Marketing* 27 (January):51–56.

Carroll, J. D. 1969. "Categorical Conjoint Measurement." Meeting of Mathematical Psychology, Ann Arbor, Michigan (August).

————. 1972. "Individual Differences in Multidimensional Scaling." In *Multidimensional Scaling Theory and Application in the Behavioral Sciences.* Vol. I, ed. R. N. Shepard et al. New York: Seminar Press.

Cliff, N. 1966. "Orthogonal Rotation to Congruence." *Psychometrika* 31:33–42.

Copeland, M. T. 1925. *Principles of Merchandising.* Chicago: A. W. Shaw.

Dommermuth, W. P. 1965. "The Shopping Matrix and Marketing Strategy." *Journal of Marketing Research* (May):128–132.

Green, P. E. 1974. "On the Design of Choice Experiments Involving Multifactor Alternatives." *Journal of Consumer Research* 1 (September):61–68.

————. 1975. "Marketing Applications of MDS: Assessment and Outlook." *Journal of Marketing* 39 (January):24–31.

Green, P. E. and Carmone, F. 1970. *Multidimensional Scaling and Related Techniques in Marketing Analysis.* Boston: Allyn and Bacon.

Green, P. E. and McMennamin, J. L. 1973. "Market Position Analysis." In *Marketing Manager's Handbook,* ed. S. H. Britt. Chicago: The Dartnell Corporation.

Green, P. E. and Rao, V. R. 1972. *Applied Multidimensional Scaling: A Comparison of Approaches and Algorithms.* New York: Holt, Rinehart and Winston.

Green, P. E. and Tull, D. S. 1975. *Research for Marketing Decisions.* Englewood Cliffs, N.J.: Prentice-Hall.

Green, P. E. and Wind, Y. 1973. *Multiattribute Decisions in Marketing: A Measurement Approach.* Hinsdale, Ill.: The Dryden Press.

————. 1975. "New Way to Measure Consumers' Judgments." *Harvard Business Review* 53 (July–August):107–117.

Green, P. E., Wind, Y., and Claycamp, H. J. 1975. "Brand Features Congruence Mapping." *Journal of Marketing Research* (August):306–313.

Green, P. E., Wind, Y., and Jain, A. K. 1972. "Preference Measurement of Item Collections." *Journal of Marketing Research* 9 (November):371–377.

————. 1973. "Analyzing Free Response Data in Marketing Research." *Journal of Marketing Research* 10 (February):45–52.

Holbrook, M. B. and Howard, J. 1976. "Consumer Research on Frequently Purchased Nondurable Goods and Services: A Review." In *Synthesis of Knowledge of Consumer Behavior,* ed. R. Ferber.

Holton, R. H. 1958. "The Distinction between Convenience Goods, Shopping Goods, and Specialty Goods." *Journal of Marketing* 23 (July):53–56.

————. 1959. "What Is Really Meant by 'Specialty' Goods?" *Journal of Marketing* 24 (July):64–67.

Johnson, S. C. 1967. "Hierarchical Clustering Schemes." *Psychometrika* 32:241–254.

Kaish, S. 1967. "Cognitive Dissonance and the Classification of Consumer Goods." *Journal of Marketing* 31 (October):28–31.

Kleimenhagen, A. K. 1966–1967. "Shopping, Specialty, or Convenience Goods?" *Journal of Retailing* 42 (Winter):32–39, 63.

Kotler, P. 1972. *Marketing Management: Analysis Planning and Control.* 2d ed. Englewood Cliffs, N.J.: Prentice-Hall.

Kruskal, J. B. 1965. "Analysis of Factorial Experiments by Estimating Monotone

Transformations of the Data." *Journal of the Royal Statistical Society*, Series B, 27:251–263.

Miracle, G. E. 1965. "Product Characteristics and Marketing Strategy." *Journal of Marketing* 29 (January):18–24.

Shepard, R. N. 1974. "Representation of Structure in Similarity Data: Problems and Prospects." *Psychometrika* 39 (December):373–421.

Stefflre, V. 1968. "Market Structure Studies: New Products for Old Markets and New Markets (Foreign) for Old Products." In *Application of the Science in Marketing*, ed. F. M. Bass et al. New York: John Wiley & Sons.

Trout, J. and Ries, A. 1972. "The Positioning Era Cometh." *Advertising Age* (April 24, May 1, May 8).

Urban, G. L. 1975. "Perceptor: A Model for Market Positioning." *Management Science* 21 (April):858–871.

Wind, Y. 1973. "A New Procedure for Concept Evaluation." *Journal of Marketing* 37 (October):2–11.

_____. 1975. "Multiperson Influence and Usage Occasions as Determinants of Brand Choice." Paper presented at the American Marketing Association Conference, August.

_____. (In press.) "Brand Choice." In *Synthesis of Knowledge of Consumer Behavior*, ed. R. Ferber.

Wind, Y. and Robinson, P. J. 1972. "Product Positioning: An Application of Multidimensional Scaling." In *Attitude Research in Transition*, ed. R. I. Haley. Chicago: American Marketing Association.

Winer, B. J. 1971. *Statistical Principles in Experimental Design*. 2d ed. New York: McGraw-Hill.

Epilogue

C. West Churchman

Rationality

One of man's great intellectual dreams is to think rationally about the world he inhabits. Typically, man believes that Nature behaves in a consistent manner and that he should be able to understand the reasons that events happen as they do. Furthermore, he often believes that he himself should act in a rational manner and that if he is inconsistent, then this is a sign of intellectual weakness.

Man has always sought ways to become rational and criteria that will help him to decide when he is behaving irrationally. Sometimes he can detect inconsistencies very easily. If a person asserts that A is so, and a few minutes later asserts that non-A is true, we say that he is inconsistent. But sometimes it is not easy to decide that someone's behavior is irrational. A person may say that he thinks that A is very likely to be true, but later on he acts as though A were false. Is he inconsistent? Perhaps not because he may be shrewd enough to see that the safest course open to him is to act as though A were false unless he is absolutely confident that it is true. For example, A may be the assertion that a certain water source is uncontaminated. A prudent man, lacking any testing equipment, might put some chlorine tablets in the water he drinks even though he believes that the water is very likely to be pure.

182

Models

A model is a device for helping man to think rationally. Sometimes men build physical models to help them think about reality. A wind tunnel or the model solar system one sees at the planetarium are examples. These physical models are designed to have many of the properties of the real objects. Furthermore, one can manipulate the models and determine the consequences of certain changes if they were to occur. Some models strip away large parts of the real event and display only the characteristics of interest. A so-called *communication map* of a company is an excellent example. Such maps display by arrows how messages and other means of communication are transmitted in the company. The map does not show anyone talking to anyone else, and yet one can easily determine from the map which persons communicate with each other. The map helps us think about communication system and possibly helps us to think how we should modify it.

Finally, there are models that are expressed in terms of a very rich language that enables us to discuss reality in a precise way and to use fantastically ingenious methods to predict the consequences of proposed changes in the real world. It is these so-called mathematical models that will concern us in this epilogue.

Reliability of Models

We wish to discuss the reliability of mathematical models. It is true that models are devices for thinking about reality. But are they reliable devices? When we go to the planetarium, we assume that the pictures that unfold before our eyes are accurate accounts of the manner in which the stars and the planets behave, unless the announcer tells us otherwise. For all we know, the directors of the planetarium may be pulling off a marvelous hoax. But in the back of our minds is the thought that such tricksters can easily be punished because any member of the audience can check this model with some other authority. Besides, in this instance, the cost of being tricked may not be very great.

But when the model tells us that a bridge is safe, that a building won't collapse in an earthquake, that a new product will sell, or that a weapon will deter an enemy, then we have every right to be concerned about the model's accuracy. It may be telling us how to think incorrectly and the conclusions we reach may be fatal.

It should be apparent from the discussion that everyone uses models in practically every activity of the day. We use a model to decide where to eat lunch because we construct some assumptions about the number of available places, the kind of food served, and the time required to get served. A manager trying to decide whether to buy a company uses some kind of financial model in which assets and liabilities are weighed, and the alternatives are assigned some rank order. Hence the question of the accuracy of models is a universal one. We are always on the alert to determine the reliability of the models that we use to think about reality.

The problem of reliability becomes especially acute in the case of mathematical models. Mathematical models, we said, are models that use a very rich language. The language is rich because it enables us to derive rather subtle and often completely unexpected consequences of the assumptions. The language can do this because it permits us to be very precise about what we say and to be very rigorous about the consequences of our assertions. In other words mathematical models are powerful devices for thinking about reality. Now one trouble with mathematical models is that their language is not universally understood. Whereas the average visitor to a planetarium can understand most of the things that are happening in the model, the average citizen cannot understand what is happening in a series of mathematical expressions. The planetarium visitor can check the steps of the model, if he wants to, by consulting some such source as an encyclopedia. A manager cannot check the steps of a mathematical model because he doesn't know what the steps mean.

Hence there must be a real concern about the reliability of mathematical models. Their danger is that they may lead us to think in a precisely wrong manner. With great rigor we may deduce unrealistic consequences. Because mathematics has become so revered a discipline in recent years, it tends to lull the unsuspecting into believing that he who thinks elaborately thinks well. Actually, one great risk of being able to think rigorously is that we may continue to go down the wrong pathway, forgetting the assumptions that started the thinking process in the first place. The elegant feeling of deriving clean-looking theorems may lead us to forget that the assumptions were totally unrealistic.

The Model of Geometry

In order to discuss mathematical models and their validity, it will be helpful to tell a historical story of geometry. It recounts one of man's greatest masterpieces of model building. It also describes the tortuous way in which man, for over 2000 years, tried to understand the problem of the reliability of geometrical models. Finally, it will enable us to ascertain the nature of models in a very precise manner.

The story can begin with Euclid's monumental *Elements*, which was written about 300 B.C. This work was the culmination of centuries of thinking about spatial properties. What Euclid did was to systematize this work in a very elegant manner. He first provides the reader with a set of definitions of points, planes, lines, circles, and angles. Then he sets down a list of assumptions. One part of his list tells us how to deal with quantities, e.g., "Things equal to the same thing are equal to each other." The other part makes some assumptions about space. These assumptions appear to be very obvious and require no proof. The first three are called the "ruler-and-compass" postulates because they assert (in effect) that in any part of space, one can draw straight lines connecting points, or extending beyond points, and one can draw circles of any radius. Obviously we can't actually draw these lines and circles in many practical situations (e.g., we can't draw a circle with Mars as a center). But the assumptions say that such lines and circles do "exist." They are part of the reality of space.

The Parallel Postulate

There are other assumptions, but the one of chief interest in this story is called the *parallel postulate*. As Euclid began to derive theorems from his assumptions, he ran into a peculiar situation. He was thinking about the special characteristics of intersecting lines. He had been able to prove to his satisfaction that if two lines intersect a third at right angles, the lines will never meet. This is equivalent to saying that one cannot form a triangle when the sum of the angles exceeds two right angles (180°). But now he wanted to prove that if one of the lines intersects at a right angle and the other does not, the lines must meet. In other words he wanted to prove that in this case a triangle must be formed. If he succeeded, he could then prove that the sum of the angles of a triangle cannot be less than 180°. Hence he would have been able to establish a very precise measure for spacial figures; namely, that the sum of the angles of a triangle is exactly 180°. From this he could easily determine the exact measure of the angles of various straight-edged figures in a plane. In other words, using some rather obvious assumptions, Euclid could measure an important property of space. He could do this without using any "measuring rods" or laboratory equipment, but merely by thinking about it. To illustrate, suppose First Street cuts Market Street at a right angle, but Second Street slightly "angles in" so that the intersection isn't quite a right angle. Euclid wanted to prove that First and Second Streets must intersect somewhere, even if it's out beyond Mars. Since he could find no way to prove this from his other assumptions, he postulated it; that is, he *assumed* that it must be true. Therein hangs the tale. For almost 2,000 years geometers tried over and over to prove what Euclid felt he had to assume. The source of their concern is easy to see. It is not quite obvious that the lines must intersect, especially if one cuts in at very nearly a right angle. Perhaps this not-so-obvious assumption about reality can be proved from more obvious assumptions.

Non-Euclidian Geometry

At last, in the seventeenth century A.D., a monk by the name of Saccheri decided, as he put it, to "relieve Euclid of every blemish." He took a direct attack on the problem and argued in this fashion: "If Euclid is right (and clearly he is), then if we assume the opposite of what he says we ought to get a ridiculous geometry that reason will reject outright." Fortunately, Saccheri was a cautious man and went at the problem in a very systematic way. He let First and the slightly errant Second Streets never meet, and studied the consequences. The consequences were astounding. They constituted in fact a whole new geometry, although it took another century or so before men realized that this was so, and Saccheri died with the feeling that he had properly cleansed Euclid's remains.

By the beginning of the nineteenth century, geometers realized that there was no rational objection to the non-Euclidian geometries of the type that Saccheri studied. That is, no contradiction results from making non-Euclidian assumptions. At first these geometries were regarded as mathematical oddities. They were the kind of thing that geometers might play with, but they were thought to have no relevance to reality. In reality, people said, lines behave like lines and only intersect when they're supposed to. But early twentieth-century physics cast some doubts on this way of thinking about reality. Specifically, if one can assume that space obeys some non-Euclidian laws, very convenient results can be obtained that explain otherwise unexplainable facts.

The innovations of one century tend to become the commonplace of the next, so that it is hard for us to appreciate the great insight that occurred in man's thinking when non-Euclidian geometries became real possibilities. It was a change in man's living as dramatic as the changes brought about by his explorations, including those to the West Indies and the moon.

Choices of Models

What is the lesson to be learned from this story? The most obvious one seems to be that geometers placed too much reliance on the obvious and did not know how to let their minds explore beyond the frontiers that reason or tradition seemed to establish. In other words, it is important to think about a problem in many different ways, including the radical ways that most men would instinctively disagree with. It is futile to insist that there is one clear and obviously correct model for each problem. Instead of being shocked at the idea that straight lines that come closer to each other may never meet, one should accept this idea as a realistic possibility, only to be rejected after examining its consequences.

This is certainly an important lesson for the student of management problems. Consider, for example, a manufacturing facility. One might be inclined to argue that there is just one way in which one can model how the facility works, and this is to describe its "actual" operations. Thus orders come first, then job specifications, then production schedules, and so on. These assertions are a set of "postulates" that describe the plant, just as Euclid's postulates describe space. The lesson to be learned from Euclid's story is that one ought to investigate other models in which these obvious postulates are contradicted. Perhaps production schedules should come first and orders should be generated in accordance with the schedule's demands, not vice versa. This, of course, is the model we often use to describe assembly line operations where we consider an "order" as a requirement of a part at a certain time. Perhaps the same kind of thinking is appropriate for other types of manufacturing facilities.

The "many model" approach amounts to introducing flexibility into an otherwise rigid way of thinking. People like patterns; they often like to have their thought processes laid out in a determined way and they resist any attempts to change them. The resulting inflexibility keeps them from even considering some realistic possibilities. Thus a marketing division will lay out its monthly operations: so much for advertising, so much for sales promotion, etc. It may never consider a serious revision of its operations because it has never tried to set down its basic postulates and never tried to explore changes in them.

Explicit Assumptions

The second lesson is that Euclid showed how thinking could be formalized in such a way that the basic assumptions were all displayed in a clear manner. One difficulty with becoming flexible in one's thinking is that one becomes sloppy as well. Unless the assumptions are made explicit in advance, it is easy to end up in contradictions or to fail to consider a hidden assumption. But if the postulates are all there, we can explore each one in as much detail as we want.

Furthermore, the postulates all work together jointly in the development of his theory. This joint development is what makes his theory so powerful that it can prove things one could never guess by drawing figures or using hunches. Even if one of his assumptions were changed, we could hardly guess what the resulting geometry would be like. We'd simply have to explore this possibility by the rigorous methods of proof that geometry demands. This happens because each of his assumptions is very intricately involved with the other assumptions.

Hence when we talk about model building in marketing, we're contemplating the possibility of changing assumptions in a very subtle way. To do this successfully, and to do it in depth, we require the kind of thinking apparatus that mathematical language provides.

Realism of Thinking

We have been discussing the value of flexibility in thinking, for this is one of the chief lessons we can learn from history. However, we must also realize that flexibility carried far enough leads to mental chaos. We can't explore all possibilities. We haven't the time or money or patience. A man who dwells only on possibilities is mentally ill because he never does get in touch with reality.

A final lesson to be learned from Euclid's story is the manner in which we should talk about the realism of models. What do people mean when they say "this is unrealistic"? Being unrealistic these days is even worse than being dishonest or crooked. It's amazing how often people are accused of being "totally" unrealistic, which must be as difficult a thing to accomplish as being totally realistic.

The rather obvious way to explain what is meant by being "realistic" is to say that there is a reality "out there." A model is realistic if it corresponds to it, and unrealistic if it does not. For example, a picture is realistic if the objects in it appear as they really are in the "outside" world. A model is realistic if it depicts the real situations accurately.

But this account of realistic models is very unsatisfactory, for it doesn't tell us what reality is. It is common sense to assume that there is some sort of fixed reality beyond the stream of consciousness that each of us experiences. But what is this reality? If we say that it is something "outside" of experience, how do we know what it is? Indeed, anyone who asserted that a model was unrealistic in this sense wouldn't know what he was talking about. He couldn't have any idea of the reality outside of his experience.

Facts

A more adequate way to explain what is meant by being realistic is to say that a model is realistic if its consequences agree with the facts of experience. This definition still leaves us very uneasy, because now we have to be sure we know what are really the facts. "Fact" is as overworked a term as "realistic." It is true that facts arise out of our experience. When we say that x is a fact, we mean that we have seen it, or read about it, or heard about it from some reliable source. But is something a fact simply because it has been experienced? For example, much of human experience is highly dramatic, and we tend to have some experiences planted deep in our minds. In this case, the "facts" are as difficult to remove as the stubborn weeds of a garden. Thus a manager, somewhat against his better judgment, tries out a new twist in his product. It fails miserably. It's a "fact" that it failed. It's also a "fact" for him that any such attempt will fail. He believes that any model prescribing a similar change in some other product is "totally unrealistic." Yet most of us would challenge this "fact" he believes so strongly. The "fact" has become embedded in the manager's mode of decision making.

Sometimes the embedding of facts becomes a beautiful thing to behold, as when an intelligent man has spent forty years in the same occupation. The lawyers, doctors, foremen, sailors, salesmen who "know their business" know what reality is, and can detect an absurdity at a glance. The attitude of these men might be taken as the definition of reality were it not that they themselves sometimes differ so strongly. The researcher bent on developing flexible yet realistic models must take these attitudes seriously, but he learns not to be deceived by the mere forcefulness of the opinions of an experienced man. He must seek for some more satisfactory definition of "realistic" than the so-called facts of those who have lived long in the job.

This difference in the perception of facts makes one of the most serious differences in outlook between the manager and the scientist. The manager has lived with his enterprise many years and has come to recognize the practical facts of its existence. If anyone asserts the opposite of one of these facts, he is apt to think them naive or downright foolish. The scientist, on the other hand, is very cautious about what he accepts as a fact. Not being deeply acquainted with the business, he is apt to develop a set of hypotheses that may not agree with the manager's facts. The scientist does this because this is his manner of working.

In order to understand the scientist's approach to facts, we must discuss in greater detail one aspect of Euclid's system that was mentioned earlier, namely, his theory of measurement.

Measurement

We said earlier that if Euclid had succeeded, he could have measured the size of the angles of many figures with absolute precision. Whether or not he succeeded, he was able to define the fundamental measures of such figures: the area, angles, and lengths of the sides. But the history of geometry seems to show that one cannot measure any of the properties, singly or collectively, without resorting to experience.

The reader may have felt all along that he could have properly advised the geometers of the past. If the total size of the angles of a triangle is open to doubt, then measure them precisely. Don't just think about it; use experience to tell you what is correct!

Now if we were to set about measuring the angles of a triangle, we would discover a very peculiar and disturbing thing. Presumably, we would have to draw a perfectly plane triangle with perfectly straight sides. Furthermore, we'd have to develop an instrument that measures angles. Luckily enough, this last task can be accomplished if instead we develop an instrument that measures lengths because (under certain assumptions) we can easily set up a critical experiment in which the size of an angle depends solely on the lengths of certain lines. But to measure length, we require a straight-edged ruler with precise markings so that we can compare any given line segment against these markings.

At this point we may begin to sense the fundamental trouble. How do we create a "straight" edge? We might try by exerting opposite forces to the extremities of a flexible body, such as a string. When the body became "sufficiently" rigid, we would argue that the center of its body represents a "straight line." Alternatively, we might try shooting a light beam from a "pin point" source and argue that the center of the beam traverses a straight line. In either case, we might obtain our straight edge, but only by assuming certain physical laws: that lines of force, or of light, are straight. Therefore, in order to measure angles and thus prove whether Euclid is right or wrong, we need to make other assumptions about reality.

Worse still, we would rather quickly come to realize that to produce our measuring rods we would have to make certain geometrical assumptions. We would have no way of measuring lengths, for example, unless we assumed the underlying geometrical structure of the measuring rods. Also, the proper use of lengths to measure angles depends on specific geometrical assumptions.

This fairly simple example from the history of science indicates that the so-called "facts" of science exist only because the scientist has been bold enough to make assumptions. We can't measure velocities without assuming a lot about the physical world. We can't measure velocities without assuming a lot about the mechanisms of clocks.

The more we want to know about a particular thing, the more we have to assume about the whole world. If a man is satisfied to experience Nature in a gross way, he can be modest about his beliefs. *The more he wants to learn about Nature in a precise manner, the more he must be willing to extend his power to believe.*

Hence, we have arrived at a conclusion about the manner in which the models of science are tested and, therefore, become realistic. As the tests become more precise, the need to assume more about reality becomes greater. The more realistic a certain aspect of a model becomes, the greater the need to make assumptions that have not been tested.

"The more you want to know about one thing, the more you have to assume about everything." Suppose we call this principle of scientific method the principle of the "maximum loop." The point is that as a scientist digs deeper into a problem, he must "loop" through more and more of Nature.

The maximum-loop principle tells us that to breathe more life into our models, we must have the courage to assume more about reality.

The rest of this chapter consists of an attempt to apply the principle of the maximum loop to the problem of breathing life into marketing models.

Prediction versus Prescription

At the outset we must recognize a very significant difference between physics and geometry, on the one hand, and marketing on the other because this difference is relevant to the definition of reality which each discipline recognizes. At the present time the ultimate test of the physicist is a certain kind of agreement among his observations. He struggles to find a theory which will enable him to adjust his observations so that they become acceptable to him and his peers. But one ultimate test of a marketing theory is not the acceptability of the theory on the part of market researchers. Instead it is its acceptance by marketing managers.

The reason for this difference is quite obvious once one considers what the marketing theorist is trying to do. He is chiefly interested, I think, in prescribing rather than describing. For the physicist, there is a world, and he wants to describe (or predict) its properties. For the marketing theorist, there are many possible worlds, each created in part by the manager's decisions. He wants to tell the manager which of these worlds is "best" relative to certain objectives.

Reality of Objectives

It is the objectives of the manager that pose one of the most fascinating and puzzling problems of model construction in marketing. The aim of the model builder is to become realistic about what is wanted as well as about what is happening. How does he accomplish his aims?

One answer to this very critical question about reality might be called the *engineering concept*. The answer says that the model builder can become realistic about the objectives of the manager only if and when the manager makes his objectives very clear. If the manager doesn't know what he wants, then the engineer cannot work satisfactorily.

But this concept of being realistic is very unsatisfactory. The goals of the manager are a part of the model according to the principle of the maximum loop. If we ask him to be precise about his goals, we are asking him to construct the model. He cannot become factually accurate about his goals without making certain assumptions. If someone says that G is his goal, he assumes that there is a feasible pathway to G. He assumes, further, that when other goals intervene, he will not divert his energies in their direction. However, if he is diverted by other goals, he can forecast the intensity of their attraction for him. In effect, he becomes a theorist of his own behavior. Furthermore, the more he tries to understand his own goals, the more he realizes he must assume about the goals of others with whom he associates. He becomes a theorist of his society's behavior. For still greater understanding, he must become a theorist of urban, state, and national behavior. To ask the manager to give the scientist a "realistic" picture of his objectives is to ask him to spell out all his convictions about human behavior.

But typically the manager does not try to gain greater precision of fact, simply because he hasn't the time. A far better reply to the problem of determining the real objectives is that manager and scientist must "work together." This very vague prescription can be stated more precisely from the point of view of the scientist. Traditionally, as we have mentioned, science has taken fact finding to be the ultimate test of its models. As we have shown, the validation of a model depends on a very subtle relationship between observation and theory. In the case of a science of management, one fact is central to the test of any model, namely, whether the manager accepts it.

Tests of Prescriptions

This statement about tests of models will sound strange to a scientist who is used to thinking in terms of the acceptance by his scientific peers only. He may find it quite distasteful to think that acceptance by nonscientists is a necessary condition for the validation of his models. But it is clear why we must argue that acceptance by managers is needed. We are considering models that realistically serve the manager's objectives. The manager's own behavior is one source of evidence we use to determine his objectives. Hence, if the manager doesn't act as the model says he should, then something is wrong, and until the error is explained the model cannot be "accepted."

Having said this much, we must hasten to add that rejection of the model by management does not necessarily imply complete rejection of the model by the scientist. The point is that the scientist needs to ascertain a fact about an organization: did the organization accept or reject the model? As the scientist digs deeper into this question of fact, he comes to recognize that the answer is a matter of degree: to what extent has acceptance occurred? In order to measure this degree with greater precision, the scientist must enlarge the loop and explore more and more about the organization and its environment.

First, there is the scientist himself. Perhaps he forgot an important variable or estimated something incorrectly. Perhaps he had personal reasons for suppressing certain information. Or some person who is important in the plan may have become alarmed about his own security and, therefore, opposed any change. Or someone may have misunderstood some of the scientist's arguments. In any or all these cases, the scientist must make assumptions about the organization that permit him to estimate the degree of acceptance. Thus considerations of anxiety or misunderstanding should be as much a part of a realistic model as considerations about the functioning of machinery.

In the present state of the art, the scientist does not understand how to combine organizational assumptions with other assumptions into one model, so that he often has to separate these considerations. He first develops a model of the firm's operations and then crudely tests its acceptance. But this simply means that the scientist is not yet able to determine a suitable way to make assumptions about organizational behavior.

Ignorance in Model Testing

Now there is one thing that may block acceptance of a model that deserves special attention: this is stupidity or ignorance. The manager may be incompetent to understand the implications of the model or he may be ignorant of some things the scientist has discovered. In either event, the scientist would not want to say that his model was invalid just because the manager didn't accept it.

This is a very important and difficult aspect of the reality of models. The scientist claims he is right in saying that his model is valid even if an ignorant manager doesn't accept it. He may admit he made a mistake if he ignored the anxieties of persons in the organization because he ignored their personal objectives, which, it turned out, were important for the firm. But if a manager doesn't understand the complexities of his operations or doesn't know something he should, then is it not a mistake to omit his ignorance in building the model? Should or should not the scientist build into his model an estimate of the manager's ignorance?

The reply that seems most satisfactory is the following: the manager's ignorance is as real as anything else about his organization. Therefore, it should be considered. But it is clearly one obstacle that ought to be removed since it has no value in itself unless the manager wants to be ignorant. But if ignorance has no value and can be removed, then the model should include the steps by which it is removed.

Here again the loop principle forces us into assumptions about the process of learning of an organization as well as the economics of learning. To be realistic about our models, we must assume how the organization can learn and what is the most economical learning procedure.

It thus becomes apparent that realistic models of the firm describe processes by which the firm can be transformed from one state to another. A part of the process consists of removing obstacles that are of no real value to the firm, and ignorance is normally an example of such an obstacle. Hence we *can* say that acceptance is an ultimate test of the validity of a model. The test is a test of whether, once the obstacles are removed or reduced, the firm does become transformed into the state that the model prescribes. The more precise we become about acceptance, the more we must assume about the firm.

The Comedy and Tragedy of Acceptance

If we could accomplish a fuller understanding of the process of acceptance, we would create a very beautiful thing to behold. The manager and the scientist would "work together" in a very intricate and elegant way. For the manager, the scientist is an essential part of his management activity. He comes to recognize, in fact, another way of managing. He comes to see that science can be perceived as a management method. The scientist, on the other hand, finds another way of validating his theories. He comes to recognize, in fact, another way of inquiring. He comes to see that management can be perceived as a scientific method.

Now that we have so happily wed the couple, we should introduce the inevitable note of tragedy that will go along with this comedy. Tragedy arises from basic and irresolvable conflicts. We have already hinted at one in stating that ignorance may be of value to the manager. The manager may want to be ignorant, i.e., to ignore knowledge. The scientist, too, may not want to maximize profits. The firm may not want to develop further refinements of the model because the additional costs don't "pay off." Worse still, the firm may want to cheat customers, lie to the government, ruin a community. What happens to a scientist serving a Hitler who expected to completely destroy Leningrad and all its citizens in order to immobilize the USSR? Is such a scientist "realistic"?

"Realistic" has sometimes been used in a destructive way by narrow-minded pragmatists of our day. They pretend that "realistic" means "getting the most out of the present situation." For them, it's realistic to cheat the customer if a profit can be made, even though this implies disaster in their industry. These are the moral charlatans of the business enterprise, who have no clearer idea about reality than they have about honesty.

Realism versus Idealism

We can, therefore, end this essay on realistic models by recalling one great, tragic conflict that men have faced over and over: the conflict between realism and idealism. Realism says that there is a world outside of man and his wants, and that to be realistic about this world is the basic prescription of the rational life. Idealism says that there is a world of ideas and ideals, and that this is the only real world there is. A form of realism argues that one should seek what one can to satisfy one's wants in the world of today. A form of idealism says that each should conduct his life so as best to serve the ideals that give life meaning. We all know the contrast; it is the contrast between a Caesar and a saint, between an experienced and practical manager and a doctor in the jungles of Africa. Who can say to the practical politician, "be more holy," or to the social worker, "be more practical"? It is a contrast between science and management. Who can say to the manager "be more theoretical," or to the scientist, "make more money"?

And yet this is not a trivial contrast that one can resolve by merely advising each to "live your life as you see fit." Realism has often threatened to destroy the world because realism cannot adequately distinguish between good and evil.

An evil politician can convince his country that the good of the world consists in murdering, in repression, in exploitation. He can do this by appealing to the realities of the situation. The idealist may say that such a man is totally unrealistic. But idealists can be evil as well. They can believe that man's ideal is the segregation of races or the suppression of art or of science. Under the banner of Freedom or a God, they can march to destroy man's deepest values.

The moral is clear. In some ultimate sense we have yet to learn what being realistic means. It may be the last thing that man will learn. If a note of optimism will help, we could think that humans are now trying, in a way they never have before, to "live together" with other humans. "Living together" does not mean being cooperative, or pleasant, or conciliatory. It means seeing one's own decisions as aspects of the other man's decisions, just as earlier we said that a manager might see the scientist as a manager, and the scientist might see the manager as a scientist. It means creating a larger and larger loop in the process of trying to understand ourselves.

The basic principle can be stated as follows: *a point of view, or a model, is realistic to the extent that it can be adequately interpreted, understood, and accepted by other points of view.*